Jeremy Sandford has lived most of his life in Herefordshire and the Welsh border country. He was educated at Oxford and in a touring military band. His TV film *Hotel de Luxe* (1963) was the subject of a famous court injunction; his *Cathy Come Home* (1966) focused public attention on the plight of Britain's homeless, won many awards and played a part in the initiation of Shelter; and his *Edna, the Inebriate Woman* (1971) won four awards, including the Critics Award and the Best Play of the Year.

He is the author of *Synthetic Fun, Down and Out in Britain, In Search of the Magic Mushroom, Tomorrow's People* and *Smiling David*, and he was for many years the editor of *Romano Drom*, a newspaper written by and for Britain's Gypsies. He is also a sponsor of Shelter and The Simon Community, a Governor of The Cyrenians, and in the past has worked closely with the Gypsy Council.

Jeremy Sandford

GYPSIES

ABACUS edition published in 1975
by Sphere Books Ltd
30/32 Gray's Inn Road, London WC1X 8JL

First published in Great Britain
by Martin Secker & Warburg Ltd 1973
Copyright © Jeremy Sandford 1973

This book is sold subject to the condition that it shall not, by way of trade or otherwise, be lent, re-sold, hired out or otherwise circulated without the publisher's prior consent in any form of binding or cover other than that in which it is published and without a similar condition including this condition being imposed on the subsequent purchaser

Set in Intertype Times Roman

*Printed in Great Britain by Hazell Watson & Viney Ltd
Aylesbury, Bucks*

But what did they fight for and why did they die?
For freedom to wander around.
But where can we wander; there's no place to go
For they're closing our camping grounds down.

> From 'The Hawker's Lament'
> by Mr Duncan Williamson, a
> Traveller from Fife

Contents

Preface 15
Introduction 17

PART I
Prince Nathaniel Petulengro Lee – The Duckerer 29

PART II
Travellers in Trailers
  Mr Tom Lee 53
  Mrs Geraldine Price 58
  Mr Jim Riley 61
  Mr Johnny Sheridan 70

PART III
Travellers in Bender Tents and a Varda
  Mr Russell Bilton 81
  Mr William Merchison 83
  Mrs Ethel Anderson 86
  Mr Ezra Price 90

PART IV
Travellers in Kers
  Mr Jimmy Penfold 95
  Mr and Mrs Alec Stewart 105
  Mr Francis Barton 111
  Mr Tommy Lee 117
  Mr Joe Cooper 126

PART V
Water Gypsies
  Mr and Mrs Humphries 129

PART VI

Mr Johnny 'Pops' Connors
   Seven Weeks of Childhood – An Autobiography   135

PART VII

Further Information – Some Notes on Britain's Gypsies   199
Gypsies   201
Information in Government Reports   216
Education   221
Travellers and Social Security   226
Legal Provision For and Against Gypsies   232
Effectiveness of the Caravan Sites Act – A Policy Statement
   by the Gypsy Council   236
The Story Brought Up to Date   239
Select Bibliography   247
Some Useful Addresses   249
Glossary   250

Acknowledgments

I acknowledge my thanks to the many members of Britain's Gypsy community to whom I have spoken while compiling this book, both those whose conversations are included in this book and those who had to be excluded for want of space.

And I and the publishers would like to thank the following for permission to reproduce illustrations: George Marriott, 2; Michael Wallace, 3, 4; Adrian Loveless, 5; Paul Hill, 6, 10, 11, 12; Hugh Gentleman, 7; A. D. S. Macpherson, 8; *The Scotsman*, 9; Sue Gee, 14.

For the section on Mr Johnny Sheridan I was given a great deal of help by Ivan Geffen and Barry Roberts of Walsall. And, in the section on Jim Riley, I was able to draw on a transcript of a conversation between him and Phillip Donnellan. Jane Kingshill provided the section on social security. George Marriott was helpful while I was writing the book, and so were all the many people, both Gypsies and non-Gypsies, who were involved in the production of *Romano Drom*, the Gypsy newspaper, of which I was editor during this period. Dr Donald Kenrick and Dr Thomas Acton helped weed out inaccuracies.

List of Illustrations

1 Prince Nathaniel Petulengro Lee
2 Mr Johnny Connors, family and young friends
3 Travellers stopped in South-west London
4 A typical caravan interior
5 The problem of life beside the road
6 In the Industrial Midlands
7 A typical urban camp-site in Lanarkshire
8 Evening in a bender tent encampment
9 A Hatchintan in winter
10 A Gypsy at Appleby Fair
11 At Appleby
12 A trotting race at Appleby
13 The old horse-drawn varda
14 A local authority site

Anthem of the Gypsy Nation

Gypsies Arise

We travel on, travel on
Along the eternal road
Everywhere meeting happy Gypsies
With their tents on happy roads

... Oh men of the Gypsies and young men of the Gypsies

Once I had a great family
But the Jackboot Brigade took them away
Now is the time, Gypsies arise
If we act now
We can achieve many things

... Oh men of the Gypsies and young men of the Gypsies

Upre Roma

Djelem, djelem
Lungone dromenca
Maladilem bahtale romenca
E carenca bahtale dromenca

... A Romale, a chavale.

Vi mansa e kali legija
Ake vjama usti Rom akana
Men hudasa mishto kaj kerasa

... A Romale, a chavale.

Ah faith, what would I give, this very tormenting minute, to be able to sit and have my natural freedom like the fox, badger, and partridge. I can only just memorise what it was like to have the ould barrel-top wagon pulled by the side of a grassy road and a clear spring river running like quicksilver along by the side of the ditch, and the rainbow and brown trout showing off, jumping out of the river as if they had not enough freedom in it.

Mr Johnny Connors

Preface

Our Gypsies in Britain today are in graver danger than at any time in the many centuries that they have been with us.

They have always been vulnerable to attack from those who, perhaps from envy of their free and easy ways, want to drive them out from our hedgerows, commons, and public places. To this constant threat there has now been added legislation which, it is not too much to say, effectively outlaws their entire way of life.

The Town and Country Planning Act, the Caravan Sites Act and the Highways Act are the principal instruments of this destruction.

The effect of this legislation on their way of life will, if it is not changed, be as disastrous as would be legislation in *our* lives which enacted that we must no more go to an English school, no longer work at our particular jobs and, above all, no longer live in any form of house, and keep moving most of the time.

It is my desire that this book may help change the public's attitude towards Gypsies so that the law will be changed before it is too late. I hope it will not be just a record of another priceless part of the British heritage which it was in our power to have preserved and profited from, but which instead we chose to sacrifice on the plastic altars of standardisation and expediency.

Against the odds, I still hope that time will bring a climate more favourable to our Gypsy citizens, and they will be accepted for those valuable things they have to give us, and that their suffering will approach its end.

There is little time to lose. Before our eyes the fabric of this entire and unique culture is in the process of being dismantled. It is a crime to which every one of us non-Gypsies in this country are accomplices.

Now, as the power invested in local authorities in the Caravan Sites Act (Part II) begins to grip, a new type of suffering is being added even to that suffering which already exists. It is a suffering whose extent is hard even to conceive let alone describe in words. Let us make change soon.

Jeremy Sandford

Introduction

To arrive at a Gypsy camp-site in the evening. To pick across the rubble or mud towards the caravans where they stand so snug and inviting, lit through their pink vinyl curtains by yellow Calor gas; to see the pretty Gypsy girls returning home with their gleaming jugs full of the evening's supply of water; to see the men come back in their huge lorries piled high with scrap, lurching back towards their home; to see smoke begin to rise from the chimneys ... How often have those of us who have become involved with Britain's Gypsies felt our heart turn over at this moment, turn over perhaps with some stirring from inherited memories of the time when we were all nomadic, or perhaps with the realisation that ultimately in this life nothing is fixed; there are as many life-styles possible as there are people around to live them. That is one side of the picture ...

To be with a group of Gypsies squatting and sitting by an open fire where a huge tureen of stew is brewing, drinking bottled beer, passing the evening in conversation and song, watching where, propped against the embers, a battery-powered portable television is transmitting the Hughie Green Show. That is another side of the picture ...

The child needlessly crushed to death during an eviction at Dudley; the three children who unnecessarily died during an eviction at Walsall; the two children burned to death in a tent in Lanarkshire on the same day that their grandfather was killed by a car; the many other Gypsy children who died not through anything as simple as an eviction but because the Gypsy life is hard – they died of exposure or malnutrition. That is another side of the picture ...

There are many Gypsy people who die unnecessarily. Proportionately, for every seven of us who live over the age of sixty-five, there is only one Gypsy.

Extermination has been suggested as a solution to the Gypsy problem by a Midlands councillor, and as a solution to various problems by a chief of police. In this we can see a tragic echo of that German policy which resulted in the extermination of 300,000 Gypsies.

Once already the British have harassed and exploited a part of our race to the point that they finally have left us, taking with them that spirituality and grace which was so necessary to the stolid ones. I speak of the Irish. They declared autonomy for a place of their own. But the Gypsies, to whom the British have behaved far worse than they did even to the Irish, have nowhere to go. And, unless existing legislation is changed, there may well soon be many parts of Britain in which they will be permanently outlawed.

'Travellers' is the name by which they now like to call themselves. They also like the name of 'Rom' – short for 'Romany'. The closest they have ever got to anywhere suitable to go is in the concept of *Romanistan* – that where a Gypsy happens to be standing at some particular time, that is where his nation is; small consolation as police and security strongmen drag Gypsy homes yet once again through the mud, or arrange for their enclosure once again behind wire mesh, concrete poles, barbed wire. They have not heard of *Romanistan*; nor has the education they have received done much towards making them aware of concepts like this one. The Gypsies will remain here. There is nowhere else. But whether they remain as people with their culture intact and something positive to give us – something *Romantic* – or whether as zombies crushed and relegated merely to a sub-life on social security in social twilight – *that* decision is ours.

The picture that emerges in the conversations that follow may be unexpected to some. That is because we refuse, many of us, to accept that Gypsies have changed with the passing of time. When we see the caravans of today's Gypsies parked in the mud by the roadside it is hard for some of us to understand that this is what Gypsies have become. When we think of Gypsies as they are described by D. H. Lawrence and George Borrow, many may be disappointed when they meet real Gypsies. But, theirs is the loss.

Gypsies have something to give us as they are, not only as they used to be. What they are has relevance to modern life. What they were has not, although it has influenced it.

And it is important to ask: how many British people have actually *talked* to Gypsies, as opposed to talking *at* them? Many decisions have been and are now being made for them about how they should live or be. And yet, until more dialogue has taken place between us and them, it may well be arrogant for British law-makers to think that they know the answers.

I travelled through Britain, talking to Gypsies. Some of the conversations that follow seem to me to be redolent with the smell of wood-smoke, the scent of the grassy borders of our twisting country lanes: these things that used to be so much a part of the Gypsy life. But the book also contains conversations which reflect the other side of contemporary Gypsy life – the squalor of the rubbish tips and refuse dumps on which Gypsies often find themselves, the endless series of evictions that still make horrible the lives of so many of them, the sprawl and concrete of our local authority sites.

Gypsies have rejected much of our culture, not in an intellectual way but instinctively and always. There are many things in this book from which we non-Gypsies should be able to learn. Many people are thinking of how an alternative society could be created, and it is worth noting that the Gypsies have had an alternative society of their own for centuries, a society which intermeshes with ours, but which is also different in almost every way. Those of us who are discontented with existing available life-styles may find many things to ponder in this book.

Most people still expect them to be like they used to be – exotically dressed, racially pure, whiling away their time in step-dancing and fortune-telling. The reality is less romantic. Many have been harassed to the extent that they are desperate, and they have shed much of their folksy colour, as have we all.

It would be as unreasonable for us to ask them to conform to what they were as for them to ask us to put on clogs, drink mead, and do morris dancing in the streets or live in half-timbered houses.

The number of Gypsies still exceeds by a vast degree the number of places for them. The lot of many of them is to be hounded, to be reviled, to be exploited, to be accused of crimes they never did.

There are still little more than a hundred local authority sites in Britain, with an average of fifteen places on each. The Gypsy Council has estimated the minimum requirements to be three hundred and fifty sites. Until that number is reached, many Gipsies will continue to spend winters without dignity or security, in the mud by the road.

There are thought to be about 25,000 of them in caravans and another 25,000 in houses who might return to the road if conditions got better. Some have intermarried with non-Gypsies and they still continue to do so. Some of those on the road would like to be in houses but most cling to their right to a wandering way of life.

They converse in English, with a sprinkling of Romany words, which are in fact of Indian origin. India is the place from which their ancestors came. In some parts of the country there are other 'secret' languages.

Most of them now live in trailer caravans which they pull behind lorries. Most of the caravan interiors are spotlessly kept, lit by Calor gas. They love ornate china and highly polished silver and the windows are often fringed with exotic lace curtains.

Most now deal in scrap and they contribute hundreds of thousands of pounds worth of scrap metal to our factories – metals which otherwise would have to be imported.

The sorting of scrap results in the land round where they stop being often piled high with what non-Gypsies often refer to as 'rubbish'. To Gypsies it represents, of course, their working capital; this difference in attitude results in friction. Non-Gypsies usually don't realise how much the Gypsies contribute to our economy in salvaging scrap iron. And Gypsies say that if they were given the same refuse collection facilites as non-Gypsies (which they would be prepared to pay for) then their stopping places would be clean. They point to the fact that many streets of London during the dustmen's strike became far filthier than a Gypsy stopping place – and far quicker. They also point to our slag heaps, our urban wilderness, our factories, our telegraph poles, our slums. In their opinion we are more filthy than they.

Gypsies conform in many respects to non-Gypsy standards of a hundred years ago. They marry young, die young, have large families, and infant mortality is high.

They are contemptuous of the fact that non-Gypsies do not cherish their old folk, and that our girls are often not virgins when they marry.

They also are contemptuous of the way that most non-Gypsies work for someone else, and also that we draw Social Security. Their life-style is closer to the Victorian ideals of self-help and private enterprise than it is to the Welfare State. Their typical unit tends to be the extended family rather than the ice-box twosome of non-Gypsies.

Many feel sick or claustrophobic when in a house and most of those on the road hold that the open air is healthy and 'indoors' is unhealthy.

They believe in living 'for the moment' and despise us for our concern with the mortgage, the nine-to-five job, the pension, and all the other sacrifices that many house dwellers make to the gods of security and property.

For centuries they have camped on our roadsides and commons. Their right to this is as good as most of ours to houses.

They have been harassed so much that they are suspicious of all non-Gypsies and also, sadly, are divided amongst themselves.

Clearly such people, with standards so different from those of the majority of British people, are sitting targets for persecution and discrimination. At one time 'being a Gypsy' itself carried the penalty of death.

The first reference to them appears to have been in the twelfth century in Perth. But most of the contemporary Gypsy culture seems to have come over with Indian Gypsies in the sixteenth century. Later they were joined by others to whom the wandering life appealed: by Scottish people defeated at Culloden and Glencoe, and by other homeless people, the dispossessed, and those they married.

They have as much right to be here as most of us. And they have fought and died for us in wars. Indeed, their vast families have provided prolific cannon-fodder. Their nomadic life-style goes back further than our settled one. They represent our remote past in human form. They are worth all the churches, all the museums. They are a unique part of our heritage.

Mrs Elsie Carter, a Gypsy now living in a house, writes to me: 'I left the road when I married and now live in a council house with my husband and teenage daughters, but in spite of all the things I hold dear to me on this side of the fence, part of me remains out there with the people I grew up with ... the people who are more law-abiding than many I meet among the so-called Christian civilised people ... Members of my family are still out there somewhere fighting for survival, uneducated and unprotected by the present law ... If you are born with a label that says "Gypsy", you are condemned from the moment that you peep at life from that tiny caravan window; you soon learn that you are different to other people and can never be a part of them or their way of life, because you're ignorant and uneducated.'

There is discrimination against Gypsies embodied even in the law of our land. The Highways Act makes it a criminal offence if 'a hawker or itinerant trader or a Gypsy ... encamps on a highway'. Gypsies are still prosecuted under this, and sometimes have paid many pounds in fines or gone to prison for it.

This discriminatory law is shocking and should be amended. It is much harder to persuade pubs to take down their 'No Gypsies Served' notices when it can be seen that the Government is itself discriminating in a similar way.

Extermination, forcing them to be licensed and to carry these licences with them, and locking their caravans to the ground, these all have been suggested recently by elected councillors as a solution to the Gypsy 'Problem'. Most Gypsies did not receive census forms; thus even proof of their existence is left vague.

They have been referred to as 'a gentle pilfering race'. But a government report which questioned the chief police officers of various areas said that in nearly every case the crime-rate among Gypsies was no higher than in other deprived parts of the population. What happens often, so it seems, is that the arrival of Gypsies in an area is a signal for local criminals to get to work, knowing that the Gypsies will become scapegoats.

Gypsies are still often harassed and driven from place to place to the extent that they can neither eat, feed their children, sleep, nor stop for long enough to earn a living.

The vast majority of Gypsies are illiterate, and the National Gypsy Education Council and ACERT (Advisory Committee for the Education of Romany and Other Travellers) have been sending non-Gypsies out to scores of Gypsy sites and stopping places.

The reception given to volunteers and a few professional teachers on sites has been good; children welcomed it.

Mr Jim Penfold, a Gypsy who toured some of the schools, said: 'In the vast majority of cases it was very successful. But there was one school where the teachers were drawing nude women on the children's arms, which was offensive to the parents. Volunteers must be taught more about Gypsy reticence and traditions.'

Mr Tom O'Doherty, a well-known Irish Gypsy living in the North country, spoke of the feeling of some Northern Gypsies that volunteers must be making a lot of money from it. He was urged to point out to such people that they nearly always did it for free.

The principle, agreed with certain counties, that a whole county should be considered as a school in itself, was mentioned. The needs of the Travellers' children in that county could then be assessed and teachers and a headmaster be allotted, who would move from site to site rather than teach in classrooms.

Those involved in a summer school at Wisbech wrote about it as follows: 'For the teachers there emerged a feeling of immense satisfaction mingled with frustration; frustration at the restrictions of time-scale, satisfaction from involvement with extraordinarily appealing, affectionate, intelligent and responsive children, unharmed by conventional ideas and methods, whose initial reaction made us suspect that they had felt unhappy in other more formal educational contexts; and a realisation of the success of methods based on family units, fluid structuring, and mutual involvement of teacher and child.'

But, even if education can be taken to all Gypsy children, and even if every local authority provides sites, the Gypsies will still remain a threatened people.

Local authorities who have provided sites are given even more stringent powers to harass Gypsies not using them. Sites usually strike at a Gypsy's pride and ability to survive by depriving him of any way of making a living.

The day when our roadsides are finally cleared of Gypsies, when the last trailer goes on to a site, will be a sad day.

Deprived of their life-style, on barbed-wire protected sites where pets and scrap dealing are forbidden, the Gypsies may well be in grave danger of being forced into degeneracy. Deprived of their autonomy, liberty and pride. No longer allowed to roam through Britain. Forced against their own desires, fair and square on to Social Security for the rest of their days.

A note about how I have arranged these conversations.

Part I consists of a conversation with Prince Petulengro Lee, the fortune-teller, who lives in a caravan in North London. This man is an exceptional person – both for the vividness of the stories he tells and also for the things that have happened to him.

Part II consists of conversations with Travellers living in trailers – their word for the modern motor-drawn caravan. This now represents the commonest form of home for the roadfaring Traveller all over the British Isles, and at least 20,000 Gypsy people live like this. Some move around fairly constantly, others stay put. Of those who move around some move largely because they want to, but the majority make most of their moves because they're forced to.

Part III is about Gypsies living in bender tents and a horse-drawn caravan. There are now not more than a few hundred Gypsy people living in horse-drawn caravans, and not much more than a thousand living in tents – mainly in Scotland and Northern Ireland. They now represent the poorest class of Gypsy.

To approach the squat form of a bender tent in the dusk is to experience something very strange. Especially if there are animals standing by, and a wisp of smoke coming out through the iron chimney that sticks through the top of the tent.

I think the reason for this is that this sight may evoke an inherited memory of man's first home; when he bent over tree boughs and covered them with animal skins, securing the skins around the foot in the same way that the modern Gypsy does his tarpaulin – with heavy stones.

The impression that I took away with me of those Travellers living in tents was one of sadness and demoralisation. But this may tell us something about Scotland, rather than about those Gypsies who live in tents. Or it may be that those Travellers I met were not typical. And there are also those many Travellers living in tents in Northern Ireland whom so far I have not met.

The one Traveller I met who was still living in a horse-drawn caravan was a wise and happy man.

In Part IV, I speak with Travellers who are at the moment living in a house, or ker.

People who are unfamiliar with the Gypsy scene may be surprised that I take up space in this book with interviews with Gypsies in houses. But the more I've got to know about them, the more I've come to realise how important are these Gypsies.

Two of the house-dwelling Travellers I talked to were vehement that they would never return to the road. The others said they would like to go back on the road and one of them has actually bought a piece of land and plans to return there.

Such statistics as are available, and my own experience, indicate that there is more interchange of Gypsies between houses and the road than most people realise. The interviews with the last two of the Gypsies in houses are sad, but this is partly, I think, because they are old folk. They can see only the hardship of the road and don't have the young man's resilience shown in many other people in this book, the young man's realisation that injustice *can* be stopped, that hardships for the Traveller *could* be ended.

Part V contains an interview with two water Gypsies. I wanted to include representatives of this type of Gypsy since in some ways their wandering culture, life-style, even the décor and arrangement of their cabins, are similar to the pattern of land Gypsies. There was another reason for including them. There are few of these once so numerous old narrow-boat Gypsies any more on our waterways. The two I spoke to may be among the last that will ever live this life. We could have no better portent of what might happen to our land Gypsies if we're not careful.

Part VI is perhaps the most important part of this book. In the course of my conversations I have met many people with a gift for poetry or song but most were not 'scholars' – they couldn't read or write. When I met Mr Johnny Connors he mentioned that he knew how to write. What is more, during a period in prison he had written the story of his youth, calling it *Seven Weeks of Childhood*.

I found it hard to read this book at first since it was scrawled in spindly capitals in prison exercise books. With Mr Connors's permission I had it typed out into a more conventional form and, a page or so after I had begun to read it, realised that this was a masterpiece. It seemed quite wrong to print an account of my conversation with him when this vivid work of his own existed. So, with his permission, I have included it in full – with the regrettable exception of certain books of it which were confiscated when he left prison, and others which he has sent to the Council of Europe.

I chose the Travellers I talked to largely at random, going into some particular part of the country and asking Gorjio friends to introduce me to Gypsies they knew; then speaking to those Gypsies who were interested in helping with the book.

The two things that struck me most were the humour and fortitude of the people I spoke to, and the prevalence of tragedy in their lives. I must emphasise that I didn't choose people because I knew their lives were tragic. Rather, as I continued on my journey through Britain, I had the increasingly sad feeling that, whatever caravan door I knocked on or tent I squatted in, there I would inevitably unearth tragedy. These people have had a bad time. Let there be no doubt about that.

But there is also an epic quality to many Gypsies' lives.

The Gypsies of the caves and natural shelters of the Carpathian Mountains and the Balkans ... Gypsies living in tents in Albania, sheltering from the wind that they call 'the devil sneezing' ... the Bulgarian women pulling at their pipes that are filled with herbs and dried leaves ... other foreign Gypsies who feel an aversion to washing (one of them said 'If I give myself a wash I no longer feel the man') ... the Kalderash who dress and wash their dying just before they're dead so that the dying man has the satisfaction of seeing himself well-clothed for the journey ahead ... the Troglodite Gypsies of Spain ... the French Gypsies who gather at Les Saintes Maries de la Mer ... the 300,000 Gypsies who just thirty years ago were dying in Hitler's gas ovens ...

The British Gypsies are a part, and not a humble part, of this larger Gypsy nation – ten million strong – which stretches round the world.

Part I

Prince Nathaniel Petulengro Lee
The Duckerer

Prince Nathaniel Petulengro Lee

'My birth certificate is on an oak-tree somewhere in Spain'

Prince Nathaniel Petulengro Lee lives in a trailer caravan which is usually parked in a cul-de-sac in North London. He is a fortune-teller or 'duckerer' and travels to visit fairs and markets for a week or so to ply his trade.

'Do you live alone?' I asked.

We were sitting on a couple of wooden chairs. Opposite us was his caravan, beneath which lurked dogs. The Prince, a stocky man of seventy, wore a scarlet bandolero on his head, and a gold crown engraved with the words 'The First Gypsy Prince'. On his fingers were sovereign rings that had belonged to his parents, also a wishing ring which, he told me, is in demand among Gorjios to wish on. 'These are all symbols, you see,' he explained. 'And when I die they'll either be buried with me or passed on to me sons.

'As you see I also wear bright beads and bright colours because we're a bright race, we don't like anything drab.'

In fact his trousers were of pink corduroy, he wore a scarlet silk waistcoat and a sports jacket. His head was surrounded with a blazing halo of white hair.

'Yes, I live alone,' he replied to my question.

Beyond the wall at the other side of the cul-de-sac a train hurtled by. We were by the main line to Paddington Station and at intervals during what followed, conversation became impossible as further trains thundered by.

He thrust one stocky arm down behind his chair and leaned in towards me.

There came a taunting voice in the darkness, 'Gypsy Lee! Gypsy Lee! Gypsy Lee!'

'Ugh,' he muttered, and his lips formed a silent curse.

Beside Mr Lee's caravan there was a smaller caravan, and also the motorised trailer that he uses for fortune-telling away from home. This trailer says on the side in lettering that he did himself:

He is Here
The famous
Prince Gypsy Lee,
Palmist, Astrologist,
and Clairvoyant.
As Seen on T.V.

Gypsy Lee was just back from Nottingham where he had been engaged to put a spell on the Festival, to ensure fine weather for five days. The spell worked. Those five days were scorchers, despite the counter-activities of an African witch-doctor.

'In one way, I've always been on my own,' said Gypsy Lee.

'I was about seven years of age when our family was broken up. My Daddy had taken some grais to a horse sale. He didn't come back that night. Next day a muskra came up to the varda.

'He was climbing up the steps and a dog went for him, tearing his trousers. My Mammy called the dog off of him and then the muskra said that my Daddy was in starry. He'd been given twelve months because they said one of the horses had been stolen.

'Them times was hard. My mother had to support us with only her basket of clothes pegs for sale, and her lace to sell to the Gorjios. Times were hard because we were twelve chavvies to feed.

'As for me, I used to help out too. I used to go with my brother and me father's pony and trap, and collect watercress, mushrooms, and other things to sell to the Gorjios.

'My sister, she sold violets, snowdrops, and primroses, and other wild flowers. I used to sell the watercress. And many a time we was chased by the muskras.

'But things still were hard and one night, as we was sitting round the camp-fire waiting for our bit of grub, up come two gavvers and some other Gorjios and they took us into what they call care; my brothers was sent to a home for boys and my sisters to a home for girls, on the grounds that my Mum couldn't support us.

'I was about nine years aged at that time, I'd never lived in anything else but a varda, never been with Gorjios or lived in a house. So I found this children's home irksome. Because I'd always been like a bird before, free like a bird.

'It was a Catholic place, very religious. And I found it hard, 'cos I was nine years of age and never been away from the family before.

So me and me brother we planned to run away, but we never did it. But we often planned it.

'In this place there was about forty of us sleeping in one room, and in the morning we had to get up at six of the day. Then we would have to stand by the beds while someone inspected the beds to make sure we hadn't wet the beds. And at this time also, there was prayers.

'And my young brother, he was uneasy there. He longed to be free, so he felt uneasy, so he wet the bed. And he was made to stand in the corner of the room while we others had our breakfast. He was made to stand there with the wet sheet over his head.

'And all this praying which there had already been was before the main bit of praying which was morning Mass. That was at seven-thirty of the day and it was one hour.

'There was much marching about and much exercise in the course of the days. And much lessons. We didn't feel free as birds no more, my son.

'And then one day as we was playing in the grounds I saw me father and mother. And when there was no one looking they come up to me and they told me they was come to kidnap me, to take me for always.

'That was a change to be back living the Romany way of life. Daddy had a chavvies' roundabout of twelve little wooden horses, and he put me in charge of it. But it took me a while to get used to being in the outside world again.

'And still, times were hard. In those days when I was a chavvy there was no such thing as National Assistance, you see. Always there was the fear that they'd send you to the workhouse. And in the workhouse they'd give you so many loaves of bread, so much tea, a pot of treacle and the boys were dished out with a pair of short corduroy trousers and a jacket, a kind of uniform which was a stigma, and people would say, "Oh, they're living on the Parish."

'See, it was like in the days of Oliver Twist, kind of thing, and it was a stigma.

'And I've seen my Mammy going round scrubbing public house steps in the winter when she couldn't get a bob or two, and she'd scrub the public house steps and the windows.

'Every country has its persecutions. Hitler persecuted the Jews and the Gypsies, America persecutes the Negroes. And in England,

I'm sorry to say, they still persecute our people. Whereas our people could be an asset to them. We could pay our rates and our taxes if you give us a camping place, give the children a chance to be educated, but no. You just treat us as scum.'

A powerful train went rattling by the other side of the wall, shaking Prince Gypsy Petulengro Lee's varda.

The Prince went into his varda and busied himself with making a cup of tea. When he returned he said, 'So now I will tell you how, when I became a father, the same thing happened to me and I lost me chavvies just as me father had done.

'It began with a dream. We were at Bethminster. And we had been hounded all the way from Severn Bridge. We were dead tired. And I had a dream. I dreamed that I was driving me caravan along a main road, looking for a camping site. I was just entering a little village when there was a terrible accident and suddenly there was blood everywhere. I had this dream at five in the morning. I was so alarmed that I went and woke my wife and told her about it.

'I said, "I've had this dreadful thought of a girl with Technicolor hair and silver spurs and a golden jacket, and she's in a pile of blood." And she was terrified that it might foretell a disaster for one of our own chavvies.

'A few days later, the terrible dream came true. We were just entering a village when a fifteen-year-old Gorjio girl riding a chestnut grai came on to the road in front of me suddenly.

'She had beautiful black hair hanging down in ringlets, and she wore a black velvet cap and a bright red riding habit with silver buttons, riding boots and jodhpurs. The pony reared. I swerved the trailer to the right and slammed on the brakes. The girl tried to quieten the pony but it became wilder. Then it bucked, and threw the girl on to the ground.

'I was just getting out of my seat to go to her help when the caravan was hit a great bump from behind. The lorry behind had been unable to stop in time and it had pushed me over the body of the girl as she lay there.

'I went to the back of the lorry and I saw the girl crushed beneath the rear wheel of the lorry in a pool of blood, and the other lorry with its engine driven right into the back of my caravan.

'It was a drunken man who was driving that lorry. He said he'd been unable to stop because he had a floating load of twenty ton.

'And he went and rung up for his boss to come down in a big car. He said, "Everything all right?" "Yes, everything under control, governor." So they brought in a case of accidental death.

'Well, after that they had it in for me, you see. And some days after, they kidnapped the chavvies. They thought: All right, the girl's lost her life. We can't prove who did it but we have our doubts, so we'll take your kids, and that's my opinion of it.

'And after that time, things got increasingly harder for us all the time, do you see. And my wife Elsie. She was in a state of shock from the accident and in fact she gave birth to Daniel just three days afterwards.

'The police towed us to a gravel pit in the New Forest and told us we must stay there till after the inquest.

'We didn't have much for food there, but I told a few fortunes, and the children picked blackberries and wild flowers to sell to the passing Gorjios. And our dog, Prince, caught a few rabbits.

'There came the inquest; verdict, accidental death. But from then on we were persecuted because people believed I was responsible for the girl's death.

'And that was the start of my disasters.

'I'd had the caravan fixed, and the bumps knocked out and trailer-bar mended from where the lorry had run into it.

'We pulled it down into Southampton and I found a bit of waste ground there. I took my Nathan to the school but the gavvers come and told us to move along. I said, "But I can't move now. My boy is in school."

'But they made me go and fetch him from school and then they made us move on to the road. So we moved off. And at the garage where we were getting some petrol the man said, "Why don't you park over there, there's going to be a fair there soon, why don't you park there?"

'So that struck me as a good idea and I pulled on to the ground that he'd said, and I took the wheels off so they couldn't tow us away. I was hoping to earn a pound or two there for to feed the wife and chavvies, with a bit of duckering, as we now were very short with all the misfortunes we'd seen.

'But the police still wanted to get rid of us. They took to coming round to the varda and I got so annoyed that I painted on it in foot-high letters: "THE BIRDS OF THE AIR HAVE THEIR NESTS, THE FOXES HAVE THEIR HOLES, BUT THE GYPSY AND HIS WIFE AND CHILDREN HAVE NOWHERE TO LAY THEIR HEADS. WE ARE BRITISH REFUGEES, DISPLACED PERSONS."

'Perhaps it was not wise to do that but I felt so chuffed.

'And next day the gavvers got more angry. They escorted us with two police cars right out of the city and on the road to London. And at that time I can tell you we had a loaf of bread, two bottles of milk, eggs, a box of Quaker Oats, a pot of jam, and a pound of sugar. We travelled all that day, it was twelve at night when we pulled into Staines. We were all very tired and very hungry. I went across to a house where there was a light on and asked for some water. But the lady there said, "I'm not giving you water this time of night. And I'll see you're not here long."

'That was not a pleasant night. The new-born babe was sick, and we none of us got much sleep. I was up early in the morning trying to get some water for the chavvies, and I was walking up the lane to buy some food and a big black car with two lady gavvers in it passed me. And a sergeant and a policeman.

'So I didn't know whether to go back or go on. But I knew the chavvies were hungry so I decided to go on and get some grub although we now were so short of money that I didn't have much to spend.

'But I had hardly got to the shop when Madeleine, my eldest, came running up behind me and she was shouting, "Daddy, Daddy, the muskras jav chored de chavvies!" That is, "The police have stolen the children."

'It seems the police had got a summons for something I'd done that had been passed on by the Southampton police. And when they got to the varda they realised the kids were near starving, so they took them away, or that's what I think happened.

'I'll tell you the ages the chavvies were when they were taken from me. There was little Danny, he was only six weeks old when they took him out of the missus's arms out of the caravan at eight o'clock in the morning. Then there was Beanie (our name for Albina), she was only two years old, and there was also Lindra, she was seven year old and there was Rodney, he was five year old. And then there was Nathan, he was eleven year old, and Madeleine, she was thirteen.

'So I went along to the police station just as fast as I could go.

And I'd no sooner got inside but I heard the sound of chavvies crying, screaming, and then a policewoman with a sheaf of papers in her hand came out of the room.

'I stood in front of her and I said, "Where are the children? I want my children."

'She opened the door of another room and she said, "Go and sit in there and wait. They're upstairs, having some breakfast."

'I'd not been in the room for more than five minutes when I heard the sound of a car outside. I ran out quickly into the back yard of the police station and at that moment saw my children being pushed into the back of a Black Maria.

'Then I became very tearful and very hysterical when I saw my eleven-year-old with the baby on his lap next to a policewoman, along with the others, Lindra, Rodney, and Beanie.

'Now the wagon began to move and I made to go and throw myself in front of it but the gavvers grabbed my arm and held me back while me children were driven away.

'Then they took me back into the station and the sergeant put his hand on my shoulder and he said, "Don't worry, old man, you and your wife have got to appear in the children's court at Brentford tomorrow, but it may only be temporary. You'll probably get them back."

'So the next morning we got up early and we went to court and we were told to sit on some benches and then they called out "Mr and Mrs Lee", and we went into the court.

'And the policewoman said that the police had been told that there was a Gypsy family on the green. They had got into the caravan and they found the children in bed and the mother with a sick baby in her arms. And that my wife had said that I had gone to look for a doctor and buy some grub. She said that the children were dirty but they looked in good health. And she went on to say that I was a good father and that I looked after my children well.

'And the magistrate asked me had I anything to say, and I explained that we'd broken down and been towed now from one place now another from pillar to post, till we got to Staines, and I'd gone out to buy some food for the children. The magistrates put their heads together and started whispering to each other. Then the magistrate says to me, "We can see that you have no money and no prospects in the future of getting any, so therefore we're going to take the children into temporary care till such time as you can get settled accommodation and can look after them."

'And then I saw red. I cursed the magistrates in Romany and I cursed them in English and I cursed the policewoman in English. I said, "You'll regret this to your dying day. This is my curse upon you. May you never rear another child of your own as long as you live."

'At that a policeman grabbed me by the arm and showed me out of the court. And my wife followed. They gave us some forms to sign and they said that they were for us to say that we would be prepared to pay 2/10d each week for the children while they were in care. But I upped and shouted, "I'll be damned if I'll pay. You've kidnapped my kids and now you can bloody well support them."

'At that I ran down from the court to a room underneath where I found the children and a birthday cake with six candles on it. And when the children saw me they shouted, "Daddy, Daddy, take us home, Daddy!"

'I threw my arms around Lindra and she threw her arms around me. I wanted to seize her and take her home with me. But the policewoman grabbed hold of my little girl and the two policemen grabbed hold of me and that was that.

'And now I'm a very lonely man since I've lost me chavvies, and I go to bed on many a night with an ache in my heart and a tear in my eye, especially after I've had a day duckering in the market when I've seen happy families and Mummies and Daddies with their little chavvies. To get my chavvies back, that's all I live for, and then I'll be a happy man before I die. For now I've nothing to live for, me life is empty. They've took me kids and me soul and me spirit. I loved them, I loved me chavvies and therefore they've hurt me very much. Children which is part of me spirit, part of me blood, they've put me children in a prison, children that were free and happy, and these are sad days for me. There was a time when folks believed that Gypsies used to steal children. That's the way they said it was, but the truth is, Gypsies have to be protected from the Gorjios who take their chavvies away.

'So then I put a curse on this whole country and the curse has worked. Britain has indeed gone to the dogs, everything's inflation, there have been strikes, money has lost its value and things have gone from bad to worse. There's been disasters on the rails, disasters in the air, disasters on the sea.

'Yes, I had had a lovely wife at that time and a lovely life and six little chavvies. But the time came they were taken from me as I had been taken from me Mum and Dad. They were put away till the time we got a house. Well, I got a house, but there was no bath in it, no toilet, that was in the yard, and that was their excuse that I couldn't have them back and since I've been in London I've got me name down on the list and I've found a tidy number of houses, and they said the authorities would see that I got a house, "You get your chavvies back with you and you can have a house." Then I went to the people who had the chavvies in care, and they said, "Get the house and you can have the chavvies."

'So after that it was a tug of war between the two, and the house people said I'd got to have the chavvies, and the chavvy people said I'd got to have the house, and meanwhile my chavvies have been brought up as Gorjios, been brainwashed, they don't know a bit of Romany, they can't rokra Romany, and they've been exploited. They brainwashed my boy, especially.

'And when they took the chavvies, my wife was very very distressed. She was so distressed she had to go to a mental institution. Because when a bird loses its young, when a cat loses its kittens, such animals go berserk.

'And now she's living in Aldgate Street, living in shop doorways and getting a shilling or two wherever she can, anywhere. Recently she's got a job working in a clothing factory for twelve shillings a day, cleaning, and they call it temporary work. They pay twelve bob a day and they make it up to a pound on the Friday. She doesn't work on a Saturday. She spends most of what she gets on the children. She's suffering from malnutrition and she's almost finished. Well, that's what they have done to us. They've come near to destroying her. They have accomplished what they set out to do. So can you wonder why I, myself, is very bitter?

'I fought in Nazi Germany, I fought for this country against the Germans, but I don't think the Germans as they are now would do such a thing, or the Russians would do such a thing. There is an old saying, an eye for an eye, a tooth for a tooth, and often I dream of revenge. I'm not a vicious, vindictive man but what would *you* do if they walked into your home and kidnapped your children and took them off you?

'Well, in my opinion, they'll be punished. I have put curses on many of them. I've seen two or three go under already: a judge, a solicitor, and one or two others that's done bad things to me.

'And the story of violence didn't stop there.

'Because, now she hadn't got the children, my wife became very distressed.

'And one day, when I was coming back to my varda a little early, I found her having intercourse with an Indian. I was deeply shocked but I think it was because she was so unbalanced by what had occurred.

'I went a bit berserk, and I don't know really what I did. But I had some petrol with me that I was going to use to put in a man's lorry who was going to tow my varda for me.

'And with me striking her, suddenly the Tilley lamp burst into flames and this caught the trailer and in a moment it was all on fire.

'And she was screaming to get out, I pulled her out through the caravan window, but I pulled her on to a pile of milk bottles and they broke and this harmed her so that now she was cut as well as scorched and scarred. And they said later that I'd hit her on the head with a piece of wood. That wood I'd been using that day to chop a sheep's head off with a knife and the bloodstains on it were the bloodstains of the sheep's head.

'And the police came, and they said, "Now we'll see you go down for a long, long time."

'And I collapsed and I was taken to hospital.

'And of course the detectives magnified it. They had three or four charges against me.

'First they said they were going to charge me with arson, that I was deliberately trying to set me wagon afire. But why should I do that since it wasn't insured; it was the only hope I had since the bus that I also lived in was now broken down through the accident.

'I woke up in a hospital bed. They dragged me out with the hair of me head and out of me bed and they took me to court, they said, "Sign this paper, you won't have anything to worry about." I said, "I'm signing nothing and I'm doing nothing."

'And they brought the Tilley lamp, they brought every bit of evidence they could find and he blackened me, the detective blackened me, he said, "We're going to send you down for a long, long time." They were true to their word, they sent me down for six years.

'When he gave me the sentence, the Justice asked me, "Have you got anything to say?"

'I says, "Yes, your Worship. Before this sentence is expired you'll be dead and buried with your shoes on."

'And he died a month to the very day on holiday in Switzerland.

'Many people suffered for the sentence that I was given for this passionate crime. And not only them.

'God works in a mysterious way, if there is a God.

'Of course, my wife had her excuses. She told me she'd done it to get money so she could have the children back. But I don't think that was the reason. I think she done it because she was deranged.

'And so I done my time after these series of disasters. I'd been given six years, but I was let out after four because of my good conduct. I came out of prison with nothing and now I've got a couple of thousand in the bank because the world of fortune-telling is getting fashionable now. I've got money in the bank and all I want now is a home for my chavvies, where we can be together.

'I'm saving up, I'm still saving up, till we can get a house where we can be together. It has to be a house now because they've been brought up as Gorjios, now they need to live as Gorjios. Until the summertime come and we go out in the varda.

'That's what I'm working for all the time. That's what I'm saving up for.

'I'm often an unhappy man still. When I see people at Christmastime, shopping, I get choked off to think of my kids fastened up in that Home. Me and the wife went up there at the back end of March, at the time of the little boy's birthday, took him some toys; and we caused him to come out of school, and he says, "Mammy, Mammy, I can't stop, can't stop, I'll get into trouble, I must run back into school." I've never seen a child so frightened in my life. We asked to see the superintendent of this Home.

'We had a row. And the upshot was, he barred me from going to see the kids alone. And he took me to the Children's Welfare Officer and I had to sit there with a man present all the time that I was talking to my kids.

'Why don't they let me have my kids? It costs so much to keep them in care. Whereas they could in the first case have given us a house. It's costing ten thousand pounds a year to keep these kids in care. It's costing you Gorjios all that money and has done since 1961, that's £100,000. All you ever had to do was give us a house.'

I asked Prince Petulengro Lee to speak in more general terms about being a Gypsy. He said, 'There's a very big distinction entirely between what the Gypsy wants out of life and what the Gorjio wants out of life. You see, the Gorjios are trying to mould our people into their way of life. And we're rebellious against it. They won't let us hatch in the places we used to, and they won't give us a house.

'I'd like to have a house. I'd like to have a house so I can send me chavvies to school during the winter months. I'd like to have a house for that. But I'd be away in the varda as soon as the blossom comes, and the thrush begins to sing, then I'd be back again on the open road.

'That would be cushti, real cushti, because it's got to be in Rome do as Rome does, and it's very difficult in the country to get a living. So you have to live in a town and in winter have a house in a town. In the town, in the city, the girls can peg their wares, the artificial flowers they make, do a bit of duckering with the cards for the Gorjio women, and the men could do a bit of tarmacking or a bit of scrap dealing or anything where they could make an honest pound or two. That's why it's useful to have a house for a base in a town. But a Traveller must be on the road.

'These local authority sites that they've built, they've built sixty such sites so far, but they're not very good because they're only for a chosen few, and there's not more than say a dozen vardas allowed on any site. They have a licence for so many and no more, and when a Gypsy gets a place on one of these sites, he holds on to it because he knows how hard it is to get a hatchintan anywhere.

'Here, for instance, where I am now, it's impossible to get a place on a site. There's the Wormwood Scrubs fairground and they're fencing it in but they're fencing it in to make a site not for the Romany Travellers, they're making it for the Gorjios that come over from abroad for a holiday. And my idea is, you see, that that will be coming to an end in September or October, and it'll be empty in the winter, so why not get the council to let it off to our people? So that our people can hatch there through the winter and fall away in the spring when the birds begin to sing and the blossom comes on the trees. And then, as the Romanies move out, the tourists can move in and put up their little tents.

'In the olden days the Romanies could hatch up a cul-de-sac or a lane, but you see the public health has made certain Acts that there must be toilets and running water, for health reasons.

'And take it from me, you never see any Romany chavvy going into hospital with any smallpox or chickenpox which the Gorjio chavvies pick up. I've never seen the little Romany chavvies with lice in their hair and nits and all that kind of thing because the Gypsy believes that cleanliness is next to Godliness.

'You may think that, in this urban place, there are not many Gypsies around here. But, actually, there are Travellers everywhere. I need a tan for a start. As you see, I'm actually near the railway, next to the gasworks, and it's becoming obsolete very shortly, this place where I am, and they're pulling the gasometers down here, so I'll need a place. And there are quite a number of Travellers round here, but mainly in houses.

'And out there on the Scrubs there's about twenty acres. What are they going to use them for? I've been here two-and-a-half years but it isn't ideal. We're right against the railway and until recently it was alive with rats. Of course now my Alsatian jukels keep them down, but I need to be here because of the market; it's handy for the Portobello Market where I can dump my duckering tan. I've got a hatchintan at this market where I put my little motor caravan and I can do business with the Gorjios and they simply love it, and of course it means that if I were to go somewhere else I'll have to start all over again and work up another business. And it's dispiriting to contemplate that because I'd probably be only there a few weeks before being moved on again. And Gorjios are not called on to move their homes from their jobs. So why should Gypsies be?

'There are a few other Gypsies in this area. There are one or two settled in caers and sold their wagons, but then it's probable they'd like to be back on the road.'

'There are various types of Gypsy. There's the true-blooded Romany Chal, the blackberry Gypsy. And there's the Tinker, which is from Ireland. And then there's the Didecoi, which is very rare, a Tinker girl marrying a Romany Chal, and you get the Pikie which are Tinker and Romany mixed blood.*

'I myself am a true Romany Chal. I rockered the Romany language fluently, I abide by the Gypsy laws and traditions, I live up to them, although I've been tried to be made a slave to convention with the Gorjios, it is very difficult sometimes.

'My mother was a true Romany Rackley and my father was an Españolo Gitano. My Mum was a cushti duckerer and her great grandmother was burned as a witch.

'And me, like them, I've always, always made my living by duckering.

'My uncle was Petulengro who was famous for his duckering. So any duckerer that has Petulengro blood, he makes the most of it.

'Some display their birth certificate. But when I was a boy, there was no such thing as a Romany Chal having a birth certificate because our birth certificate was carved on a tree. My birth certificate is on an oak-tree somewhere in Spain.

'So sometimes it is very difficult for my people when they become slaves to environment, hatching in the city: "What's your child's name? Where's his birth certificate?" says the law and the health inspectors ... you can't produce the bloody oak-tree, you see.

'Duckering hasn't changed much. In the olden days it was the country girls and the country boys but now you get the coloured people that's very superstitious, the Irish people, and they go to any means and any end to get to see a good duckerer or palm reader time and time again.

'For instance, myself, I've told 'em many a time how many chavvies they have, how old they are, what sex they are. I've told 'em in a roundabout way about deaths I foresee – like death on a motor-bike, for instance. But you mustn't tell them straight.

'You can't learn to be a duckerer. It's bred in you. It's handed down from father to son or mother to son and it runs in the family. People have been amazed when I've told them that they're married and have got two chavvies and I tell them how old the chavvies are, and what sex they are.

* Other Travellers have slightly different meanings for these words, and their usage seems to change according to what part of the land one is in. Also, Romany should correctly be spelt Romani: I preferred to keep the better-known spelling in this and some other Romany words.

'And they say, "Someone's been telling you about me." But nobody's been telling me about them because it's only the first day, it's the first day that I've pulled into that fair.

'So they come back a week or so later and say, "So and so became of what you told me, and I'm so impressed that I'd like to have the cards now." And I use the Tarot cards, the old fortune-Tarot cards, belonging to me Granny, and then I use my television that is about five hundred years old – that's what I call my crystal ball.

'I first learned about duckering when I used to sit under the table while me Granny was duckering to the Gorjios, and I used to listen, this was in the tent in the summer and the varda in the winter.

'When a person has their horoscope made by a Gypsy, they must give a date and time and place where they were born. But some of these newspapers, they give everyone born under Capricorn the same horoscope, which is wrong. Because they don't understand how astrology was invented. It was invented by three wise men. Two were shepherds and one was a Romany Chal. That's why Gypsies have always been so important in the world of duckering.

'And people have followed that Chal since then, and in the olden days they used to say: Cross the Gypsy Chal's palm with gold and he'd look into the future. As a matter of fact my Mum had two little parakeets in a cage on a brush pole and a little door to the bottom. She wrote up the horoscopes herself with a pen and stuck 'em in a drawer and she put a little parakeet out on a little perch and just by the flick of a finger she'd tell the parakeet which drawer to open and the parakeet would take out a little card with the person's horoscope written on it and then she would ducker the vass, that is, read the hand. People would play tricks on her; for instance, women would swap rings to see if she could tell you whether they were married or not, they were amazed when my mother told them that they should be wearing the wedding ring and how many years they'd been married and how many chavvies they'd got.

'My mother would say at the end of the duckering, "Do you love your husband?"

'"Oh yes, I do."

'"You don't want to lose him, do you?"

'"No."

'"Well, put yer ring back on yer hand missus, because that was put on for better or worse, till death do you part, and you've not died yet."

'So the woman got frashed to death, she said, "Oh we only did it for a bit of fun, Mrs Lee, to see if we could catch you out."

'So my mother says, "You wouldn't do that in the confession box, would you, to catch out the priest? So don't do it to me."

'When a woman comes to be duckered, it's very confidential, it's like a person going to see a solicitor, or to the Citizens' Advice. And my Mammy and myself have made many, many a person happy, and have got many people together that's been parted and mended broken marriages.

'Duckering is as old as the hills because when they opened the Pyramids they found slabs of marble with the impress of the hand on, before BC. And it now is a recognised science. I mean I've been nicked many a time, I've been fined forty pounds, fifty pounds, sixty pounds, in years gone by; I was fined sixty pounds in Manchester and I was fined fifty pounds at Blackpool; two lady police come in plain clothes at Blackpool and one behind the curtain was writing down everything I was telling her friend and she said, "We're here because you're breaking the law because there's an old Act of 1864 that it is an offence to deceive Her Majesty's subjects." But I explained to the court that people come to me of their own free will, like they go to a solicitor. I never dragged them in and said, "Would you like to come in and have your fortune told?"

'Anyway, as far as I was concerned I wasn't deceiving them. I was telling them the truth. And it was their money that they were spending, nobody else's money.

'Actually, I believe they're not prosecuting under that law any more. Because if they did they'd have to prosecute the newspaper astrologers and all the large number of people who are now duckering at every seaside, they'd have to pull in thousands of palmists and astrologers on every fairground, at every seaside in the British Isles and in the United Kingdom.

'Duckering is not just a profession, it is a way of life. The first time that I duckered was like this: I got kicked with a grai when I was twelve years old, and when I come into the hospital in good old Manchester the nurses all made a fuss of me because I was a Gypsy, something unusual, and they said, "Can you tell fortunes?" And I told one or two for the nurses and they were very pleased. That was the first time. Later, when I was put into the Children's Home in Liverpool, I spoke my first curse.

'I used to rob the orchard when I was hungry, and other naughty things, and when it came for the day's outing to Southport in the wagonette (there were no charabancs in them days, four horses and a wagon it was from Liverpool to Southport), and my name was called out, there were so many bad marks against my name, that I was barred from going to Southport. So I shouted, "It'll rain, it'll rain, you'll be sorry you ever went," and as soon as they got in the charabanc it started to rain at nine o'clock in the morning and didn't finish till eight o'clock that night. And when they got back they were very angry. The boys formed up in two ranks and I had to pass between them, and I was kicked and punched till I was black and blue all over and they said, "That's for putting a curse on us and being in league with the devil." That was the first time I did a curse.'

'All through the ages there have been people who have been cursed, you see. I mean, for example, Cain was cursed. I also have this power. People sometimes have asked me, is it right to curse people? To which I reply, is it right that a man should shoot another man that he's never seen in his life when there's a war on? So that's my weapon, my reply. I do put spells on people. People come to me and say, "Gypsy Lee, I'd like a baby boy." Then I've made a love charm and they'd have a baby boy, and that's why people have got faith in me.

'Cursing is the Gypsies' defence, similar to the defence of the porcupine which puts out its spikes to defend itself; but I would never do a bad curse unless I'm driven to it.

'Once I was up at Herne Bay, working on the pier for the season, working for the Council fifty-fifty. Then the season ended and I drew my motor caravan and trailer to Norwich market where there was going to be a fair at Christmas. We'd settled the caravans down and there was a knock at the door late at night and the superintendent of the fair and a sergeant and a couple of cops came and they said, "Come on, get this thing out of here, the fair's coming in."

'I said, "Look, I'm a travelling showman too, I'll pay for a pitch, please let me stay. I've five kids to feed and I'll pay you the same as the other people's paying."

' "If you're not off by twelve o'clock tomorrow we'll have tractors to tow you off."

'I said, "If you put tractors to tow me off, I'll put a curse on the fair because the fair is out on the cattle-market and there'll be no fair and there'll be no cattle sold on the market."

'So they laughed at me.

'So, I sent my little boy to the slaughter-house, he bought a pig's head and a sheep's head, a pig's foot and a sheep's foot and a cow's head, we got some cosh and made a little pile of fire in the middle of the market.

'And it came to pass that I said certain things when the full moon was out and put a cockerel and some blood on the fire and as sure as God's above, foot and mouth disease broke out next day and spread all over Norfolk and true to me curse no cattle was sold for three months.

'Then we travelled on to King's Lynn and at two o'clock in the morning when the chavvies were in bed they brought a tractor. The tractor towed us two mile out, towed us two mile outside the town into a lay-by. Well, I got out the wagon, and fluffed out me long hair and beard, I was fed up at that, and I cursed them. And I went and got a water can and I hammered it full of holes, filled it full of water and I made a curse that the town would be flooded for fourteen days and nights and they'd have to take refuge in the bedrooms with a ladder, and it happened.

'It's some kind of gift, you see. Gypsy duckerers don't believe, like you Gorjios do, that you've got only a good spirit. We believe everybody's got an evil spirit *and* a good spirit. If a person commits evil, commits murder, we believe that the evil spirit provokes them to do that. And if a man commits a good, the good spirit provokes him to do that good. That's what we believe. It's in our own mind, we're not taught it like you're taught about heaven and all this thing about religion.

'And of course we believe in certain things what's in our minds, you see. Everybody's spirit's in the mind and you have the actions controlled by your spirit and that's why your Romany Chal isn't frightened to die, because we believe that this life we're living is a dream and that the real life starts when we're dead, when the spirit leaves the body.

'Strange to say, I have been dead so I know what I'm talking about. You've first got to experience a thing before you can discuss it. When I was in Tangiers, in Mr Brabazon's orange grove, I pitched my tent. This Arab was there and I'd seen his shadow on my tent at one o'clock in the morning, this crouching figure, and I'd seen a brown hand coming looking for my wallet, so I just picked up a chopper which I kept lying beside me. I took one blow and I chopped his fingers off. There was the hell of a scream, he ripped the tent open and came staggering in and drove a knife right into my stomach and embowelled me and I'm blessed if I didn't have to hold me hand over it all the way to hospital. And I was on a table there.

'The doctor was giving me the kiss of life, and he told me later that I had the heart of a lion, otherwise I would not have survived, for I'd been dead for five minutes.

'I told a priest of my experience, and he said, "Promise me you won't breathe a word to anybody."

'I said, "Look Father, I've been over the border. All my ancestors were waiting, pulling my spirit towards them, and I came back."

'He said, "Don't tell anyone about this."

'I can tell you about death. Death was like a dream. I thought it was a dream. You get people dreaming in black and white and some dream in Technicolor. The one who dreams in Technicolor is psychic, and also dies in Technicolor. When I died it was as if I dreamed – beautiful flowers, beautiful trees, beautiful girls in different coloured dresses.

'Gypsies don't like anything dull or drab, even in death. At a Romany funeral, for instance, there is singing and dancing and the corpse is laid into a coffin; like me Granny was, put into an oak-tree lined with fern, laid to rest in a bright coloured frock with an ounce of baccy and a pipe in one hand and a box of matches and a box of snuff in the other. These things are to see her on her way.

'We think death should be the same as a wedding. It's a great thing. You go into a new experience, a new life. Why should people wear black? I said to my father one day, I remember I was a chavvy, I was only about seven year old, I'd seen about six coaches and lovely black horses with plumage, prancing up with these people crying in the carriage, and in front was a coffin and a glass hearse full of flowers and wreaths, so I said to me Daddy, "Daddy, what is them people crying for?"

'"Look my son," he said, "in that box they put a sister or a brother, and they're crying because they can't get up and smell the flowers that's around them. They send them flowers when they're dead, but they don't send them flowers when they're alive. The only flowers that I'd like when I die is cauliflowers, I can eat them. They don't believe in having happy funerals like we do."'

'We Gypsies believe that the Earth's been polluted with the exhaust and the oils of motor-cars. And, you know how they can inflate a balloon and send it up into the sky, and it'll go up and up, well, this world we're living in is like a gas balloon. I've heard me Mammy talk about it.

'It's all gas in the middle of this Earth, like the gas inside a balloon. They're sucking the life blood out of this Earth, and my Mammy said, "If you keep on doing it, by 1985 or 1990 this world will have nothing to keep us in orbit. It'll drop like a falling star, because they're pumping all the gas out of the earth and using it. What do you think keeps this world afloat in space? It's simply like a balloon and I'm forecasting this will happen. The Earth will fall."

'You know, I can see the day not far off when you can go to a telephone kiosk and put a fifty pence piece in and you'll see on the screen the person you're talking to.

'And I can see that this plane, known as the Concorde, in five years will be obsolete, because if the Americans are building rockets to go to the moon in a few hours, they will also be able to build a rocket plane which will get you to America in five or ten minutes.

'And then they'll have motor-cars on the road that fold their wings like a fly does and open their wings again and take off. People will get into this car and go to the Isle of Man or anywhere in this motor-car. This is the premonitions I get.

'My Granny before she died she said, "My son," she says, "I won't live to see it, but you'll live to see men with wings flying amongst the birds in the sky, you'll see men living amongst the fishes, you'll see iron horses running on rails, horseless carriages without horses on the roads and men will talk to each other thousands of miles away and see each other thousands of miles away, and they'll land on the moon, and they won't be satisfied with that, they'll want to go further out and they'll find other planets."

'I can foresee a certain day, it could be around the year 2000, there'll be one house only left in London, and in that house there'll be a little nine-year-old girl and one woman. And the child will say to the woman, "Mammy can I go out and play?" And the woman says, "But, my daughter, there's nobody left to play, there's no more children left. Go on out."

'The child goes out and she comes running back five minutes after saying, "Mammy, Mammy, Mammy, I've seen a man!" "No, a man?" Her mother is thrilled. Because that means that there are one man and one woman and one child left in London after the atomic bomb has dropped on it.

'My Mammy and my Granny was great people for predicting things and it's a kind of gift. We can't understand it. My Granny and my Mammy and my Daddy knew the exact day and date they'd die, and I know I'll live to be ninety, and I've been near to death four times, and I'm still here. I've seen stronger people than me go in the coffin, and I'm still here.

'I get a lot of complaints where I am though. It's only a blank wall at the back of these gardens as you see, but even so, I get complaints. "*We* pay our rates and taxes" – that sort of thing. "*You've* no right to be here." But we Gypsies take nothing from this society.

'I've been telling fortunes now, down the Portobello Market, for three years. You see, it's a wonderful gift, duckering, and I make good use of it.

'I've got a good name and make a good living. I was in Dunkirk, but I get no army pension, I get no old age pension. I give the Government nothing and I ask them for nothing, that's the true Gypsy way of life.

'You see, my son, what I make of this whole world is this: there's a law for the rich and a law for the poor. And one half of the world doesn't know how the other half lives and couldn't care a damn. But for one half, it's nothing but persecution from beginning to end.

'And I'd still like to have me children back with me, I still always dream of this. I'd give me right hand to have me children back with me, me son, me little chavvies back. At fresh of the morning and at balance of the day I think of it.

'God grant that one day I shall see them chavvies live back here with me again.'

When I left him, Prince Petulengro returned to his upright chair and sat there in the dusk till I was out of sight. He was the only Gypsy I have ever met who lived alone.

Postscript for 1975: And this story has, at any rate in one respect, a happy ending. Petulengro Lee has, since this was written, married a former girlfriend who, unknown to him, had conceived a child of his. He has, regrettably, still been unsuccessful in his endeavour to get his other children back with him.

Part II

Travellers in Trailers

At least 20,000 of Britain's Travellers live in trailers – their name for the motor-drawn modern caravan. These caravans are usually made for the Gorjio market and are bought by the Travellers for prices between £100 and £1,000. The typical caravan of this sort is twenty-two feet long, and has two rooms. There is usually a small stove burning coal or wood. Cut-glass, silver plates, family portraits, and decorative china plates hang from the walls. The windows are often fringed with decorative lace curtains. The caravans are kept scrupulously clean.

Those who are lucky have lorries to pull their caravans – lorries that they often also use for scrap dealing.

Little more than 120 of the sites which local authorities are required to build as a result of the Caravan Sites Act, 1968, have been so far completed. There is room for only a fraction of the Gypsy population on them.

So far official sites have usually been notable for a remarkable ignorance, in those who built them, of the Gypsy way of life. And new ones are being created very slowly. Since the Caravan Sites Act became law in 1970 the provision of sites has not been much larger than the actual natural increase of the Gypsy population during this period.

Mr Tom Lee

'All they got is site mad now.'

Mr Tom Lee, unable to find any stopping place in London, finally parked his caravan outside the Houses of Parliament.

'I want to raise the matter with them, the governors,' he informed a policeman.

The policeman replied, 'Are you aware where you are, sir?'

'Well yes, mush,' said Tom. 'That clock over there looks to me like Big Ben.'

'Well you can't stay here.'

'Who says I can't stay here. I want to talk to the folk in there about the shortage of sites for caravans.'

Tom was eventually persuaded to park in King Charles Street, SW1.

He received a visit from Lord Sandford, Under-Secretary at the Environment Ministry, but, though the situation had its bizarre side, Mr Lee was anxious that this should not blind the public to the seriousness of his mission.

'We Gypsies have been carrying on our wandering way of life as long as the house-dwellers have,' he said. 'But just because there's less of us it is unkind of them to close the verges of roads and our old stopping places to us.

'It is essential that we are given sites and stopping places close to the centres of population where we are living our lives.

'Most Travellers live from scrap-dealing. And yet central London is very poorly represented for dealers. The Travellers find it hard to travel that far.

'I call on the Queen or any owner of large public spaces to donate stopping places for the Gypsies.'

On another occasion, Mr Lee parked in an urban cul-de-sac. The local authority disapproved of this but, rather than mount a full-scale eviction, decided on the unusual policy of fencing Mr Tom Lee in. They erected a large iron bar across the road. Mr Lee drove his lorry into it and crumpled it.

Next time they put up the same again – in triplicate. Mr Lee treated it in the same fashion.

Next, a pair of twelve-foot-high steel gates was put up across the end of the street in which the trailer of the resourceful Mr Lee was parked. He borrowed an oxy-acetylene cutter and made himself a door. When I called, the various fences and gates had been taken down and Mr Lee was being left on his own. He has a dark-haired wife called Margaret, and one daughter.

'I do feel strongly,' he says, 'about the way Travellers have been treated in Britain. In some ways I can see things from a wider angle than other Travellers. One of the reasons is, when I was a kid myself, me brother died on the road, me sister died on the road and me mother died on the road and I've seen me father die on a bomb site. Well when you've been through that, that makes you think.

'They died on the side of the road, in wagons. Me brother died at twenty-four from consumption, from damp and cold; me sister died of consumption at eighteen years of age, me mother at forty-five. It's all from the same thing, dampness, wetness, rain, mud, pushing vehicles about, see what I mean?

'And if we're not careful, the kids will suffer the same way. Looking back on it, I suppose, if we had been in a house, I'd still have me family with me. So that's one way of looking at it.

'Being on the road may not be an important part of being a Traveller; but it's what you're used to. You can't say it's important, an important way of life, it's just what you're brought up to.

'The majority of Travellers don't want Government sites, they want to be left alone and travel as they've always done. Once the Government has set up the sites, in my opinion, the travelling way of life is finished, because you'll be *told* to go on to the sites, and not be able to move about any more on the roads. And it will just collapse. The travelling life will collapse, it will become extinct.

'I'm filled with regret about these sites. It was Gorjios getting the wrong end of the stick that were responsible, so I believe. The Government put the idea up and the Gypsy Council took it up and now it's all got mixed up, they don't know who's doing it. Know what I mean? See, some want sites, some don't want sites; as I say meself, personally, I don't want no sites.

'All I wanted to stop really when I became an officer of the Gypsy Council was this: to stop the aggravation of the councils and the police. Nothing about sites whatsoever. I wanted to stop the police knocking on your doors and moving you on. That's all. Norman Dodds was on about stopping aggravation, the councils, officials, police moving you on. This was splendid. But then they moved on to the idea of providing sites. We didn't want sites. All we wanted was to stop aggravation, people moving you from place to place. That's all.

'And all they got is site mad now. By building sites for us they're giving the council a licence to move the fifty or sixty other Travellers what's in the area, they'll get licence to do it, because they'll have done their part of the Parliament Act. This other sixty Travellers what's in the area, they'll then have the proper authority to summons them and to nick 'em for camping unlawfully. It will be a licence, a glorified licence.

'Already it's been happening. Take Barking. There's about sixty or seventy trailers round that area. Soon as Newham built a site at Temple Mills, nearby Barking had the council along the week after and nicked the others, for camping illegally on the side of the road.'

I asked Tom Lee for his views on education, but he passed this question to his wife, Margaret. 'Gypsy children learn to speak quick, they have to learn to fight back and that's what does it. They have to learn to think quick, and I think that if they were educated they'd be far more intelligent than lots of Gorjio children, because they've got that extra intelligence where they've learned to fight for their way of life, learned to fight for themselves and they're quick-witted with it.

'But the only way that they could be educated would be during the winter months, because otherwise you'd have to stay stationary.

'I think in the winter months, Travellers like to spend more time in one place because of weather conditions, and also you can't always find another place to stop. So any time that the Traveller was in one position for a long period, then obviously the children could have education.

'But I don't think a lot of the Gypsies want their children educated. The Travelling boys do scrap iron, they don't need education. The girls grow up, they get married very young. They bring up their children, they don't need education. I mean we've survived years without it, I'm sure we can survive a bit longer.

'Travellers are not poor as a rule. Travellers in fact do quite well.

The reason for this is that we don't have to pay out so much, I suppose that's what it is. We don't get the chance to pay out rates or tax.

'I think the way we're treated is because so many people are ignorant of us. They won't get to know us. And if only they would come to visit us and realise that we're not bad people. They've got some weird ideas that we're different to everybody else, but we're not, we're humans the same as they are, you know. It's just, you know, that we are a bit dubious of some people because they take the micky out of us. Calling us "Gyppos" and things like that. That can hurt.'

The Lees were just back from the International Gypsy Festival at Les Saintes Maries de la Mer.

'The foreign Travellers,' he said, 'they're a different sort of people, I mean you can't compare the Continental Travellers to some Travellers in England. They've travelled England, and that's as far as they've been. Scotland, Ireland and Wales, Doncaster, Lancaster, back to London – that's the extent of the travelling of some of them. They can't compare with Continental Travellers who travel the world.

'Those Travellers, they roam all over the world, and they don't care. There was music, music everywhere, everywhere guitars and lots of gaiety. I'm not comparing them with some Travellers in this country.'

'Would you like to live in a house?'

'No. When you've been in wagons for years and trailers for years, being in a house is like being in a prison cell. And that's why when you get a Traveller in a cell in prison he can't hold himself together, don't know what it's all about.

'Then again, as regards living in a house, it depends on the neighbours; you might get in a house and you might get good neighbours either side of you, then again you might get some that resent you. There is a lot of Travellers down the houses that later have come out of 'em. There's Benny Webb, he come out; he come out, Harry Smith's come out.'

'What was it made them come back on the road?'

'There's plenty of answers to that question. Often it is Travellers who have got plenty of money. They return to the road, not because it's cheaper, but because they've had enough of houses and feel more freer. But for others, it could be cheaper for 'em. Some people come out because it's cheaper for 'em to be on the road. Not because they like that sort of life, you can't go by that. Not necessarily.'

Margaret writes poetry. Here is a poem of hers.

The Gypsies

When God made the Gypsies
He said that they should roam,
There would be no need for houses,
For the world would be our home.

He would give us the grass so green,
He would give us the sky so blue,
He would give us the evening sunset,
He would give us the morning dew.

He would give us a lot of laughter,
But he would also give us pain,
For every time the sun shines,
There must always be the rain.

The Gorjios may never love us,
As long as we are in this land,
But of one thing I am certain,
God will always hold our hand.

And so I say to you my friends
No matter where you roam,
God will keep his promise,
We will always have a home.

In the time that has passed since we had the above conversation, Tom Lee's involvement with Gypsy rights has gone further and he has now become General Secretary of the Romany Guild, a new organisation based on the Folly Lane local authority site at Walthamstow.

Mrs Geraldine Price

'A Gypsy can see into the future.'

One of the new local authority sites, very tidy. The toilets are all in one block and each Traveller has a key to his particular toilet. High breasts of grass-covered slag-heaps overlooking the entrance to the site.

On this site lives Mrs Geraldine Price.

Geraldine is a blonde, in her forties, with a serene and gentle smile. The interior of her caravan is spotless.

'I've never met a ghost but I've seen – I've seen many things. If ever I've got trouble coming, I gets warned, I gets warned by one of them what's dead. This is the truth.

'There's been a ghost come when me mother or me father or one of me relations was gone and they've warned me. Comes to me in a vision or a dream and I know about these things and I know there's another world. I know this 'cos I've seed good from bad, I've seed it when my mother was dying. I've seed a vision of God upon the wall. His cross. This is true.

'A Gypsy can see into the future. A Gypsy feels these things, and they know. I know. I know when there's going to be trouble amongst my family, or anyone's going to be ill – I know. I get the feeling of it. I get these feelings, what's going to happen. No matter how far they're away. If they're taken ill I know about it.'

'Do you believe that the Traveller's curse can be effective?'

'Yes. It can.'

'Can you tell me an example of that?'

'... I don't know, you know what I mean.'

'You mean, you'd rather not say?'

'It's things like this you can't...'

'You can't speak of?'

'You can't. You get people involved in things ... and sometimes if I say a word it comes to pass.'

'... So you have to be careful what you say then?'

'I have to be careful. If I do say something, something like ...

something bad ... or something like that, then that sort of thing could come to pass. It could come. It come.'

'How much do you pay for this site?'
 'Three pound fifty a week.'
 'What do you get for this?'
 'Oh, we get a toilet, a dustbin and a slab to stand the caravan on. In between the slabs there's a lot of slack dirt. As you see, all round the site there's wire netting and barbed wire. And the other side used to be the fairground, but now it's closed, where all the Travellers used to stop on that all the winter through. I don't know why they've closed it up but they've closed it up. There's been no fair on there this year at all, last year was the last time the fair was on it. And then it was only a small fair.'
 'Are you allowed to keep pets, animals?'
 'We're allowed to keep pets but no horses, there's no room for 'em. We're allowed to keep dogs, yes.'
 'Are you allowed to have a fire?'
 'No, we can't have a fire outside like we'd like to.'
 'Can you keep any scrap?'
 'No. We can't have scrap, but they've promised us a little bit of land in time, but it'll mean more rent. At the moment there's no place for scrap.'
 'They've promised that later on they'll do a little bit at a time. Over there there's going to be a washhouse and a shower. And all those trailers at the top are fixed up with electricity.'
 'Who collects the rent?'
 'He's a rent agent.'
 'Is there a warden here?'
 'Yes. He's a Gypsy.'
 'And what's his job?'
 'If anybody was coming on he's meant to fill a form in and get it to the council, or if there's one going he's to report it to the council.'

'Do you like it here? Or would you like to have the old days back?'
 'I'd love it to go back like it used to be. I'd love to see places where a person could pull on and pay a week's rent. If there was a place in every town or two places in every town, you can go and pay a week's rent if you wanted to and pull off somewhere else when

you wanted to, when you got sick. That's what I'd like to see. More like the old days. You know, because there's a lot of people goes tarmacking and to do that they must have somewhere to keep their equipment and on these sites they can't keep their equipment so there's no more living for them. Well, I say if it was back like it used to be you could have a few weeks here and a few weeks there, you know, and if you pull on a farm and you give a few shillings he could put your horses in and you'd have no trouble then, when you're settled down in the country hop-picking, pea-picking, plum-picking, and it was lovely. All the Travellers used to get together, you know. I think they was lovely days 'cos you find no Traveller wants to be tied down.

'You have to fill in a form to go from here to somewhere else. Well I call that 'striction. And there's a lot of Travellers don't want 'striction. All that 'striction's no good. You got to let a person live their own life. Not too much interference.'

Mr Jim Riley

'A Mumpley, he understands nothing. He's ignorant to it.'

Mr Jim Riley lives with his wife and family in a trailer caravan in Herefordshire and neighbouring counties. His living comes mainly from scrap-dealing and fruit-picking.

I go first to a deserted Air Force camp on the outskirts of Bridgenorth. This must once have been a vast camp housing tens of thousands of troops. Now, rank grass grows up; there are the foundations of scattered huts and the occasional pathetic remains of brick buildings – the camp cinema, and the NAAFI – sticking up like rotten teeth.

No Travellers here.

I continue, and after ten minutes' more driving arrive at the grass verge of a little lane off the main road. A Traveller's varda is drawn up here.

'Have you seen Jim Riley?'

The Traveller says, 'I haven't seen him, but I know where he is.'

And he describes to us how to get to the farm, just off the Ledbury Road outside Hereford; he wouldn't have told me if I were alone but he does tell me because I'm with a man he knows and trusts. So we drive on to the farm, wondering at that bush telegraph which seems to enable Travellers, wherever they may be, to let each other know where they are.

At the farm there is a wide field that stretches away. At the end of it ten caravans are drawn up neatly in front of a long hedge; a dog lies tethered near to the first caravan. There is a little green square tent with a pointed top, and hanging fringed edges to its roof. The sun is shining bland across the bright green grass. Some Travellers are eating mushrooms that are boiling over the fire in a vast iron pot.

Jim is a fine-looking man in his thirties, with the easy dignity of one of nature's gentlemen. He is wearing a dark suit and a trilby hat. His wife, Carol, is beautiful.

'The lorry is respected now more than the horse. When I was a single fellow I used to have quite a few horses around me, not a big lot, say three or four, but very high-class stuff, so I could always say, "Well I'll sell that cob there for sixty or seventy quid." But I can name you quite a lot of these blokes who are rich today and had nowhere near the horseflesh I had, and now today they are rich. And these same blokes they won't stop to talk to you today; but when I had horses many of them used to come to me and they'd try to get a horse off me, you know, try to rob me of a deal when they had nothing. Well, today they're up in the air and I'm still the same way, in the same position. They won't entertain me now.

'And I'm still gone on horses. I'm very fond of them still. Me heart is in a horse. I love to see horses – not riding stuff, I like to see working horses. If I see an old working cob, I try me best to buy him but I've never succeeded in quite a long time. I do love horses and mostly I do love breaking them in. I give an extra five pounds for one horse unbroken, you know, one real wild horse that's never saw a bloke, I don't believe, two or three times, some ones that never saw a road, a hard road, never saw a motor – that's my type, that's what I like. It's my hobby to break them in. I love the fun you know of flagging it out and then getting it to work, you know, to let it know who's boss. I should like to have a job at that; but my kind of breaking-in would be no good for these riders. You see I break working stuff in. I take a day or so, but these riding stuff folks they aim to take two or three months. Well, one riding bloke I talked to, he was breaking it in in three months; I could have broken it in in a couple of hours.

'I am sorry in a way that I left the horses, but in another way, all our blokes they've all got motor-cars and you know it sort of puts one out if one's only got a horse. It seems to make out like, you know, he's got bugger-all and he knows bugger-all: he hasn't got the knowledge to run a vehicle. I wouldn't mind going back to horses but still I should still keep a small vehicle.

In the old days a bloke would be doing a bit of shoeing his pony before he went. And if he went out and got himself a bag of rags and an old mangle he was quite satisfied; get himself a quid or thirty shillings and he was quite comfortable.

'But now the Gypsies want more.'

'We're not Gypsies, you see. We are not a Gypsy, not as you know us as Gypsies. We are Romanies, what they call Romany Travellers. You see, the Gypsies originated from India, they come over from India. Like that is our right great ancestors, right back, you see. They come over and we're what they call the new population of the Gypsies. But by law we're British and we're born and bred in England. And we've took the life up from our people before us. We're true Romany Travellers, you see. Well there's the lad now come here today. He come here last night, if you remember, he's what you call a Mumpley Traveller. He's not what you'd call true-blooded Traveller, he's half and half.

'I can name you eight or nine different sorts of the different sorts of Traveller.

'A Mumpley, he understands nothing. He's ignorant to it. He hasn't got the knowledge to go out and do a day's work or to do a job of work; that's what they call a Mumpley.

'A Hedgecrawler, that is what we call a tramp Gypsy. He's too idle to wash himself. All that he wants is a fire, to lay around a fire, to eat and drink and smoke; that's what they call a Hedgecrawler.

'An old Didecoi, that there is a true travelling bloke. He can turn his hand to anything. I do believe there's not a job on the face of the sun that I couldn't do – I'd have a try – I've done quite a few jobs in my time. I am a Didecoi.

'They're trying to make us sites now, but there's a disadvantage to this. They only want us to go on there and stop there permanently and then they only want on the site a certain amount of us. Well, say now if me mother now is coming here tomorrow. Well if I went on that camping site and they only wanted a certain amount, say there was only me allowed on, you see me mother wouldn't be able to come on where I was. We wants a site where anybody can come on. We'd like an open site free to go, fresh to come and go when we like, come when we like, and as many as we like.

'Travellers keep in contact by meeting each other. When we meet each other, it's like a telegram from each one to each.

'It's like that bloke I met in Leominster today, Denis Smith. I had a chat with him. He asked me where was me mother-in-law staying; I told him. And he told me where such and such a person was; if I wanted to go out, I should just get in the wagon and drive straight to them. We always meet someone and every day we hear fresh. A bloke was here last night who told us all about his brothers and his uncles, what fresh things they'd got. That's the way it goes from one to another.

'When we had horse wagons we used to leave signals. That were when somebody were coming on behind us and he didn't know the road. But you see now when you've got a motor-vehicle, no sooner than a minute and you've gone out of sight. The signals we used to always lay would be a clod of grass or a clod of dirt. If we were going to go on to such a place, well we'd put two clods; if we were turning to the left, we'd put three clods. Say if we wasn't sure of what's coming behind that might sweep it away we'd put four or five clods. We'd put some this side of the road and some up farther so he could see. We'd always leave him plenty of track, plenty of markers which way we'd turned off and, you see, he'd know then how long we stood there for; he'd just look where the grass had been stood and he could always tell by the horses' hoof marks how long we'd stood there by the horses trampling about.

'But now with the motor-vehicles, no sooner you walk on with the vehicle, give me half an hour like, you could be forty or fifty miles away in the caravan. It's impossible. Give me an hour's start with a car, no one couldn't tell. But with horse wagons we could always tell. Say a horse-drawn wagon went from here and I come here say two or three hours later, I could partly tell to half an hour what time he left here by the fire. I'd just rake the ashes and feel the ashes in me hand. If the ashes was warm I'd say he'd be gone for two to three hours. If the ashes were still alight I'd say he'd be gone half an hour. You see we could partly tell; we used to go in the road, and rub our hand in the road across the road you know where the hoof marks have been, and if the hoof marks were on your hand he hadn't long gone, you see, because the track rubs them off.

'I don't know a lot of Romany, we don't speak it now between one another. We used to, years ago, we used all that sort of talk between one another but it isn't today, not like they used to years ago. They don't teach the little ones like they used to. I've got a sister, she won't entertain our kind of talk, if you know what I mean. She says, "Everybody's looking at you, you're talking in Romany, everybody's looking at you, you ought to talk out in English so that I can understand you." She'll walk away from me she will, she won't listen to me if I'm in a town and I say "Joller" like, you know, "Joll" to me, she won't look at me, she'll keep walking on, she won't bother with me.

'Travellers are superstitious. I wouldn't move on a Friday even if I had a summons, without I'd moved the caravan on a Thursday. If I hadn't moved all through the week I wouldn't have him took up on Friday not for all the money in the world. You know I've got that belief that it's bad luck would follow it.

'A bird going in the caravan would worry me to death. If it's gone in there I get sort of upset; I believe in something going to go wrong if a bird goes in the van.

'If me eye itches, say, which probably yours would do sometimes, I'd say, Oh, before the week's out I'm going to cry, and I usually do – it's funny isn't it?

'If me eye jumps I say I'm going to see a stranger.

'I don't believe in fortune-telling though. I don't believe in that sort of thing because I think what's on its way you'll have and that's it, ain't it? I mean some people have got that side. Me mother-in-law's a very good one at it. What she says is true, you see, but I'm not one for it.'

'When cooking I don't hardly use any Calor gas, I don't bother with it. I don't like gas lights. The weather must be very bad before I use the gas. I mean, when you've got to make a fire to fry and cook outside it's very cold and very bad in the snow. But we're used to cooking outside, we don't find it a hardship because we've been bred to it.

'Your oven-cooked food doesn't taste the same. I'd rather fry a piece of bacon, roast a piece of bacon with a stick through it than go in that caravan and light that gas; you get the fume of the gas on to it and it doesn't taste the same.

'We eat a lot of hedgehogs. I've had millions and thousands and I shall eat more before I die too. Their fat is a good thing for a bald-headed person, and Carol puts their fat on her hair. You get a hedgehog, open him out, peg him out, stick him in the fire, chuck some salt on him, give him a good wash first, soak him overnight in some salted water, and then give him a good wash again; just peg him out with a stick like a pig, you know, like you're carcassing a pig; and put him there to cook.

'A lot of travelling people, now, they use saucepans. Well, I don't believe in the saucepan. We cook in a pot, and we have a pot there now, you know, which you can't get for love nor money the type of pot we use.

'It's one of those cast-iron pots, but mostly now, you see, they uses all aluminium saucepans, but we always use the iron pan on the fire. Never believe in those little saucepan things, you see.

'I generally cut a stick out of the hedge, stick a piece of bacon on it, and stick it over the fire; or just chuck a piece of steak straight on the fire. It tastes beautiful. But they don't believe in that now, that's dirty to a lot of the travelling people. They say, "Oh I couldn't be bothered with them dirty pots," and they'll have them crumbled, they'll have their little cast-iron pots crumbled you see, but they're still using the pot but they don't know it, because when it was crumbled it went to make one of the small kind.

'When I'm totting, I never go to one particular place; in my line of business you haven't got to be fussy. Of course you've got to go, like, where you think you can get something, like, you know. But of course it doesn't happen all the time like that. You may go a day, you may go two, you may go a week. I always have been in this line. I do other jobs in between like farm work, farm labourer, painting, decorator. I never saw a job yet I couldn't do or try to do. But all me majority is scrap, I've always been on it. I know a good many folk don't like it. But it's what you take to. I used to do a lot of car-dealing once, old scrap cars. But I've gone off that now; too much hard work.

'However, it's a trade that's dying out fast, scrap; every year it's getting worser. It's getting harder to get, there's a lot of modern stuff coming, a lot of plastic taking over. One time of day you'd see all these landings, fettering, water tubing; now it's all plastic. Same as on the drainpipes they had, well, they've done away with all the scrap for that. It's the plastic that's taking all over now. But as years goes on it will be harder to get but the price will be better.

'I picked the trade off me parents, that sort of thing. We was reared to it. We used to go around with me parents, and of course you hear them talk and you hear them chat. You pick it up. But each one of us has got a different way of going around; each one have got a different saying.

'Being moved on, we always have been moved, but it's been worser since we've had the vehicles than when we had the horses, 'cos you had an excuse with a horse, but with these lorries you haven't. When you have a horse-drawn vehicle after hours, you see, the police knows very well that you could not travel. You could easy say, "Well this horse has come a long way and it's worn out. I've got to stop twenty-four hours," and, see, that's where we got the vantage of them.

'I remember one time, we'd been moved on all hours. A knock's come on the door at dusk in the morning, about seven o'clock in the morning when it's been snowing and freezing bitter; and we've had to move straight away. We've got the little girl up without any breakfast, we've had no cup of tea ourself. We've just had to back the vehicle on and move. We've been stuck in the road skidding, spinning, you know.

'And, of course, I'm a bloke that quick gets upset with any Government bloke. I've been in trouble many a time. Carol always had to correct me. We've had the council come to move us off, we've left half our equipment behind, couldn't find it in the snow, and that's how they get us. It hurts us in the winter.

'We don't mind in the summer so much. If anyone comes now and say I'd have to go now, I'd say, "Well I'll go in the morning." But when it's bad we don't like it; when it's cold.

'Just around here they know me.

'Back in the winter I pulled that caravan in the road there, I'd no time to get off the road but a police car was behind me.

'So I'd got to get off the road, I pulled in the side, he said I'd got to shift. I told him to come out the way, to move his mini-van. I told him to move it or else I was going to move it for him, I was going to pull over.

'So he said, "You've got to go."

'So I said, "I don't think so, it's getting late," I said, "and I've had no tea and my little girl's very hungry," I said. "She wants to get ready for bed."

'It come to a bit of an argument so I pulled over.

'He said, "You won't go?"

'"No." I said.

'So I was here for a week after.

'He come again, I told him to get off, and we was here for seven weeks, wasn't it? We was here after for seven weeks. It was the snow that kept us here.

'So he come again, didn't he?

'I said, "When the roads is clear." I said, "When the roads is clear, I'll get that caravan on the road, and the wagon, I'll go, but not before." But they never bothered us after.'

'This is a good life, I mean I wouldn't change it, I've had the offer to settle down. Mind you I like settling down in the winter and I likes to move off then as I please.

'I like to be free. I like to be me own boss – when I'm on this job I can take orders and I can give orders. I just like to be me own free boss; do what I like, go when I like, come back when I like. So long as I just get a bit of living I'm quite happy. I ain't a rich bloke and never will be. But we can manage, me and the missus and the little girl; we're quite happy.

'Sometimes you touch, sometimes you don't, you see. That's how it runs. There's an old lady she's got some old copper geysers. I tried to buy them Tuesday but I failed to buy them. They told me to call back, it was still no good, got to wait again. That's how you get it, you see, up and down, up and down. To know which is the good, which is the bad.

'I live a lot decenter than some of these housewives. I goes around some of these houses – oh Christ – they ain't fit for a dog to live in. Well my caravan it's fitting for the Queen to come and live in.

'I'll admit some of us goes about dirty looking, but our bodies is always clean. We are free from any vermin or anything like that and we're very healthy. And it's very rare you see us travelling folk ill unless it's a natural illness like, but everything else we're very fit.

'I reckon it's a very rude word, Gypsy. I don't mind anybody calling me a Gypsy if I can't hear it. But if I'm in company or out in a pub having a drink and anyone calls me a Gypsy, I go ashamed.

'But I'd never live in a house. I think if I lived in a house it would be no good to me 'cos it's too close, I like the open air, that's what I like about it. And I think if I went in a house I wouldn't stay there a minute. I've had chances to go in but I couldn't.

'Instead I've travelled all over the world: Scotland, London, everywhere, Ireland. But now we've ended up here, and there it is, we're hop-picking you know.

'I don't want to be on a permanent site. If I was on a permanent site, with a trailer it's just the same as a house. I like travelling. I like a month in one place but after that I like to go again, I get sick of the same place. That's why I don't like it. I wouldn't like to settle down.

'Of course you've got to think about the children, haven't you, schooling and that. I think I will settle down in a caravan for a bit when me daughter gets older, about three or four months in one place if I can, but not to settle really, you know, all the time.

'It is boring sometimes for me; I'd love to read and write. If I'd have knowed how I'd love to have gone to school. Me mother and father could read and write but not me. Me Grandma reared me up like, and she was a real Gypsy, you know, she used to travel about. But she didn't believe in sending babies to school, you know.

'I've never voted. We've been asked scores of times to vote, but we never believe in it. I mean it's no good the likes of one of us going in to try and vote 'cos we can't. We're no scholars, I mean, we can't read or write. There's very few of us scholars.

'And, I mean, it would be no good we going in and voting for one company, one lot of Government, if it was Labour, Liberal, whatever it was, we shouldn't understand it, you see. There's nobody for the Travellers.'

Mr Johnny Sheridan

'It's harder for a Traveller to be inside than a Gorjio.'

A derelict waste in the industrial Midlands. Twenty caravans scattered as if washed up on a shore from which the tide has departed. A winding canal at one side of the area, marshy land below it. Caravans, lorries, dismembered cars, washing on makeshift poles, piles of tree branches for burning.

Two Gypsy girls pass, carrying a dustbin between them. They dump it in a ditch, then depart. A man sitting outside a caravan sorting out something. A few open fires burning. In the depths of the canal old iron lies rusting. Beyond it all a huge factory with shunting chugging noises coming from it, smoke pouring out of its chimneys. And you can see how all around the trees have been hacked about by people in search of firewood. Two Travellers are approaching with a pram along the canal bank. The pram falls over. They right it and continue towards me. A girl scooping up water from the canal in a plastic bowl. Two Travellers who are peering into the canal perhaps to see if there's anything of value.

A man at the local school had told me, 'The land that the Gypsies camp on is derelict, an unsightly land, it's been derelict for ages and it shouldn't have been allowed to be so. This is exploited country. It's fucked-up. It's the most fucked-up countryside in the world.'

There are hundreds of Gypsies in the area. This Gypsy stopping place is one of many similar to it. Towards the back of the caravans stopped here stands the caravan of Mr John Sheridan. It is kept spotless. John's living comes mainly from laying tarmacadam drives for Gorjios. He invites me in and we get talking.

He refers to his attractive tiny wife as 'little un' or sometimes 'short un'. He has short crew-cut hair and is a broadly built man in his twenties who, on the night I call at his caravan, is wearing a grey shirt with rainbow-coloured slashes let into its sides. As we speak he snatches the cigarette from his wife's hand, just as she is about to smoke it. 'Don't do that,' she cries. But I can see that it is a gentle teasing way that they have of expressing the relationship between them. He asks me if I'd like tea and says to her, 'Fill the kettle.'

The pretty girl says, 'Go and do it yourself.'

A fierce row develops. At length their friend says, 'All right, I'll do it, to settle the problem," and goes out to fill the kettle. They are full of these rivalries, and in them seem to express something loving and compassionate to each other.

Later we go out for a drink and as we drive in his lorry, she's constantly watchful, warning him when he's likely to run into something, warning him, 'There's a car there coming, Johnny . . .'

As we are talking, she listens, saucy-eyed, her bright eyes rimmed with black mascara, and tosses her blonde hair, looking at herself and opening her mouth to look into its pink interior in one of the mirrors that line the caravan.

I ask him, 'Would you like your children to grow up as Travellers?'

'Oh yes, it's a life that you was brought up to, we do it the whole time, you know. We'd never settle down in a house.'

'What's the longest you've ever stopped your caravan in one spot?'

'The longest was twelve months. In Wolverhampton.'

'I believe that one trouble Gypsies face is getting hold of water? Have you ever had trouble getting water?'

'Yes. We've been refused from garages and been refused from houses. We've had to drive miles and miles to get water. Some places they'll charge us five shillings a churn for water, see what I mean, different places. Some garages will if you put petrol in first, then they'll probably oblige you to give you water. Sometimes they won't give it to you.

'Every time we go, we hear, "The police have told us and warned us not to give any water." The police is doing all this. The police is telling the people in the houses not to give us water. Why the police is doing this, I don't know. And the police warns them all. When you go to buy in a shop you have to show your money and they're watching you all the time. I can't understand these policemen.'

Afterwards, in the pub, the other Travellers are buying them drinks because a relative of theirs has lost a child. There's talk that they're all going to pull out in the morning to go up to the funeral.

'Are you with John?' they're asking me. 'Here's a drink for you.' And rums and pints of bitter are being handed around in great numbers.

Johnny is a popular man. A member of a tightly knit extended family that, left to itself, would always, so you'd think, support him. They were not left to themselves. Johnny Sheridan was falsely accused, falsely imprisoned, humiliated, suffered alone in prison the pain of learning that his family were destitute, tried to kill himself by swallowing razor blades; was given cotton wool to eat and, in solitary confinement, given the 'freeze' treatment. When six months of hell were over and he was finally released, was given recompense that was a farce.

None of this would have happened, so I believe, if he were not a Gypsy. As it was, his lot was injustice – injustice of a particularly blatant kind. He had professional friends and he was lucky in this. If he had not, like many another Gypsy, he might be falsely in prison yet.

What happened was that on the evening of Friday, 14 February 1969, two policemen in a police car 'keeping observation' on a van parked by the road, saw two men come round the rear of some buildings carrying a gas boiler and some piping. They put these things into the van – later events disclosed their value as about £5 as scrap. They had been taken from a derelict building.

The policemen claimed that they had got a close view of both men. They drove up in their car and got out to question the men. One of them ran away, and was chased by PC Brown. The other man, Mr Felix Doran, was arrested.

Two days later the two policemen together with a sergeant went to a stopping place of the Gypsies and they got some information from the first man, Mr Felix Doran, now out on bail. While they were talking to him, Johnny Sheridan went past. He was immediately claimed by the two policemen to be the man who had run away.

And so Johnny Sheridan was arrested and the sergeant told him that the two policemen identified him as the second man concerned in the theft of metal. Johnny replied that he didn't deal in metal.

Later at the police station, an ignition key was claimed to have been 'found' on him which fitted the lock of the rear door of the van. Sheridan couldn't understand how this key had come to be in his pocket. He was charged and he then said, 'Honest to God, it wasn't me, sir. I never deal in metal, sir.'

Johnny explained it to me like this, 'I told the police, "You've got the wrong bloke." I knew they had me for the wrong bloke. So I told them about this, they wouldn't listen. "Oh," they said, "you're the fellow, you'll do for him."

'They already had Felix Doran there, the other fellow inside the cell he told the police, "What you brought him in for, you've got the wrong bloke there."

'He said, "Oh never mind about that, he'll do, we'll accuse him of the same thing."

'So they had me a week on remand. I had witnesses where I was at the time of the theft. I had six witnesses altogether. They wouldn't listen to me. Two policemen swore blind I was the man. That was it. They took my coat, shoes and tie off me and left me in a cell. About an hour later three policemen came in. One of them said, "These officers recognised you in connection with the larceny of some metal."

'I said, "Are you rightly sure what you're talking about? You're making a very big mistake here. You must have me for someone else. You want to get your eyes seen to. You must be going blind."

'One of them said, "You'll do well enough for now."

'And they went out.

'Half an hour later they gave me back my shoes and brought me upstairs to the CID. They started questioning me about this stuff and I told them that I knew nothing at all about it, I was innocent. I said, "There are more blokes at that camp similar to me. You want to go back there and make sure." They wouldn't listen to me.

'They had some tea brought in and tried to sweeten me up. They said, "Plead guilty to it and it will be O.K. You've got nothing at all to worry about. Plead guilty and you'll be out of court in the morning."

'I said, "I'm not stupid or daft. I'm innocent. I know nothing at all about it."

'Then they took me back to the cell and locked me up.'

Johnny's alibi was not believed. In court, Mr Felix Doran pleaded guilty to the theft of this almost worthless scrap from a derelict building, and the jury appeared to believe Johnny was the man who had been with him.

'It's harder for a Traveller to be inside than a Gorjio. Gorjios have friends inside but a Traveller can't get outside to where his friends are. I think it's twice as hard for a Traveller to be inside any time. Well, a Traveller, like, he hasn't got things he can read and write, like the Gorjios. I couldn't write, you know, to the wife. And this makes you feel very lonely.

'It is lonely especially when a Traveller's been free all his life and is put within four walls, it's miserable. This was the first time I've been inside four walls. I've never lived in a house before, and it was very bad. Enough to drive you mad to be quite honest.

'There's another difficulty I think: the Traveller likes to be his own boss. Whereas in prison everybody's bossing you around. I mean you're locked up all the time. You have to do what you're told, and if you don't do what you're told it's bread and water, you know.'

Subsequently the solicitors appearing for Johnny, and Johnny's relations, continued to reiterate his claim that he was falsely in gaol.

And they took a statement from Mr Felix Doran saying that it wasn't Johnny who was with him. It was a man called Mr Patrick Purcell.

'They transferred me from Shrewsbury to Walton prison in Liverpool. Then I felt terrible. Very sad. So I swallowed a packet of razor blades.

'They gave me some cotton wool and some porridge to eat. Then they locked me in a cell alone, stripped naked with just one blanket on me for three days. That was what they did when I ... tried to kill myself .... They gave me this cotton wool to eat and stuff, you know, to get the blades out. They had me there for two weeks. Then they had me back to Shrewsbury.

'Soon after that the court case come up.

'The way I felt that when I went to prison if they just turned round to get a gun to shoot me it would have been better. I'd sooner be dead than be in there. It was just like a nightmare.'

The next thing that happened was, one day, in a very battered state, his face covered with blood, Mr Patrick 'Paddywhack' Purcell, the man who was really guilty, appeared in the office of Ivan Geffen, Johnny's solicitor. Looking out of the window, Mr Geffen saw a crowd of members of Johnny's family standing outside. Mr Purcell described the incident and said that he was the man who had been with Felix Doran, had taken the stuff, and who had run away and it wasn't Johnny Sheridan, who had nothing whatever to do with it.

Mr Geffen urged Mr Purcell to go to the police, and he did. A detective sergeant made this report, 'With regard to the statement made by Purcell, I have discussed it with PC Brown and the facts mentioned in it appear to be unusually accurate. The only mistake made by Purcell is in saying that the tall policeman, PC Denant, went after him when in fact it was Brown. The description of the ground over which this took place is remarkably accurate.'

Once again there were long delays, and then, at last, the police decided to charge Purcell and he finally appeared before the Justice. He pleaded guilty and he was sentenced.

Months had passed since the police first heard of Mr Purcell's confession. During all this time Mr Johnny Sheridan remained, an innocent man, in gaol.

They said that perhaps there was a third man at the place of the crime (no one had ever suggested this before). Perhaps Johnny was him.

There were further delays. Finally Johnny's case came up for appeal. And the police *still* maintained that he was guilty.

The man who ran the appeal, Lord Justice Phillimore, denounced them all:

'Today, when Sheridan's appeal comes before this court, we have Counsel for the prosecution saying that he is instructed to help the court, but in fact maintaining that Sheridan was properly convicted.

'This court thinks that this attitude on the part of the prosecution is utterly wrong. And we think that a proper attitude on the part of those responsible for the prosecution should have been able to recognise this months ago and to have been anxious that this matter should have been put right and that any question of injustice should have been avoided. Not a bit. That is not what has happened ...

'Mistakes are inevitably made from time to time, but when it is appreciated that there is a risk of a mistake being made then every attempt should be made to put it right, not to preserve the error. That's what has happened here.

'This court is quite satisfied that this conviction is, to say the least, unsafe and unsatisfactory and this man ought to be released immediately.'

'What did you think the first day you got out of prison?'

'I thought I was in a different world, I thought I was walking on air. I just couldn't believe it.'

'Was your trailer where you expected it?'

'No, it was in a different place, being moved on the whole time. While I was in prison the wife had to pay £2 each time to get me caravan moved on. And all me tools I had to go to work with, those had all gone. She had to sell them. She had to sell a £500 caravan for £50. The day of the court, my wife went to court, so I'd know where to come back to the caravan. I had no money. Me money was all spent. I'd nothing. They give me money to go to the Assistance, but we never go to draw any. We never go to the Assistance. We like to fend for ourselves.'

Though Mr Sheridan was now at last set free, no effort had been made to compensate him for his six months inside.

Extract from a letter from his solicitor, Ivan E. Geffen, to the Secretary of State, dated 28 November 1969:

... I have been asked to approach you for compensation for Mr Sheridan for the loss of his liberty. In this context I draw to your attention the fact that the actual offender, when he appeared at Aldridge Magistrates Court on October 13th, was sentenced to a small monetary fine and costs totalling together less than £26. While the innocent Mr Sheridan's records are different. The discrepancy between the punishment imposed on the two men is startling.

Nothing seems to have come of this letter, or of another, or of a third.

Extract from a letter from Mr Geffen, this time to the Home Secretary:

... My client is a working man, who was deprived of his liberty for over six months, as a result of a wrongful conviction. Within days of his conviction at Stafford Quarter Sessions, a confession signed by the actual wrongdoer was forwarded to the Registrar of the Court of Appeal (Criminal Division). Despite this, bail was refused to my client, pending the hearing of his appeal and when the matter actually came before the Court of Appeal, the prosecution were sharply censored by the court for the attitude it had taken.

While he was in custody, my client not merely suffered the loss of his liberty; he was also very much upset by the hardship endured by his family. Mrs Sheridan is unable to read or write, and instead of receiving help from the offices of the Ministry of Health and Social Security, she was sent from one to another and throughout the period of her husband's imprisonment she was able once only to obtain any assistance. This amounted to £6.

To put it bluntly the treatment of this man has been scandalous, and I trust that you will now intervene personally to ensure that something is done to right the wrong done to him and his family.

Finally, after yet another letter, it was agreed that Johnny should be paid. But the sum offered, £750, was in fact less than he would have earned if he'd stayed at liberty. There was no recompense for the indignities he'd suffered or for his loss of liberty; or for the fact that his wife had had to sell most of his possessions for a pittance.

Extract from a letter from Mr Geffen to the Home Secretary, 30 December 1970:

I have seen my client today. His financial position is such that although the amount which you offer represents the exercise of power over right, he has no alternative but to accept the sum of £750.

Johnny blames some of all this on the fact that he is illiterate.

'It helps to be a scholar, it helps to be a scholar very much.'

I blame it on the fact that he is a Gypsy and that justice in the traditional British sense is not yet available for Gypsies.

Part III

Travellers in Bender Tents and a Varda

I wanted to meet some of those Travellers that live in the traditional Gypsy way – either in bender tents or in horse-drawn caravans.

The tents are made by bending over branches whose ends have been stuck into the ground, tying the tops, and placing over the framework a covering of tarpaulin, sacks, or clothes and other materials. Inside, there is usually a home-made stove and straw to sleep on. Between one and two thousand people live like this in Britain.

The horse-drawn varda was the typical Gypsy home until recently, but now it is not used by more than a few hundred Gypsies.

Most of the British Gypsies in both these types of homes are in Scotland or Ireland. Bewildered by our civilisation which is so much more complicated than theirs, the bender tent dwellers are the hardest of all Gypsies to reach. They are, perhaps understandably, hostile to Gorjios, whom, in the areas of Perthshire and Lanarkshire where I travelled, they refer to as 'Country Handles', or just 'Handles' for short.

I think it would not be exaggerating to say that there is a quality of terror and dread present in their lives which it is difficult for those of us who sleep in beds to understand.

A bender tent is a vulnerable place to live even in the summertime, amidst a hostile community. In winter, when the wild Scottish winds sweep across the moors, it is doubly so.

I count myself fortunate that three of them agreed to speak with me.

The Gypsies who live in tents are the only Gypsies in this book whose names I have changed.

I had a reason for doing this.

Mr Russell Bilton

'I joined the housing list, but never got no word back from them.'

A large tent made of green tarpaulin stands amid the Scottish scrub. There is a home-made stove at one end and a hole has been made near the top of the tent for the chimney of the stove. The stove is made from an oilcan which has had a hole made in the top with a little lid that can be pulled on or off, and a square hole made near the bottom of it for the draught to go in. The floor of the tent is cold earth over which some form of carpeting has been placed which has now become the same colour and consistency as the earth.

In this tent live Mr Russell Bilton and his family. They have a double bed at one end, and boxes and chairs round the stove at the other.

They pay a pound a week for the right to live amidst the scrub. I'm shown the way there by a weak torch held by one of the boys. A wild-looking man sits behind the stove-pipe.

The earth around the place is littered with roots and branches and a scrub of trees. Behind the stove is a small corrugated iron coop containing puppies. There's a large telly on a box with a Benny Hill programme playing.

Mr Bilton, unshaven, sits on the bed and is the most dispirited of any Traveller I have met so far.

He has three children. One of them is barefooted, on this cold night, on the cold earth.

Mr Bilton: 'All the land's tooken over by the pylons and all, you know, big lairds, you know.

'If you stop nowadays, you might be there for five minutes when a policeman comes round and just puts you in the road right away. You have to go, if you don't go you'd be pulled up. And if you're not fined you'd be tooked to gaol.

'A few years ago they picked us up four times for being just camping at the same place. And fined a pound each time. They kept us in this cell from ten o'clock at night to two o'clock next day. And then they took us to court. We had nothing to eat or drink while we were inside. Just one cup of tea about eleven o'clock next day.

'Here we're being left alone though. There's not much work though, only a bit of potato-picking you get here.'

'Do you have trouble claiming from the Social Security?'

'No, they're all right.'

'Some Travellers have been saying that they think travelling will be finished soon in Scotland.'

'Well, it's coming that way now, it's dying out.'

'What do you feel about that?'

'In one way it is sad.'

'But in another way would you wish to be in a house?'

'Oh yes.'

'Have you actually joined the housing list anywhere?'

'Well, I joined the housing list, but never got no word back from them.'

'Were they discriminating against you?'

'Well, I think so. They don't want much Travellers around – some parts don't want Travellers to mix up with the local people, you know what I mean. But down South Scotland here they're not quite so bad, up North they're very particular who they take on, you know, and who they give houses to. Down South here they're not quite so bad.'

'Have you got happy memories from the past?'

'Well, at the berry-time in Blairgowrie used to be the happiest times. There used to be a lot of caelis, pipe music, 'cordion, guitars, everything. And plenty of dealing: car-dealing, horse-dealing and all this carry on.

'A lot of the old Travellers is dying out you know. This travelling life is getting finished. Well, in a few years' time I think it will all be finished.'

Mr William Merchison

'I prefer a tent to a house.'

A simple bender tent. The entrance is three feet high with a striped bit of tarpaulin to go over it. The tent is about ten feet long and at its highest is about four feet six inches.

Inside it is dark but very snug. There is what appears to be straw at one end which is then covered with blankets on which Mr Merchison sleeps. The tent is at the side of a large field. He says that he has problems from water since he's under a high bank and when it rains the water comes down 'like a burn'.

Mr Merchison is sitting by a home-made stove with a friend in the dark warmth of the interior.

'My father got lifted you see. Well my mother was due for me. They had nowhere to go and she had nowhere to go – we were in just an open wilderness. And my mother went over for my Granny for to make a bed. So about one o'clock in the morning my mother took bad and she gave birth to me. So the next morning we were at the hotel grounds in Malaig and a lady came down you see, and she saw my mother lying there. And she says to my Granny, "She's got to go. She's got to move out of here." "Sorry," she says, "she can't go, my daughter she's given birth to a baby." "Oh my goodness," she says. "Whereabouts?" So she saw the child. And they took my mother and they moved her into a house – it was an old house but she give her blankets and so forth to comfort me and, well, for ten days they kept my mother there till she was fit and well to go on the road again. And she gave my mother five pounds, she said, "That'll get something for the children and the baby and Granny." My father was in gaol. He was lifted. He'd been fined a half a crown. But a half-crown was as hard to get as what was a pound today. So they went to the police station and paid this half-crown and got him out. And I suppose, my father, he was the boss and he demanded a pound for drink. So he got the pound for drink. And he went off to get a cover so we could have another tent.

'During the time he'd been away, my mother and my Granny

couldn't carry the other cover, so they dumped it. It was too heavy to carry.

'They left it where they could find it. But when they went back it wasn't there; it wasn't there. It was a very tragic time, there's no doubt, yes. And my father was tooken away through drink. Just a quarrel you know through the drink. He just got lifted.'

'What has been the best time of your life?'

'The happiest times I recall were down picking the berries. Lots of Travellers around. Have a sing-song, a dance and so forth. I used to play the pipes then, but not now because my chest's away.

'I prefer a tent to a house. With a house it can be very, very draughty. And damp. The old houses up here, they're very damp, these old houses, they're getting very old and they're usually damp. Oh yes. But in a tent – I mean you stay there with the fresh air all the time, all the time. I mean during the frosty weather I always keep an extra fire on in the tent. Keep plenty of heat. You can't do that in a house.

'I been always in a tent. I wouldn't mind a trailer. It would be all right if you could afford to get one. Yes, but I mean to say to buy one just now, they're too dear. I had an old one here last year, but that was very old, it was damp. I just broke it up.

'This is much more cosy actually than a varda which can be very damp. And if the roof goes they get very damp, once they get wood rot.'

'To put up a bough tent like this takes, oh, a couple of hours starting from scratch. From cutting them, well you get boughs from round about, I mean, if you got to travel for your boughs that'll take you more time. But to get it up when you've got the boughs, roughly an hour to stick 'em up.

'And then you make the stove yourself. Just use a chisel and hammer, that is all we use.

'I have no horse, now. If I want to move, well you can go on a bus, but there's usually somebody to shift us around, somebody with a car.

'The things I can't take like that bit of furniture there, I just leave it behind.

'We tie the boughs together with string. Tie 'em round with string, put the canvas over the top and stones round the bottom to weight it down. Then it will never shift.

'A friend of mine, he's a gentleman and he took a copy of one of these tents and he made a – what you'd call a rose byre, and he built one like this and he planted roses up each stick and all grew up into an arbour. In the summertime he can have his tea outside in the summer and smell roses, beautiful. And he just uses it as a summer-house. It's lovely, you know, when you see the roses all growing about.

'When I lost my wife, I found it hard to start with. To keep the boys – tea and bread and cheese is no use for boys, you got to get soups and that for 'em. You've got to have a lot to keep them going.

'What's the farthest I've travelled? Oh well, I've been all over. I've been in England. Been in Inverness, Aberdeenshire, up at Ayrshire, Edinburgh. I've been all over.

'Well, I like Perthshire the very best. Perthshire's a great place, I think. Always come back, yes. I like a bit of fishing and there's some nice fishing in Perthshire.'

'Do you think that travelling will go on or come to an end?'

'Oh, I think it's coming to an end. Like, the Traveller people in the glens, they're still making baskets, tinware, and that. But you don't see 'em coming around here with 'em any more because they're all getting off the road into houses. You miss them coming around with their baskets, tinware, and that.'

'Would you be sorry yourself to see the young ones giving up the old Traveller's traditions?'

'Well, not in a way, because I mean there's nothing on the road no more, the road is finished.'

Mrs Ethel Anderson

'My husband, he's a great go-ahead.'

I am leaving Coatbridge in Lanarkshire – the scene, shortly after I was there, of the tragic triple death of three members of the same Gypsy family, two burned to death in a tent, one run over. Just before a railway bridge I turn right along a road past a factory. Then along a muddy track, past a desolate-looking farm, across a dank moor whose edges are rimmed with the distant view of evening-sodden rain-washed suburbia. Just as I'm beginning to think I must have taken the wrong turning, I see them. A collection of bender tents, huddled like huge stones together. Horses and ponies standing around, munching hay.

Mrs Anderson stands amid the mud at the door of her bender tent. She's a short woman, nicely dressed like a Gorjio.

There is hay on the ground that the horses are eating, and hazy smoke rising from the chimneys of the tents. The ground is sodden, churned-up mud, rank grass, stretching away to where, amid even deeper bogs, vast machines are constantly moving, emitting an ugly droning sound.

'Yes, they're pumping it. They're pumping water out of it. They say, so they can build more houses there. They pump the whole night through,' says Mrs Anderson. 'Keeps me awake.'

I asked whether she would ever want to live in a house or whether the travelling way of life was valuable to her.

'He'll never give it up! Mr Anderson! He'll no give it up. I would but he won't.'

'He loves it, does he?'

'Ay, it's his life. He's been used to that. I came out of a house, you know, I'm not a Traveller. I came out of a house. I'm just like you, you know. I'm a Country Handle. I find it a hard life this, right enough. I'd rather be in a house, having all your comforts and all, you know. I find it hard. But they don't seem to. They don't seem to notice it. I thought I would have got my man away from this life but I could nae manage it. I tried but it was impossible. But he's a good husband 'cos he's a good worker and can earn money. We could have nothing tonight and he'd get to work and we'd have a hundred pounds tomorrow morning.

'He's good at selling horses and buying them and dealing, you know. He doesn't go out ragging nor skiving scrap. He hasn't done that for a couple of years now. Just the horses he works with and I would rather have him out working with the horses. I don't like a man going out with the rags and scrap and that. I say it's too poor a looking thing that. I say I'd rather have him work his living with the horses. It's much better and he's richer since he got with the horses.

'He goes to the sales and he buys horses and then he sells them. Sometimes I go with him and sometimes I don't. If it's very early in the morning I don't go with him. I like to stay in bed in the morning, especially wintertime, I don't mind getting up in the summertime. Often my man's away at four o'clock in the morning, he's up and lifted with his self while there I lie still in my bed. My husband, he's a great go-ahead. But that way he gets the bargains. Oh he goes all over the place. He gets as quick as a man in a motor. Like he was thumbing lifts and things and getting in buses. He goes quick but he canna drive a motor. If my man could drive a motor he would have a motor but he can't drive one. So he has to go on the buses and things, and gets lifts with friends and that. Then he brings them back here. See he's run up a fence here, by the tents. If he gets the customers he brings them here then they get a good look . . .

'Aye, he would nae go into a house, and sometimes when we're stopping in the tent in the winter nights I says, "Now what would be nicer," I say to him, "a nice house, that's where you could have your door shut, sittin' with your slippers on and what have you, TV and bairns." But he will nae have it.'

'Do you and he have children?'

'I had two children but I lost them. That's why I'd like to be in a house. Maybe in a house I would nae have lost 'em. Travellers are good people. Travellers are happy people and very happy. Some of them are always fighting with one another, but I never bother with the Travellers, it seems to be the parents that fight with one another and not the children. That's funny isn't it. God knows why they do it. Maybe they're jealous.'

'Jealous of what? Jealous about each other's women?'

'No, jealous of each other getting on. Going daft 'cos my man is doing better than them. That sends them jumpin' mad . . . but thank God that's going away. Travellers aren't really bad.'

Mrs Anderson said that they were all very worried because the owner of the farm where they had put their tent before they came here was claiming that they had paid no rent, although they had.

'You see, my man has no record. He didn't get a receipt. We were there for about three year and the police never bothered us. Then all these other Travellers came in and they made a mess. They had big lorries and motors and they stirred up muck over the ground. And after that we all got shifted.

'You see we've only got horses and carts, you know – they don't turn up the ground. But that other lot – they made it like muck up there. They did nae care. No they did nae bother.

'The farmer says he never got any money from us. I don't know how it'll go – they've to go on the 16th of this month to court.'

'Have they got a solicitor?'

'No. There were others, brothers – they got lifted. They were told to be off the ground at twelve o'clock and they were told to be in the court at twelve o'clock. So how could they be in the court at twelve o'clock and off the ground at twelve o'clock? They could nae be. No man's an invisible man could be in two places at once. I don't know what they'll do about this, I told them that. They should have told the police that, "Do you think I'm an invisible man or something? Being down in court and being off the road?" It was either stay on the ground and go to the court or don't go to court and get off the ground. But they never went to court – they got off the ground, you see. It was put back to the High Court, you see. So I don't know how they'll get on – they're quite worried about it, seeing that it's winter and the mother so old now. She takes bad turns and all like, she's too old for just travelling about the country, isn't she? And then the boys, the boys . . . they shifted and then they got lifted . . . if they had nae shifted . . . then . . . they maybe would nae have got lifted . . .'

As I drive away from the little camp I see the tower-blocks of Coatbridge standing up sheer against the evening sky. Smoke twists into the sky above the little bender tents.

In talking to Mrs Ethel Anderson I have felt a sense of induced confusion greater, I think, than that I have found in anyone else I ever talked to.

Mr Ezra Price

'I would never eat from a tin.'

As I approach I see him standing by a deserted canal washing out a bowl, his back to me, with that apart, turned-away quality which so many Travellers have when they see Gorjios. Beside him sits a dog which is growling at me.

I go closer to him and introduce myself.

Behind him I can see his home – an old horse-drawn varda, drawn up delicately under the trees. Mr Price evidently comes from more resilient stock than the tent-dwelling Gypsies.

Mr Price: 'Gorjios are all poisoned now. Their minds are poisoned. I don't know what has happened to you in the last twenty-five years but things have got bad, the country has got bad.'

'You seem a happy man,' I said to him.

'Yes, I am happy. I've got a philosophy of life but it's the same philosophy that anyone should have who's not round the bend. Ninety-nine per cent of the country now are round the bend. The Gorjios, can't they see what's happening? Their own children are turning against them.

'And they're poisoning themselves. From the tins. I've never eaten from a tin, no, never once in my life. A cooking pot like this is the best, enough to put a couple of hares, a couple of rabbits in them. Why we had such a huge pot is so we can feed five or six people and the dogs as well. Say you had a couple of dogs, you want to let them have it since they gets them, gets them down to work at catching it.

'And the tenderest thing in the world is a hedgehog.

'Not in the summer when they've been running. They're no good then, just like dish water. No, when they're really good is in the winter when they've been asleep, laid up, that's when they're really good and tasty.

'There was a man camping, he was an earl, and I took him over some hedgehog one day, not knowing he was an earl, and he thought it was so delicious that he paid thirty pounds for a pair of dogs that I had trained to catch hedgehogs.

'It's not hard to train those dogs – you have to know where the hedgehogs go, no good training them to go for the hedgehogs that's on the road, you have to know where they are.

'We've been here for eighteen years, we have, sir, with a bit of land that a councillor gave me. He's not on the council any more. There's many has tried to move us, the Health men, and other Gorjios, they tried to poison my chickens and my horses and my dogs. And they used force on me, not in direct ways but in all sorts of indirect ways. Why can't you let us be?

'Like it says in the Bible, the poison that's in you, it'll just poison you yourselves.

'We lost one of us Travellers a couple of weeks ago, she was an old lady, one hundred and seven.

'Of an afternoon I go to get my living for there's no work around, there hasn't been factory work for some years. I do a bit of knife-grinding, that sort of thing.

'I'd sooner get a couple of swedes from the field and a few potatoes and boil 'em up into a stew, throw a bit of bacon in. The food that's around today is useless. The bread goes mouldy within twelve hours; the bacon, at one time when you bought the bacon you used to be able to hang it up for six months and it would still be good whereas now it goes bad within a day.'

I asked him whether he would like to go back on the roads.

He said, 'I am on the road.' And he said that he would like to travel farther, but he hadn't a horse right now and the shafts were broken.

'There's not many left in the old horse-drawn vardas.'

After he'd finished cleaning the cooking pot we went back to his caravan, an old barrel-topped varda, beautifully carved, with wonderful wooden horses on the front, festoons of grapes along the sides and tiny little high windows at the back.

'Nettles is good, nettles is very good for you, very good for the blood. And dandelions also, they're very good for you. Well, soon the winter will be here.'

When I asked him whether he'd ever lived in a house, he said, 'No, never been in a house, except to go with a Gorjio woman, and I've been with one or two of them I can tell you.'

Part IV

Travellers in Kers

Gypsies in houses: it is impossible to form an accurate picture of their numbers, but most guesses say that there is a Traveller in a house for every one in a caravan or tent.

The Travellers in the section that follows vary between those who are pleased to be in a house and those who would like to be back on the road.

Their houses are alike in one thing; they are crammed with the same ornaments, cut-glass, ornamental china, family portraits, lustre, candlewick, frilly vinyl curtains, that deck Gypsy caravans.

There are other similarities: children and relatives gust through in large numbers; often there is a fire smouldering outside in the garden; sometimes there is a trailer in the garden in which the Travellers sleep, only using the house by day.

Mr Jimmy Penfold

'Sometimes I want to drive and drive . . . I'm getting Gorjified . . .'

Mr Jimmy Penfold lives with his wife and family in a terrace house in Battersea, London. Like most Gypsy houses it retains many of the exotic features of a caravan. Mr Penfold lives mainly through his trade of electrician, but he is also a craftsman and has made many vardas. He was president of the Gypsy Council, and is now its treasurer.

He says he would go on the road again tomorrow if only life for Gypsies could return to the way he remembers it between the wars. He's bought a patch of land and is fighting for the right to put his caravan on it and once more live there.

Still a popular figure at Gypsy gatherings like Epsom, he has none the less become conscious of the widening gap between him and those Gypsies who are still on the road. As he says, 'I'm becoming Gorjified.

'The Gypsy philosophy is to live. Nothing else matters. The simple reason is, we understand that during a period of seventy or eighty years, give or take a few years, you must learn to enjoy every minute of it.

'Don't become clots, we say, like the Gorjios, get up at eight, work till five, watch television till ten, go to bed, get up at eight, back to work till five. Their clocks is what they serve, the Gorjios, they're automatons; well our people, we don't behave like that. We get up when we feel like it, we eat and drink when we're hungry and we're thirsty and we do what we want.

'We work to live rather than live to work. This is it. I remember as a boy talking to my grandparents, and they said, "Son, don't worry about getting an education, see, even the ignorant have got to be kept." I used to ask my Gran, "Well, what d'you mean, Gran?" She said, "You take the mental people, son. There they are in mental homes, we keep them, they don't keep us." And this is true.

'However, my children are having an education.

'I came to live in a house a few years back and I hate every minute of it, every second I live in a house. Why? Because I'm becoming like the Gorjio.

'We moved into a house because things were so bad on the road. We had twenty-seven summonses in one week for obstruction, and other offences, and I decided to come into London and get a house, which I did. And I decided to give my children the advantage of an education, even though I never done a day's schooling.

'I've earned good money when I've been on the road; now I'm being Gorjified. I don't like it, not a bit. Sometimes I dream of getting up in the morning, and just drive and drive until I lose myself.

'When you're with your own people it's a different atmosphere. And there is a feeling among Travellers against those who move into houses. When they get talking to you they say, "Where are you stopping at?" And you say, "I'm in a house." They say, "Oh, maybe you're becoming a paki," which means an outbreed, and I say, "No, I'm still what I am."

'They say, "No, you're becoming like the Gorjios, you live and you sleep like the Gorjios, dossing down in a house." And it's partly true.

'When I'm in bed, I have to be underneath the window, I can't sleep in a closed room, the windows have got to be open summer and winter. I've got to look out at the sky and when I get up and I go to work I can't be like other people, there's no interest to me there. It's like sitting down like a lump of wood.

'When Travellers go to work it's the pleasure of the work. They enjoy what they do. The Gorjios don't.

'I make vardas, don't I? Yes, I make caravans. Grandfather told me how to cut a piece of cosh, and it sticks, you never forget it. I teach my boys now. Jim's very interested, he sits down and chips a piece of cosh out; but it's dying, the art is dying fast and I don't know whether my boy will be like me and make vardas too.

'Although we live in a house we never let the children forget that they're still Romanies.

'This part of Battersea has got a large number of Gypsies living here. Some years ago when we was children there was about fourteen Yards in Battersea. We'd shift from one Yard to another. There was Builder's Yard, Cooper's Yard, Old Jack Marney's Yard in Wandsworth, Johnny Hilden's Yard in Wandsworth – there was quite a few.

'On Sullivan's Yard there was perhaps maybe thirty wagons, not all horse-drawn, but the best part of them horse-drawn wagons, benders with sheets chucked over 'em, and they were the homes of men that couldn't afford to buy proper caravans, because it was costly enough in those days, and as for now . . .

'The proper old caravans took a long time to build. It took me four or five years to build a caravan. I can build a wagon in two months easy, full time, and build it as good as the best, but in those days, you just had what they call box wagons, that was just plain wood. Grandpa used to make them out of tea chests. We used to have to go and get all the tea chests we could and these he would put them together and then put a frame round them, carve the frame, and that's a wagon. It wasn't glamorous, but it was serviceable. If you was going to move a wagon for really long journeys, you would have to build a wagon of ash, it had to be of ash or hardwood. And we'd be weeks preparing to do a journey; you never just got up one day and travelled off. You'd grease the axle, the horse had to be shod, specially shod not just ordinary shod. You'd paint the wagon, get everything ready. Your mother would be perhaps a week beforehand washing and cleaning, everything had to be spick and span, everything had to be tied down. The kettle box had to be prepared to carry all your goods, that's the box at the back, and the hayrack, which as you know is on the back, would have to be made sure that it was firm.

'This hayrack, incidentally, it's not only used as a hayrack, it's also used as a table. When we were on the road my mother used to come out, turn one of the seats from the inside of the wagon upside down and place it on the hayrack and that would be a table and that's where we would stick the old fire kettle at the back and she would cook up over the fire and then she'd call the boys to get a bit of grub.

'The favourite way of making a living in those days was hop-picking, and fruiting. And there's a break in between some of the seasons, perhaps a week.

'Well in that week we wouldn't just sit about, we'd be busy. We'd cut clothes props out of wood, my father and brother would sit down and cut pegs, well then we'd come back to London by train, go to the market to buy plants, fetch 'em back down to Kent or wherever we was at and sell them and earn a living that way. Also, we'd go totting, rag-and-boning, iron-calling. In the later days when car men come along and motors come along, it's become a lot different than it was in those days.

'Also for a living we used to go duckering. Going door-knocking and also from the tent or from a wagon. We had a tent on Hampstead Heath one year when Granny duckered, but if none of us had a tent it was done in the wagon and you'd have your wagon painted up so they'd know what it's supposed to be.

'People used to come up to our wagon and then Granny would tell the boys to shoot off out of it. We knew that when she said it that we had to get out at once.'

I asked Mr Penfold what he would recommend to a Gorjio girl who was thinking of marrying a Gypsy boy.

'Well,' said Jimmy, 'if a Gorjio girl were to marry a Gypsy boy, the first food she'd have to learn to cook is a jogray – that's a stew. It's tinned soup, Oxo, bacon, sausages, a bit of meat, plenty of onions, carrots, etc. All together, in a stew.

'The next thing the Gorjio girl would have to learn is how to cook when you're on the drom; she'd have to learn to be able to cook a hotchi – a hedgehog. When you get your hedgehog to kill it, first you got to get him open and that ain't no easy thing so you stroke him until his head comes out and you stash him on the nook – you knock him out on the nose. You just stun him, you ain't killed him, you stun him. So what you have to do is kill him while he's alive. Now for the killing you got to cut him off at the top of his head right the way round to his tail, and then you put your fingers over the top of his head slightly in underneath the belly or the gut and keep pushing and the lot comes away. Then, if you like, you nip his feet, although a hell of a lot of Travellers would leave his feet on. I like leaving the feet on meself, you never get the taste of the feet, but I think they give a bit of flavour to it. Then you roll him up into a ball, with good clay, good earth, it don't make much difference. Dig yourself a fair-size hole, put plenty of dead leaf on it and put yourself a good fire on top.

'Cooking over an open fire is something that's not so easy as it looks or it sounds. It makes things very tasty. This is in the wood. Burn a bit of cosh, chuck a bit of green cosh on and a bit of smoke will turn up into the food and this is what gives the flavour to the food.

'Here's how you do a chuchi. When I do a chuchi, I catch him, gut him, cut his head off, skin him, then I get meself a good bit of steel, run it right through him and roast him over a fire, on a spit. And then while I'm doing that, Rose, my wife, will cook a few potatoes and a few greens, then we'll sit round a fire, and roll and cut it up just like Gorjios do.

'Another thing the Gorjio girl has to do is, realise that what their man says is law. When travelling boys become ten or twelve years old, they're like small men. Because they have to earn their own living and they can judge most anything. I teach my children how to weigh up anything, they beg and buy or sell anything. They know that when they buy something they get half of it. Anything, no matter what it is.

'When a Gorjio girl marries a travelling boy it may be strange to her at first. Whatever he says, she must. When I sit in this chair, for instance, my children and my wife run about like they were slaves. They're not really slaves but they know that this is the custom. I say, "Fetch some food." See. And it's put down in front of me and she washes my hands, washes my feet, washes my face, gets my clean underclothes, gets me shirt, and puts me shoes on, and then we go to bed, and we're just like normal people.

'This is the basic sort of thing that a Gorjio girl would have to expect.

'A Gorjio girl who married a Gypsy would have to get used to having a big family too. My grandmother brought up thirty-two children. They wasn't all hers, there was sixteen of her own, sixteen of her sister's. My mother brought up seventeen of us, two of her own, fifteen of my aunt's. And then we've had Gorjio boys that mother took as wagon boys. I can remember six Gorjio boys that I taught how to buy a bit of scrap, fed them, clothed them, and they liked the way of life and they became Pikies, they married into our family, they liked our way of life and they stayed with us. That's what we call Pikies.

'Then, there's one other thing a Gorjio girl will have to get used to. When she's married she's scrutinised. We're not like Gorjios; Gorjios just take their women as they are. But our people have always been called whores and Christ knows what. Our women, when they get married they're scrutinised, they're examined to make sure that they've stayed a virgin.

'And if a Gypsy girl doesn't carry a virgin then she's discarded from her own family because she's given away the best thing that a woman can give a man.

'If a Gorjio boy wants to go out with a Gypsy girl, and he wants a bit of sex before marriage, he can't. He can't have it. If the family got to know about it and he did try to back out of the marriage they'd kill him.

'This is what the trouble was at Appleby. There was also three or four years ago the same trouble at Epsom.

'It concerned one of the young girls. Some Gorjio boys got her into a caravan. They didn't rape her but it came pretty close. This caused friction amongst the fair people; beautiful caravans, old-style caravans turned over, smashed up – it really came to murder just for the one simple reason that a Gorjio boy took Diane.'

'Now I will tell you my views about the local authority sites. Those that I've seen are fairly good. The only thing is, it's like the Indians in Canada and America, these reservations, the Gypsies on them can't move. This is why I keep recommending that we should have transit sites as well as permanent sites, because otherwise the Gypsies are going to finish up exactly like the American Indians – a race that's finished. There'll be no more Gypsies. We'll all become Gorjios.

'For one thing, with the permanent sites, you can't keep an animal on most of them, you can't have your dogs about you, and a good Traveller has to have a few good dogs, so that, when he's got no money he can take his dog out and get him a good rabbit, cook it, and get himself a meal. You can't do that on a permanent site. You're just stuck there.

'Then, you can't have a good fire outside the trailer, ain't got nowhere to sit. And, as one Traveller put it, we was borned outside and we want to bide outside.

'Then, often, you're not allowed scrap – not a bit of scrap lying about to sort it out. And that's a big loss to a Traveller.

'Personally, myself, if I was on a site and I had my relations come to see me, I'd need a site to myself. Because there would be so many of 'em. A site would be no good for me, but a house is worse. In this house I'm in now, I've got everything a man could want: kitchen, a nice home, bathroom, hot water any time I want it, everything that a man could want, if he was a Gorjio. But I'm a Gypsy, and there we are. You just can't change it, you can't put a wild bird in a cage and expect it to live. It don't work.

'And on these local authority sites, you've now become a house on wheels. This is what it boils down to. At the one at Dartford you can leave during summer to go fruit-picking, but you still got to pay for your site which isn't cheap, I believe it's fifty bob a week. Now for that fifty bob a week you pay for your own light, you got one building where you draw your water from, you got a car bunker, that's all I can call it, just to keep your one or two things in and a place to park your lorry. That's it. The one at Dartford, well, I wouldn't live on that, not if they paid me to live on there, because the way to it like is right down the side of a mountain.

'As a matter of fact, outside the site there's more Travellers than inside; they can't get their wagons in during the winter, that's how muddy it is.

'It is essential that the Government also builds transit sites. My ideal transit site would be a fairly vast area, on say an area to allow for twenty-five caravans, and it would have permanents, that is Travellers that stay there all the time and places for fifteen Travellers in transit. You'd have to have someone to keep it a bit tidy and the ideal proprietor, then, would be like Hughie Burton. Hughie Burton is known to be the best man amongst the Travellers. He's as tough as they come. This is the sort of man you've got to have, a man that they will respect, a man that won't back down. He must be a Traveller, not a Gorjio, because Travellers will never accept Gorjios. Not as Wardens.

'Now from the very start off I was on the committee that went to the Houses of Parliament and listened to the Act that was brought up, and we was guaranteed at that meeting that we would have transit sites and a Warden who would be a Traveller or Tinker or a Romany. This was all right by me, this is what I wanted. But it ain't turned out that way. Now they've started to put Gorjios as Wardens. And not such very good Wardens and before I ever met 'em the word Gorjio did it, you know, just the word Gorjio. They have ex-coppers – well, that's a bad start.

'To a Traveller, anybody carrying a brief-case, a walking-stick, is a menace, let alone a copper, and when we used to see 'em we'd say "prastie", and the word "prastie" means "run". And that's what we used to say and that's what we used to do.

'It still carries on today, if you have somebody coming along with an umbrella or a brief-case, a hell of a load of the Travellers just won't be here because they just don't want to know, because of the Gorjios and the laws that Gorjios bring with them.'

'The important time for the Travellers are times like Epsom, the big gathering places. This year was a good Epsom, but a little less good than usual, because a lot of 'em got to hear that there would be police, security guards, and the rest of it, and a lot of 'em didn't turn up that was expected.

'At this gathering at Epsom I suppose there were some five or six hundred wagons. There was about four hundred on Epsom Downs and the other two hundred was scattered around the area because of the price they had to pay. Eight pound. Eight pound to get on to the Downs at all.

'But in spite of this there was a good turn-out. There was some of each family, the Boswells, Lees, Marleys, Jessops, Davises, Penfolds, the Gilberts . . .

'There was the usual bit of violence done this Epsom. A couple of boys, a Marley and a Davis, got violent and one dislocated the jaw. There was a bit of skirmishing about it. This is something that normally happens, but the thing is that like all Traveller boys they have a fight and straight afterwards they have a good drink. It's just a way of getting rid of the excess energy.

'The authority this time was a bit unpleasant – it was piled on a bit thick; it took a hell of a while for us to cut through it.

'And there are many Travellers there with very striking horses, dogs. Young Johnnie Hilden, he was there with the best of dogs, lurchers, that I've seen. There are only two good sets of lurchers that I know of, he's got one and Peter Copper of the New Forest has got the other.

'I had a couple of dogs with me, but they weren't class of any sort. Just a couple of dogs to keep away the Gorjios.

'Appleby Fair was also a good turn-out this year. I had a letter from one of our relations and this was a girl called Simmons. She dropped us a line and told me there was a bit of trouble up there, I don't know the full story and I haven't been travelling to find out anything about it.

'Plenty of Travellers there, plenty of trading, which is what we like anyway. Trading a good horse, a good wagon, a good dog, see what I mean, a few rings, fawnies as we call 'em. And do a good trade and have a good drink, good sing-song, a good time and all.

'This is what half the fairs are about, having fun. Because we Travellers can live a way the Gorjios can't.

'Barnet was another fair I went to this year. There was some good horses turned out there at Barnet. And one or two of the boys had some good lorries. A really flash lot, you know. The boys like to have a good lorry because it's a good front, you know. When you go to a factory wanting scrap or a job or whatever it is, it's always good to have a good moulder, a good lorry. The governor comes out and he looks at your lorry and he looks you over and he thinks to himself, Well, at least the boy's got some money in his pocket because he's got a good lorry.

'But if he sees you outside with a rough old moulder, then very likely he just don't want to know.

'As well as the English meeting places, I've travelled the Continent quite a bit. I been to the worship of St Maries de la Mer. The Continental Traveller clings more together than the English Traveller. The English Roms, for some unknown reason, they broke apart. It's only been this last five or six years that they've started to come back together again because now they've come to realise that "united we stand, divided we're going to fall".

'But the Continentals, they really stick together. Of an evening there's a bit of step-dancing, there's some good violinists, some accordion playing, the French Travellers play a lot of accordions, it's as good as a show, it's like a circus.

'Perhaps you get half drunk and another family will get half drunk and then it will sort of build up, and that small group will have a party that night. The next night, or the next day, you see another party that's got a bit merry and they have a party.'

'There are many Gypsies and Travellers now living in houses that would like to go back to the road. Last night I went to see an uncle, Uncle Arthur. Arthur Penfold. His daughter's getting married this Christmas and I asked where she's going to get married at, and what sort of ceremony she's going to have, is she going to have a Gorjio ceremony or is she going to have a Romany ceremony, and he said, "I'm going back on the tramp, I've had enough of the house."

For a man sixty-odd-year-old to come out of a house and go back on to the drom, it is significant. And there are more. I was talking to quite a few and there's a hell of a lot of them coming out of the houses.

'It's because we feel the Gorjio and the Gorjio way of life is brainwashed, is finished. They're definitely every one of them brainwashed. Gorjios work to a clock, they work all the year round to have a fortnight's holiday.'

'I long for food that's been cooked in the open.

'Living in a house you can't get what you want and how you want it.

'I can see more beauty in a blade of grass than Gorjios can in a forest. To them a forest is just a load of trees. A wood is just a wood. But to a Traveller – it can be a garden of Eden.

'The world could be a garden of Eden. The whole world. If men would only live and let live.

'There's more Gorjios becoming Gypsies than ever now. Because the Gypsy way is the right way.'

Mr and Mrs Alec Stewart

'Many tell of how in Scotland the strong came over the weak.'

Alec and Belle Stewart live in a one-storey house in Blairgowrie, in Perthshire. They are typical of the thousands of Travellers who have been forced into houses but might return to the road if times got better.

Alec is a fine and sardonic man who earned his living for much of his life as a bagpiper. Belle holds herself very erect and is beautiful. She's also a fine singer.

When I first arrived they announced, 'Here's a real Scottish welcome for you.' Then Alec marched round the room playing one of his own compositions, 'The Twa Belles', on the bagpipes. And one of the many relatives who were present came striding in with a tray full of cups of tea and haggis.

They travel in summertime, but in the winter live in a house.

Mrs Belle Stewart: 'I think it would be very tragic if ever they let the old tradition die. I mean, our customs, our traditions, our way of talking and the way of bringing up our kids. It's never changed. I'm a Traveller born and I hope as a Traveller I will die. And all my family and my daughters and sons, we've all got our own language of talking which we call the Cant language. We've got our own customs as regards how we make our food, how we look after our house, how we do the dishes and one thing and another. And we've never ever dreamed it will die out.

'We don't have to use the Cant language now very much, but you see it was really a great language in the travelling people. Because when they went around the houses you know, begging, and they'd go to a shop and they didn't have much money to spend for food and that, and they would maybe see a piece of bacon, you know, or bits of cheese, they would say, "Well, let's see if we can get it cheap" – they didn't ever have much money. So they no would let the people of the shop know this. They spoke the Cant really an awful lot then. But now, in the country district here where we live, I think that Alec and I and my family are about the only ones who still do use it quite a lot. In fact, in Perthshire, and even Aberdeenshire, Inverness-shire, Sutherlandshire, there's hundreds and hundreds of Travellers and yet I have spoken words of Cant they've never even heard of. My Granny lived to a ripe old age of eighty-nine. I had an uncle that died when he was eighty-two in Perth, and when I was young and the rest of the kids would be all outside playing, I was very interested in the old cracks, as we talk about, you know. The old sayings. I used to stay inside. And I would sit with my Granny for hours when the rest were outside playing and she'd tell me an awful lot of the old Cant: and it always stuck in my mind you know.

'We've always gone to school. That's different to Travellers' children now. Oh God, it was murder going to school. They wouldn't sit beside you in the seats. They wouldn't play with you in the playground, you was always getting knocked about. Many and many a time I went home crying to my mother.

'But definitely we are more or less respected now. Alec goes around playing his bagpipes, we go away in the summertime, and we make it our business to be where the real old travelling people are, you know, on the road, and we get lovely stories from them, and I wouldn't change my way of life for nobody, not if they lived in a palace.'

Mr Stewart: 'The musical tradition of the Travellers is something which used to be very strong. Round about here you hear that much pipes that you get sick listening to them. In the summertime you hear the bands from Aberdeen, Edinburgh, Glasgow, they all go up there you see at the time of the games; it's a sport, you know, well there's prizes for the best piper, you see. And that's why they come up here. There's a lot of music anyways.

'The Travellers have played an important part in the development of pipe music in the past.

'One time there was a Gordon band in Aberdeen and everyone in that band was Travellers. The only one that was a countryman was the band leader.

'And there's a lot of them can sing all right, but they're shy. If you went to a Traveller's house and asked somebody to sing they wouldn't do it. And they're very good singers too, you know. So they'll get round a fire at night and get one person to sing and they'll all sing. That's the only way you can get them to sing.'

Mrs Stewart: 'The television is a big threat to all this sort of thing. It's the greatest tragedy that ever happened to Travellers. The younger generation just sort of more or less grew up with it, you know. It's very hard just to tell them not to listen, not to do that. But it has spoiled many a good keelie – a keelie is a get-together. They get round a fire.

'As well as the music and the Cant there was the story-tellings, you know. They lived in very remote places and of course you've heard of the body-snatchers long ago, which we called the Burkers, you know, Burke and Hare, but the travelling people just called them the Burkers. For many old lone travelling people that lived away in these wee bough tents, well, you know, they were never really seen or heard tell of again. They were taken, oh yes, many of them. Alec could tell you some tales about what had happened to his old people.

'We weren't always mixed up as we are now. Long ago, in the travelling tradition, if you married outside a Traveller it was a tragedy, the family would put you away, they would banish you from the family never to return if you married out of your own kind of people.

'Some of the people on the road in Scotland are descended from people who were evicted when they made the grouse moors and the sheep moors. They say, for instance, that the Stewarts and the McGregors (my own maiden name), all their clans were broken up. And they just took to the road. They used to be sitting at night around their fires and they would say, "Well, if I had my rights what I am entitled to I wouldn't have to be sitting by this wee fire tonight."

'Many tell of how in Scotland the strong came over the weak. They were driven out of their homes and their clans were all broken up and they took to the country and they just had to go around from door to door making a living as best they could because they were banished from where they came from.

'It used to be all tents, they didn't have caravans, and you had to be a very well-off Traveller before you could afford a horse and cart; most people had just a small barrow, or a pram, you know, or just bundles on their backs, they just wrapped up their bedding in the morning in a bundle and took down their camp which was these small bough tents, and move on to somewhere else; and they just got their living from door to door.

'The men used to work for money at the time of the harvest, potatoes, the turnips, and the women would go out begging if they had to beg, they had some baskets which the men made that they could sell.

'My people were good basket-makers. There was an old tradition that the oldest of the Gypsy family, all the money you earned was all given to him; and he'd give you just so much money, even after you were married and had a family. But that never applied to us. We never kept that up as a tradition. We got married and that was it.

'It was no fault of Alec or me that we finished in a house. I told you earlier on that my father died when I was seven months old, and if there's any other Traveller about they'll know I'm telling you the truth that a widow woman, long long ago, would never wander the country unless she had a big family, but there were only two brothers and myself and my mother settled down in a house. If my father had been alive it's understood that he would have just kept on because he'd never have thought of settling in a house.

'It was very hard for women on the road. My mother was scared. She was terrified as to what would happen. Because many many children, when the woman would be away in a village hawking or begging, if a policeman was passing that camping ground and see two or three wee kids sitting there on their own waiting for their father and mother to come home, just because there was no father or mother, they would take these kids to a reformatory school without any criminal offence. They'd just make out they were neglected. That happened to many travelling people that we know, oh many many of them; they were taught to read and write in these places and when they became sixteen they were put out on jobs. Some of them did go back to their fathers and mothers, they just couldn't give up their travelling life, but others again went out into the world and got situations. The girls became nurses and I know two men that became policemen, one was an inspector but he was still a Tinker boy at heart. And they never stopped visiting their parents, even though they settled in houses and married, they always went to see their fathers and mothers.'

Mr Stewart: 'The stigma was always there. Here is a poem I wrote about an incident at berry-picking:

> It happened at the very time
> When the Travellers came to Blair.
> They pitched their tents on the berry-fields
> Without a worry or care.
> But they hadn't been long settled,
> When some policemen came from Perth,
> And told them they must go at once
> And get off the face of earth.
> These folk of course were worried,
> Of law they had no sense,
> They only came to the berry-fields
> To earn a few honest pence.
> It was hard to make them stay there,
> When the policemen said to go,
> So they just packed up and took the road,
> To where I do not know.
> But it's a hard life being a Traveller,
> For I've proved it to be true;
> I have tried in every possible way,
> To live like Gorjis do.
> But we're always hit below the belt,
> No matter what we do,
> But when it comes to the Judgment Day,
> We'll be just the same as you.

'In some places the police will come about twelve or one o'clock in the morning. I was in Dumfriesshire one summer and they just says, "Come on, away you go, you can't stay there." I says, "We've just sat down for dinner, will you give us half an hour for dinner before we go away?" "No, no, no half-hours," he says, "get going."

'Another time we was staying in a place in a back road, and the police come, the sergeant and one of the constables, and they said, "Oh," they said, "who told you to stay here?"

'I wasn't at home, but it was my brother-in-law. "Oh," he says, "we have to come here," he says, "because my brother-in-law's wife is going to have a child."

' "Well," he says, "you must shift."

' "She cannot shift, because she's in labour, you know."

'So they went away.

'So when I came back my brother-in-law told me what had happened. Well, the baby was born there.

'The law came back. "Now," he says, "you have to go," he says. He says, "How is the wife?"

'I says, "She's just got the baby, just now."

'He says, "I don't believe it, I don't believe it."

'I says, "Well, go up in the caravan, you'll see."

'I took him up in the caravan and showed him the baby.

' "Well," he says, "I'll give you till the morning. You must get away tomorrow."

'And when I come out next morning it was hard keen frost and snow. I had a look at the roadside, and there lay our horse, it was lying with its feet in a ditch, it was dead. So I had to go and pull the wagon with my own hands, about ten mile.'

Mr Francis Barton

'The old days of starvation are over...'

Frank Barton recently moved from a lifetime on the road into a house. His views, however, were almost the reverse of those of Mr Tommy Lee, whose section of the book directly follows this one. Whereas Mr Lee regretted his move, for Mr Barton the move to a house has brought him a life far better than life on the road.

'A lot of Travellers would move, if they could, if they could get the opportunity to move into houses they'd do so, 'cos they have a very hard time on the roads. In the past I have. And now I'm in a house and I'm more than pleased, and if any of the travelling people was coming along now and wanted a house, well, I'd help them to get one. As I've already done for one of my brothers who I've helped to come off the road and go into a house.

'So now he's already done it, he's moved into a house and he's got two kids going to school and I'm more than pleased with it. And they get the school dinners every day that they never used to get before as Travellers.

'I think that every Gypsy family would really like to be in a house. Yes they would, 'cos I mean on the whole the road is really a dog's life. When you're in a trailer you haven't got no home and you don't know nobody and you're just living from day to day and it's not easy to earn money. In summertime you're cherry-picking and apple-picking, and hopping, but then when apple-picking is over you get out, and you're on the roads through the winter.

'I'm more than glad that the old days is past. Years ago when we had the horses we just had them shoed once a month, or each six weeks, and if you never had the shoe money you'd have to let them go without shoes till you earned the money, see what I mean. And apart from that the kids just went on coming into the world, being born and being brought up on the road – they never had proper clothes to wear nor proper shoes and they never had no toys to play with and as I say they never had no education. They didn't know A from B and they never know'd no songs, they couldn't sing no songs, 'cos they didn't have the scholarship, they just used to learn it from the gramophone; they used to have a gramophone, and if they liked a song they'd go and buy a record of it and play it on the gramophone till they'd learnt it by ear and then they would learn another one and that's how it would go on till they got to about seventeen or eighteen year old, and then they would meet a boy-friend or girl-friend and it might lead up to a marriage, but they would run off together, and they would have to seek for theirselves, get a job, get the money to buy a varda and then they would go on the road in the winter and then they'd probably buy a horse in the summer, and that's how they'd carry on.

'I met my wife in hopping. You see, at other times of the year you were scattered all over the country, Sussex, Surrey, but every hopping season they'd come back to the hopping.

'And they'd get to know each other, that's when they'd link up together and become man and wife, and then they'd have all the summer in front of 'em to earn enough money to buy a varda for the winter and an old pony or horse.

'I met my wife on one Saturday night; I had a car, and her farm was about two miles past my farm, where I was hopping, so eventually she said, "Could you give me a lift home?"

'I said, "Yes."

'So I dropped her back to her farm.

'So I said, "I'll see you tomorrow night."

'She said, "You will?"

'I said, "Yes."

'She says, "All right, it's number ten along the other end."

'She was a Gorjio girl from Bethnal Green. A lot of Cockneys used to come down in those days. That was the best part of the year, the best time we had was hopping-time, that's when we used to mate and link up.

'But we never had plenty of money. We used to have a drink, we used to enjoy ourselves. Somebody used to sing and then somebody else used to sing, and of course it was quite a nice time while it lasted really.

'I was singing this night, chucking myself about like I used to when I was young and really I suppose she fell for me, and eventually after the hopping was over, we sort of come together. I asked her if she wanted me, and she said yes, so I went and bought a varda then and it started from there.

'The varda cost fifty-five pounds. It was a lot of work, a Churchy wagon, it were – that's a sort of wagon that's made in Reading somewhere, a Reading varda, they call it. The top of the door is round; the other vardas have got a square top to the door, but this is round over the top of the door, like a church door, they call them Churchys. We used to buy 'em off a man called Jimmy Tildley, he comes from Hounslow in London, I think; he used to make 'em and we used to buy 'em off him very cheap.

'Then we got a very good horse for twenty pounds. He was a little heavy, about fourteen to fifteen hands high. Not a cart-horse, not a race-horse; it's in between, a cob type, a little heavy "banner" they call it, a cob about fourteen to fifteen hands high.

'My girl never smoked, she never drank unless I took her to the pub. And of course she was taught to save every penny she could get hold of. She always liked the idea of marrying a Traveller. Really, Travellers, they used to marry one another, but as I say, in the first place they didn't know nothing else, 'cos they couldn't read nor write and they only see'd one another from year to year so when they did meet one another they had to run away you see, 'cos the father might not like this boy, you know. "Well I don't want him over here, he's got to keep away."

'So eventually when the girl got a chance they just runned off together. That's what I done, yes.

'There's quite a lot of London girls, Gorjio girls, marrying the travelling blokes. They then move into houses, you see. I should say, eventually, in this coming ten years, there won't be many Travellers about. They'll all be in houses. And I think it'll be a good thing for 'em. 'Cos when you get old like my grandfather, he was seventy or eighty, nearly a hundred I should say, we had to take him along the road till he died, and it was tiring for him, I mean old people don't want to be pulled about every other day, do they. They want comfort; just to go to bed, get up when they like.

'When I fetched my wife down to this part of the country we moved from farm to farm, and she liked that. She saw different people and we seemed to get on all right. And when we was moving she seemed to like it. She liked all the change and different types of living. She enjoyed it.

'And then we got rid of the horse-drawn varda and I bought a motor-trailer, I actually chopped the varda away for it, and I've still got it now. I still keep it. Sometimes I sleep in it. Sometimes I take it out still when I go cherry-picking, I take it with me.'

'I'm glad now that my children are having education. I'm pleased, more than pleased. It's the main part of a man's life. I've had the offer of jobs during the war, and I had to turn 'em down just because I couldn't read or write. If I could have read and write I'd have been a top man, I'd have been a big farmer, but I just couldn't do that. That's my downfall.

'Travellers that have learnt to read have done very well. Some of my sisters, they got Gorjio husbands, and they can read, see what I mean? They can pick up a paper, they see a thing in it going for fifty pounds that's worth a hundred pounds. I can't do that you see.

'And if I have a letter I have to have somebody else to read it. But not now, because the wife's a scholar. If she hadn't been a scholar I wouldn't have married her. I wouldn't marry a Gipsy girl for this reason; she couldn't read and she'd have been as silly as what I was. Because there's times when insurances have to be switched over and you have to fill the forms in for the car and, oh, different things, you know, you have to get other people to do it, they just won't do it for you.

'But now, when my car wants taxing she'll just get the pen and ink out and send it off and there you are.

'I was at Sittingbourne the other day and the police said, "Is this your lorry?"

'I said, "Yes."

'He said, "What's the number?"

'I said, "I couldn't tell you, not if I got down and looked."

'He said, "You can't?"

'I said, "No."

'He said, "Well, is it your lorry?"

'I said, "It is, I've had it two year." Honestly, I couldn't tell him the number. This is the problem, you see.

'And, say I wanted to find Blyth's shop in Bergot Street, Canterbury. Now anybody can see the sign "Bergot Street", it's right up in big letters; but I have to say to someone there, "Could you tell me where Bergot Street is?"

'They'll say, "Just down here on the left."

'And then I'll go right along in front of Blyth's. I'll have to stop somebody else and say, "Excuse me, could you tell me where Blyth's is?"

'I know it's Blyth's then, because I've been told, but otherwise I'd never find it.

'All this was a bit too much really, being on the road, being stopped by the law. When you've had it all your life it's a bit boring, you've got no home, you don't know anybody, only see them once a year or betimes, and eventually when I picked up with this woman I thought to meself, I'll get meself a place, so I could go out the morning and come home at night. And that's what I done. I bought a piece of ground and I put the caravan on it and one day the Council come along and said, "Have you got a licence to stay here?"

'I said, "No, never knew you had to have one."

'He said, "Oh yes, you have to have a licence."

'I'd bought this land with money I'd saved from fruiting and hopping and log-wood selling, for a hundred pounds.

'Seven years after I got the land, I come into more money, and I said to the wife, "I'm going to have a little bungalow put up here on this land." So I went to see a bloke and he said, "Well, you go to Canterbury see the architect," he said, "and they will draw the plans, what shape you want. Then," he said, "they will put it before the Board, the Board of the Council."

"So that's what I done, and it come up one Monday and they turned it down. Then about three or four Mondays after it come up again and they turned it down. And then all of a sudden the Council man come here and said, "Well I'm afraid that you won't get no house on this piece of land 'cos it's in the green belt, and you'll have to clear off."

' "Well," I said, "I'm determined to have a house to live here, I've been roaming the country now for fifty years," I said, "I'm determined to end my days here."

'So anyway, another three or four months went by so I see'd this Mr Ball, the architect from Canterbury. He said, "I'm having it up on next Monday again." So he had it up the next Monday and it was passed.

'Was I pleased! I went in to see these two builder blokes and arranged for them to come and do it weekends over the rate of six months. And I bought all the sand, ballast, bricks; I got me own lorry to carry the stuff, and gave a bit of help where they wanted, and that's how the house got built. And I'm very happy there. It has inside toilets, and it has two big rooms, and well, I don't really get any longing to go back on the road, now. I don't think so, not now. No, not now, no. Well, you see, my children eventually they will marry to Gorjios. 'Cos they are going to school every day with other Gorjios, Gorjio girls, and they're getting to know each other, but I never had that chance. Later on, my girls will marry those Gorjio boys and my boys will marry the Gorjio girls.

'They're pleased, they're more than pleased to be going to school. They're up every morning, you know, ready, just waiting to go to school.

'Those old days of starvation are over. See, years ago you couldn't get no support; well, now, these old people, they can go to the Social Security and they can get support, you see, five or six pounds a week, whereas when we was kids we couldn't get nothing, really, we never had no shoes to wear, no shoes. And often we went four or five days without anything to eat.

'If every Traveller could do the same as we've done and have a house, they'd be more than happy. But they don't know this. And if you've got one redress it's far easier to get another.

'Once one Traveller gets a place he's got an opportunity; if another place is for sale his friends can go and buy it because he's got a redress to come back to – he's got a redress, you see, like I've got. Well see, if I was travelling I ain't got no redress, see what I mean?'

Mr Tommy Lee

'Travellers are particular. They are among the most particularest people in the world.'

Driving down a leafy lane near to Canterbury in search of Mr Tommy Lee. He is a Gypsy who moved into a house six months ago.

He's sitting outside his old-fashioned brick cottage on the ground on a bus seat, a wisp of smoke from an open fire drifting up beside him. A shed behind him and to his right, an apple tree.

Mr Lee apologises for not rising to greet me, saying that he has been poorly and that the doctor has told him to stay in bed. 'But I knew better than that. I knew I'd do better to come out in the open air, get some air in me.

'I know better, you see. I know the air is more healthy.'

He prods the fire with his foot and says, 'I've had a couple of heart attacks, you see, the doctor told me I had to get a house. But for me own self if it hadn't been for what the doctor said I wouldn't have had it.

'And really, if the Gorjios would leave us Gypsies alone, if we could bide our ways by the road, the same as Gorjios do in the houses, there wouldn't be no problems.

'Yes, I moved into this house for the sake of me health, now I don't think it's any better. They kept on at me about it being healthy in a house, and at my age I ought to be in a house, but I don't think it is. They said I'd have more space to wander about in, more room, but I don't know what to think. It may be better in the wintertime, but in the trailer you have all the fresh air in the world; it's a good life, and I don't think it's so good in a house, really. It's the Gorjios that are messing it up all the time, the gavvers and that. But I mustn't tell a lie now, the gavvers aren't so bad as they used to be. Well, it wouldn't do me no good to lie. When I was a boy they would be asking us to move up till one or two o'clock in the morning. When it was dark they'd come along and if you wouldn't move, you'd get beat up, but this was never made public knowledge. The children was hurt, yes sir, they was, yes sir, they was, they was hurt. Often.

'They're not so bad to you today, you see.

'They say, "How long do you want to stop?"

'You might say, "A couple or three days or till tomorrow morning."

'They come along and say to you, "Well, have a clean up, and make a move."

'They do let you hang about now, till the next day. They ain't too bad. This is in Kent, of course. In other places it's worse, so they tell me.

'But there's a lot of Gypsies today they leave a lot of motors and a lot of old things around, they're just messing up the roads. Well then the policemen they come along, they ask, "Who stopped there?" But life ain't too bad for the Gypsy, it's one of the best lives.'

I asked Mr Lee what the change from horse-drawn varda to trailer had felt like.

'Well, in a sense, there's no difference when you're laying down but there's a difference when you're roaming around.

'With a motor you is here and you is gone. But when you had a horse and varda you sat on the foot-board and you took note of everything you know, as you passed along. And everybody came around to talk and you was known everywhere. People stopping round to talk to you. And you'd stop the old horse and stand to have a talk.

'But with a motor, it's soon gone. You never see nobody. Never see the country or nothing. But around and around with horse and varda was the cushtiest time in the world.

'Here's another thing about the old horse, when you're with the horse, he was your own. You were out with him there grazing, and when he was grazing, you were out there with him. It occupied your mind. A horse took a lot of worry off your mind then.

'The favourite horse I ever had was a horse whose name was Bryn. He came from Ashford. And I bought him when he was five years old. When they ran him up and down at the auction I knew that he was the one for me. You know, the typical auction; there is forty or fifty of them there and you have to look to see if they've got any faults, like whether the horse has any splits or marin bones or spavins; then you'd wait till the horse you wanted came up.

'The auctioneer would stand up and he'd say, "What would you give for number so and so," and you'd bid for it, see. Somebody would say, "I'll give ten pound for him," and you'd put your hand up to bid eleven. And then when somebody else would say twelve, and you'd stand and bid till you'd bought it, you know. Bryn was a nice horse, he was a good horse he was.

'I like horses better than dogs. There's no point saying I don't like horses best, 'cos I do. But I like dogs too, I like the dogs.

'They're good to animals the Gypsies are, very good.

'It was me kids, me children, decided me to have a trailer instead of a horse-drawn varda. They kept on about having a trailer. I had a twenty-two foot trailer and then I had an eighteen.

'But I didn't seem to find the room in it, as much room, as in one of them old vardas. Also, you didn't seem to have the comfort.

'You won't believe this, but come the wintertime you are more comfortable with a ten-foot varda in them little lanes than you are in the big trailers.

'The vardas was very carefully made, well done made. When you went through the door there was a bunk where you put your clothes and there was a lid on it, you took the lid off and put your clothes in it and then you put the lid back on and you could sit there. Go on farther and you come to the bedside. You come along the other side and there's a nice bath and a bath-tub, whichever you prefer, then you come back farther, there's the stove and then you come back towards the door there's wardrobes hanging down. And in some of the vardas you get beds with mirrors both sides of them.

'Many a time we travelled in the night-time in the old varda. We used to have two lamps that we put candles in. But most of the things we used to have were smashed up when my father died. We smashed them all up. The main reason for this was so you wouldn't go along and see somebody else every day driving the thing that had been your Dad's.

'I lost one of my boys when he was seventeen. He was a lovely boy and I bought him a lovely piebald pony and a van. I burnt that van and I had his pony killed. You see you never forget 'em. You never forget the dead, I reckon.

'So that's why we burn the vans, so at the time you might forget 'em for a little while. So you don't see somebody else driving his varda.

'Travellers are particular. They are among the most particularest people in the world. For example in childbirth. I've done it many a time, gone to get the midwife, then you want plenty of hot water ready for her. All the towels and everything. It's just the same as a Gorjio does. Travellers always use the Gorjio midwife. I've heard of a woman giving birth to a child and getting up the very next morning. A proper Romany, he'd call that "nogany", dirty filth. He wouldn't have that.

'My Dad was very particular. See that cup of tea I've just drunk now? Before he'd drink out of it again, he'd wash it up again. What's made it so bad as regards the Gypsies' reputation is actually the Gorjios. The Gorjios that marry Gypsies. I've got a couple of aunts that married Gorjios. So then these Gorjios marry Gypsies and they think they *are* Gypsies. But they ain't. They ain't because it's born in you to be a Gypsy.

'One way that you can tell the difference is in the question of courting. This long courting. I don't think that's in the proper Gypsy line. They like to marry quick. In the old days the old folk didn't *ask* who you went with they *told* you who you went with. However, if a girl of mine came up and said she was going with a lovely Gorjio, and that she was in love with him, I'd say, "Go ahead." If somebody loves somebody then they must get married to them, that's my opinion. Although I don't ever want to see my girls get married, I'd like to keep them always with me. You know.

'Me and my wife, we met at cherry-picking. She was a young girl, and I went to see her a few times at the cherry-picking and then we started to go with each other and court each other. We courted each other for a month or two, we got married, bought ourself a horse and a caravan and we went roaming around, you know, only in a different way. We used to travel all around Sussex up as far as Belvedere where the wife comes from. We roamed around at that time and we've been at it ever since.

'When I was young, Travellers used to know remedies from all the things in the hedgerows. For instance, if you had earache or a headache or blue chronic or something wrong with your eyes, my father would know what to get to set you right. And the pity is that they couldn't read nor write, and when they died, the names died with them. If you had anything wrong with your eyes, my father would go and get some ivy and he'd boil it, and he'd pulp it and he'd bathe the eyes in it. In about a week he'd have them right.

'And if the chest was bad or your temples or anything, or if you had skinheads, he'd go and pick some marshmallows, boil them, strain them off, then wash your face four days running in the water of the mallows and all the skinheads would come off – you'd never believe it.

'The same with stinging nettles. He had a remedy with them. If your bladder was out of order he'd get a nice lot of stinging nettles and boil them, give them a nice wash, and then give them you to eat with a bit of pepper and salt. You'd have these boiled nettles on the corner of your plate when you had your meals, and you'd eat them like you would candy. He also had remedies for things that Gorjios use pills for.

'You never see a sick Traveller. Take me. I used to weigh fifteen stone. Then I had these two heart attacks. I passed clean out with one of them. And then I became a diabetic. It's unfortunate, I mean you never see Gypsies with it. Gypsies never used to call the doctor. They didn't call the doctor 'cos they didn't want to have 'em, if you'd seen what I've seen, you wouldn't think the doctors do any good. We used to take from the hedgerows, and that did us good. But now you get people taking thirty or forty pills a day, and still as bad as when they started. You can't convince the Gorjio doctors that the open air is better than inside; but it is. Travellers know it.

'One time of day I used to get up at four o'clock or half past four in the morning. I could run or jump or do anything you mention. But today I'm useless. I can't do nothing at all. Today I lays in bed till nine or ten o'clock. Unusual for a Gypsy. I should never have moved to a house. So at any rate, I get out here in the open, out of the house and into the open.

'And I make a fire up and after I've been sitting outside by the fire for a while, I feel different, better. I spend a lot of the day out here in the open. I say that, if you stay indoors you might as well drop down dead. In the house, I've got a lot of oxygen that the doctor gave me to take when my blood goes bad, but I don't stay in the house or take the oxygen. When I come to be short of breathing I get out here straight away. And I feel quite different again.'

'The Gypsy ways are the best ways. I always said I'm a Gypsy. That way, people know who you are. I say to my children, "Never disown yourself." If people say, "What are you?" say, "Well, I'm a Gypsy."

'My children never had Gorjio education. No. They never. I reckon Gorjio education destroys a lot. I do. That's my belief. Neither one of my kids can read or write, but I can send them anywhere, trust them anywhere. The boy wouldn't go to a pub without first coming to ask me. The girls, they won't go to the pictures without coming to ask me. Their ages? Well, the girls are twenty-four and twenty-two. And it don't matter what job I send them to do they can do it. They can get their living, see what I mean. It's my belief that too much education's about. Too much of it.

'The young people today, the moment they sit down they've got to have a book in their hands. It's all wrong. I don't reckon that a lot of any education is any good. If you've always got a book in your hand you ain't got no time to do anything else. I've seen a lot of travelling children being educated, I've seen a lot of it. But I reckon they should be left alone. I reckon if a Gypsy wants to be a Gypsy, if he's going to be a Traveller, let him be.

'Travellers have a different attitude to their womenfolk. A Gorjio man says about his wife, "I've got to take notice of her." And to a Gypsy, it's all wrong. A Gypsy man loves his wife, he lives with her and he does everything he can to help her. But it ain't the case for the woman to become the Traveller. She ain't. It's the Gypsy man that's the governor.

'Gypsies think very bad of divorce. They don't like it at all. Before we get divorce we get out and hit each other, like, if she done anything wrong I'd clout her for it. Say she started trying to live with another man. And she'd clout me back. See what I mean? Now that's a proper Gypsy custom it is you see.'

'The worst time was ten years ago. Things weren't so good and plentiful. They come along and they push you along, they'd go out and have a few drinks then they'd come along and move you along. Well then you'd begin to beg, you've done this business of begging. They'd come along and knock you up, you had to get up and get your things up and if you didn't want a clout you had to be civil. I've clouted one or two policemen in my time but it's no good. They get you for assault, yes, they do. They do, sir. They have no right to do it, but they make out they have the right to do it. Yes they do, sir.

'You had to keep going, on and on and on. You was never two days in a place. We might start from here, and we'd go right down to the coast, along to Portsmouth, Southampton, all the way round. We had to like, you know. Today, it's much better now, you know. Not that I'd ever want to stop too long.

'To be honest with you, I wouldn't stop any place more than one week. This is a beautiful house here, and we have everything we want. But if I had my way we'd be out of here tomorrow. My wife, she'd be with me. We ain't had it all smooth all our life. But, you know what I mean, it's been a lovely life.

'You know, you hear people say it's one of the roughest lives in the world, but it's not. It's one of the best. Say you have a load of logwood, you sell it to some Gorjio and you take four or five pounds. You know that there's a couple or three days' food there, you can relax. You can poove down in the same grassy bottom.'

I asked Mr Lee if he'd seen local authority sites.

'Yes, yes sir, see a lot of 'em. And I don't go much on 'em. They ought to make a plot, you see, put a fence around it, and say, "This is your plot of ground," and the trailers spaced out.

'Not like they do now when they put 'em on top of each other with no privacy at all in it. If someone has a bucket of dirty water it's just there like, on these sites. Well if you was a decent way away you wouldn't have that smell would you. You see I reckon that's where they're wrong. And they should make the place like if they went out to shift logs like, there'd be the space to shift the logs, see what I mean.

'And then have a man to go round every fortnight and expect them to see if their places is kept clean. That's how the sites ought to be.'

'When the Gypsies used to go to town in the old days, people used to run out to come and see them. We used to pull up behind the pub and people would come running out – "Tommy Lee". Everybody knowed us. That was a nice life.

'It was the gavvers messed us up. It just messed me up like, you know. When the policeman worried me and they brought my sickness on.

'We used to travel all the roads. Down to New Brandon for the pea-picking and we come back up through Chichester and then we come back up the Ashfield, and we moved every day like, you know.

'So if you wouldn't hurt your horse, you do about nine or ten mile a day. Your horse is one thing you had to look after.

'You'd go about walking pace, you would. You'd never get a horse with a caravan trotting. You just had a walking pace all the time. You walked along beside him holding the reins and let the old horse walk along comfortable, never hurried him. You'd stop to have a bit of dinner, and then done what you wanted to do.

'Some days you did a bit more, but generally you did on an average ten mile a day.

'With a horse, you've got to look after them. In the evening we used to put them into the field for a bit of pooving. And in the morning we'd get them early, and then harness up and away.

'We'd give them a bit of hay in the wintertime, you had a place made on the back, what they call a rack on the back of the varda, we call 'em a rack with hoops. Well, you can get a couple of bags of hay on the back of it. Sometimes we used to have a wagon for hay as well but then you had to have spare horses.

'When we got them all together we had as many as fourteen horses.

'Maroon and yellow, that was our colours. That was the colours of our varda.

'A nice colour for a varda is grain. You get the varda painted plain yellow and then you get an oak stain and you grain over the top of it and then put a bit of red colour in with it, it looks lovely.

'It was a good life whether you had a tent or a varda or whatever it was, it was a good life. With the old bender tent, you could make it warm and comfortable. You got a couple of big army blankets to put over it and then you got a waterproof covering for it and it's comfortable as anything in the world, you'd never believe it. You have the fire outside. You *can* make 'em with a fire inside, but you'd have to have a big door to it; and then you'd have it like what they call the wing-wong, one of those Indian styles. We used to call 'em barricades. And they were one of the comfortablest things you ever laid in.

'The best wood for making a bender tent out of is hazel, young hazel. You can make the tent so high you can walk in it. The door, it's a bit of sack. You get a bit of cloth, and you make it six foot high.'

As I was leaving, Mr Lee asked his little grand-daughter, 'What is you? Tell this gentleman what you are. What is you?'
 'A travelling girl,' said his little grand-daughter.
 'That's right!' said he, with approval. And, turning to me, he said, 'I always tell them never to disown theirselves.'
 It was only as I was leaving that I realised that Mr Tommy Lee was a sicker man than I had thought.
 His wife said, 'Yes, and the doctor said if he had another stroke it might be dangerous and of course he had this new stroke early this morning.
 'So we're all sad. We sent for the doctor at once and he said that Tommy must go to bed and stay there, and must on no account go out of doors. And he must keep the oxygen by him.
 'But of course Tommy reckons that he's better sitting out here, by the old yog.'
 I was appalled. I had been engaging him in conversation, when he was in this state.
 But Mrs Lee said, 'Don't worry, dear. I think it's done him good. He's right. Things are better for him outside than inside. And it's been good for him, talking to you.'

Mr Joe Cooper

'I'm at an old man's home now.'

Mr Joe Cooper, an upright, white-haired, handsome man, recently moved, after a lifetime on the road, into an 'old man's home'.

'We put in for a house but they wouldn't give us one. So in the end me health cracked up and I'm at an old man's home now, and I'm very pleased of it. Yes, very pleased. It's very warm, very dry, very comfortable. They're good nurses and good doctors.

'Sometimes you get restless, wish you were out on the road. Well, if you do you just got to put up with it. The only thing you misses is the company. You miss the sort of travelling people. Well you do, like, miss one another, but still now that's getting forgot a bit. I'd sooner be in a house now than have a caravan.'

Part V

Water Gypsies

On the canals of Britain there are still a few descendants of those water Gypsies who once operated the longboats along Britain's network of waterways. Their exact relationship to land Gypsies is unclear. Some claim that the cultural similarities are the result of similar solutions to similar problems, rather than anything more direct.

1 Prince Nathaniel Petulengro Lee, the duckerer

2 *Top:* Johnny Connors, family and young friends, Hertfordshire

3 *Above:* 'The horse is still the Gypsies' best friend'. Travellers stopped in South-west London

4 *Top:* Cut glass, family groups, and a typically spotless caravan interior. Travellers stopped in North-east London

5 *Above:* The problem of life beside the road. Travellers stopped in Sussex

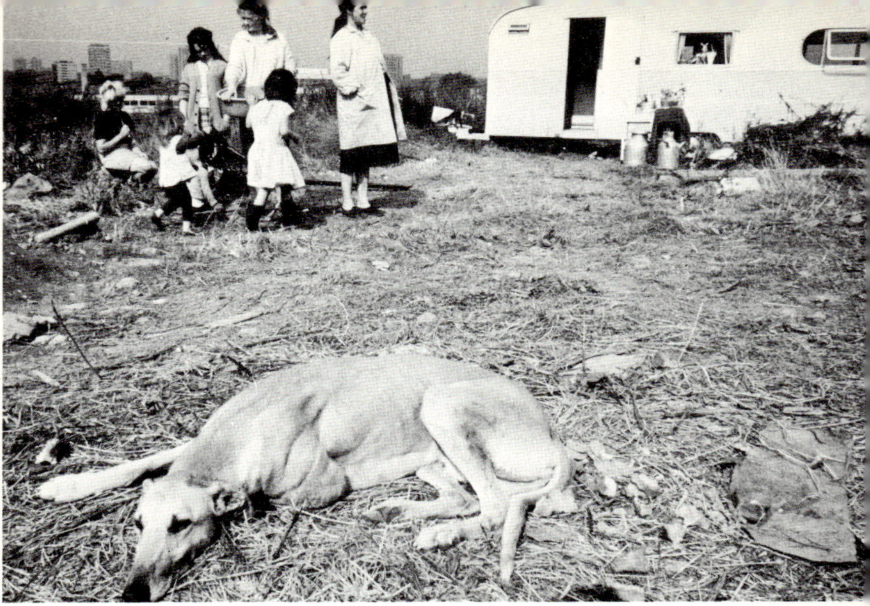

6 *Top:* In the Industrial Midlands
7 *Above:* A typical urban camp-site in Lanarkshire

8 *Above:* A typical bender tent encampment in Perthshire

9 *Left:* A Hatchintan in winter, Perthshire

10 and 11 *Right:* Two Gypsies at Appleby Fair in Northumberland

12 *Below:* A trotting race at Appleby

13 *Top:* The past: the old horse-drawn varda
14 *Above:* The future: a local authority site

Mr and Mrs Humphries

'Boat girls make good wives and all . . .'

Their longboat, beautifully picked out with castles and roses, is moored alongside the Grand Union Canal.

Mrs Helen Humphries: 'I could never live in a house. I'd rather be on the water. Things are more peaceful there. All of my family were born on the water. My daughter, Pansy, she's on the land. The land is foreign ground to me. Not Pansy, she married a dealer. When we go to see him he comes to pick us up in his car. I couldn't get there on my own. I'm a stranger on the land. There's a big shop on the corner, there's a pub with a lion on top of it, well I couldn't say more near than that, but he's a shop-owner, *important*.'

'How many of you boat people are there now?'

'Oh, not too many. There's a load of boat folk up at Daventry. They're moored up. Waiting for houses. It's like that now for most boat people.'

A group of boats pass by – vast barges pulled by tugs, not lived in, with names like *Eureka, White, Vial, Blackwell, Ben Hope, Blue River*.

'The cargoes we take now are only lime-juice. We used to take lime-juice, fruit, coal, wheat, wood . . .'

Helen paints the longboat. She paints the big red ace of hearts on top of the hatch, and the red clover leaf. Then she paints the cream base to the deck, lets that dry, then puts a wet coat of golden brown on its top, and runs a comb through it to give an appearance of stippling. She paints the roses on the water cans, the castles on the cabin doors. She polishes the three brass rims on the black enamel chimney, a beautiful cylindrical chimney whose height has been yet further increased with the help of a Nestlés milk tin. The decorations, even the dimensions and arrangement of the cabin, are very similar to those of the old horse-drawn vardas.

Tom: 'In the old days I had me own horse. Used to take coal to the old age pensioners at Oxford. That was sweet.

'Used to be a lot of barges, but now it's all going off. They worked and made the roads and that way they ended the canals. The boat people is dying.'

Tom gets out a collection of photographs.

'Here I are coming into the old 98 Lock. Here I are with Pat, the brindled dog. Here I are moored for the water fair at Banbury.'

Downstairs is the cabin – the bed at the back, a shelf occupying the whole width of the boat, screened off with white lace curtains. In the nearer part, by the doors, white fancy-bordered plates hang thick like leaves.

Barges like these have their own oil-fired motors and reckon to do three miles an hour, including locks.

'Boat people are industrious. My daughter, she hasn't got an idle bone in her body.

'This cabin is registered for man, wife, and four children. But we smuggled more in than that, as they arrived.'

'Can your children swim?'

'Oh no. Nor the wife. Every so often they fall in. Then I are diving in to get them out from the reeds.

'But I think children on a canal are good behaviour. You can take 'em into the street, you never see 'em gawpin' through the windows like town folk do to us people. There's always town children coming here, gawpin'. And they do spitting at you, beating up, punch up, throw stones at you as you go under the bridges.

'Boat girls make good wives and all. There's a load of boys from the towns married boat girls. My daughter married that feller on the shore. She's good in a house, good in an office, good at the cooking, and what's more, good on the water.

'In the summer it's too hot. Winter is better. Then you can always work to keep yourself warm.

'The winter is rough. But I don't mind because we can't always have it sweet. Must take the rough with the good. There are bits we have to go on the Thames. When the Thames is full it's not very sweet.

'I remember the old horse best from the old days. Yes, it's funny, the best thing I remember is the horse. When we'd moored up for the night I used to saddle the old horse and ride about on her. You'd see so many people. And I remember Banbury one day, Banbury Fair. There was twenty-seven pair of boats laying there I remember, for the fair.

'I had to make an early start, at six. There were thirty horses there, waiting to go through the lock. And I had to make an early start to go on four-days' journey up to Liverpool.

'So, for they hid my horse's collar under a truss of hay, I couldn't find it nowhere. I couldn't find it, search though I may. They'd hidden it. That was a laugh.

'Well, I'm glad I saw you coming. I don't like most of you fellows. I don't like house people. When I see house people coming I shut down the hatch. That's not very sweet.'

Part VI

Mr Johnny 'Pops' Connors

Mr Connors lives in a trailer caravan on a series of patches of derelict land in the industrial Midlands. He also returns periodically to Ireland.

During a recent visit to prison he wrote his autobiography – a work of very exceptional merit. It concerns life in the old horse-drawn caravans in Ireland, and also the present days in the Midlands.

Rather than print a record of my conversations with him I preferred, with his agreement, to print this work in its entirety with the exception of some historical sections and other sections which were confiscated when he left prison, and others which are now in the possession of the Council of Europe.

Seven Weeks of Childhood – An Autobiography

'We are the mysterious people in the world; history knows nothing about us.'

Just before World War Two my father and mother were camped at a roadside camp at Locklington, County Dublin, Eire.

My mother got a kick from a donkey or horse. I was still in my mother's womb at the time. Seven days later I was born.

During them times my father made tinware such as buckets, kettles, pots, pans, basins, beakers, mugs, plates, baths, etc. It was very hard times for the Tinker in those days and, to make it worser for both me Dad and me mother, it was the wintertime of the year.

There was eighteen children in our family and my father would have to make a lot of tinware and sell a lot of tinware to keep us all going on food and drink. Into the bargain, we would be shirted by the local authorities and police sometimes as often as five times in one month.

When I was a child I was a terrible mischief-maker. I can honestly say I broke every cup and plate that came in front of me. I hit a very wicked and peevish pony with a stick on the legs and the pony kicked me over a hedge. I still have the mark on my left cheek to prove it.

When I was five years old a minister ran over me with a Baby Austin car in Banbridge, County Down, Northern Ireland. The Minister gave me a white five-pound note when I was coming out of hospital. My Daddy is very superstitious and he did not want to take blood money from the Minister. So my Daddy would not handle the five-pound note. And he told me to buy boots and shoes for the other travelling children with the five-pound note. I was brought into a shoe shop and I bought boots and shoes for all the children except my sister Mary. I had no money left to buy her boots.

'What about my boots, Johnny?' said my sister Mary to me.

'Oh well, I have none more pounds left to buy you boots, Mary, you will have to wait till another of God's motor-cars knock me down.' Mary never got her boots.

Food rationing started and the Travellers had no ration books. The only way we could live was to smuggle our food across the borders, food we could not get in the Free State. We would go over the English border and buy it on the black market plus some kinds of food we could not get in the English part of Ireland. We would buy it in the Irish Free State. But sometimes we were caught smuggling over food. And the people that were caught doing this would be fined a lot of money and sometimes they would be sent to gaol. Still we had to keep on smuggling our food and risk being gaoled or fined by the Courts. We just had to smuggle to keep alive. If we did not smuggle we would have died with hunger. We also risked being shot on the borders. It was very rare we went through the Customs. We always used the unproved roads. By using the unproved roads we could travel freely from the Irish Republic to the North without being seen by the police or Customs officials. Some nights we would travel through the fields with our wagons to escape the authorities. Also, I can well remember, it was not a very pleasant journey to travel in a wagon over ditches, hedges, bogs, rivers, especially in the dark. Many's the time I got slapped against the floor or sides of the wagon when we would be travelling over rough ground. To look out of the door of the wagon on a dark night and see the steam from the horse's sweat rising towards the blue sky and not a sound could be heard, only the breathing of the horse under the shafts of the wagon, an odd burst of the dogs through the hedges after rabbits and a death squeal from the rabbit in the terrier's or lurcher's mouth. This was the only noise that broke the stillness of the night. Low whispering voices outside and all of a sudden a stupid cow said 'maue' to the top note of its voice. Everybody jumped, and I scream so blue murder with the fright.

When we were well over and safe away from the Barons we pulled out of the land and on to the by-roads. All the wagons and carts were tied, pulled in along the side of the grass on the verge of the road. The poor jaded-out horses, the lathers of thick white sweat frothed out of them, would be unyoked from the wagons and carts. The horses would be that tired and worn out from pulling the heavy wagons and carts all night; they would just move very slowly out from the shafts.

When they had been unharnessed, the horses would be let loose to find their own sweetness and taste of grass. The camp-fires would then be lighted, the pots and kettles filled with water and they would be put on the fire to boil. And then we would all sit round the fire and have a tablecloth spread out on the grass as a ground table. When the food was cooked you could hear the voices of the children say to their mother, 'Give me mine first, Mammy. I want more soup, Mammy. I want more poppys, Mammy. You never gave me none. What about me, Mammy?'

And other of the children would get angry and say, 'You would, you big face,' or 'Ya, I was before you.'

'You were not, with your fox's nose.'

'I was first, badger's eyes!'

'Old look-at-yourself, bull's mouth.'

And the voice of a very small child could be heard saying, 'Soup, me want soup. Give me, Mammy.'

The sweat would be dropping out of their mother trying to serve them all with food. Including me, of course. I was very fat. I used to eat a lot of fat meat and butter and potatoes and cabbage and I would go to sleep in the grass when I ate my victuals.

The next morning I would wake up in the wagons and would dress myself and then go outside with the dogs. The kind of dogs and the breed of them would be lurchers and terriers. They would kill that many rabbits and hares I would not be strong enough to carry all the rabbits and hares home. Two rabbits or one hare was the most I could carry or drag. The dogs would carry one apiece in their mouth. It's surprising I never got lost in the land. I was always able to find my way back to the camp. Sometimes the dogs would kill a pheasant or partridge. Or go down a fox's den and kill a fox. Badgers were very hardy and they are really good fighters. It's not every dog that can kill a badger. Many a good dog the badger has killed. But two good wire-haired terriers will bolt the badger from its den and when the lurcher gets his long mouth around the badger's neck one of them will have to die because they are both game animals.

Young badgers are lovely little animals. They make very good pets and so does the fox cub. But when the fox gets big he won't stay domesticated, he will always run away to his wild and open life. I suppose nature made him to be free and that is the way he wants to stay.

Well, Travellers are like nature. Their nature is similar. They don't want to live in a house. But they do want to settle down on a site with their caravan or wagon or tent. This is their way of life and it has been that way of life for thousands of years. They still like to be free to go and come as they please.

I was always ever fond of fishing and one way I like to fish is with my hands in a trout stream. Even when I was five or six years old I caught big trout, eels, pike, bass, roach and perch. And many's a bite I got from a pike or eel under a bank or under a bridge or stone in the river. How I used to fish was to put my hand under a pocket or hole in the bank, run my hand very lightly along the side of the fish till I got my fingers near his gills, then I would squeeze lightly on his gills with my thumb and forefinger and then I would pull him out and he would be mine. Many's a bite I got from a rat or snap from an otter under a bank. But I always managed to get my three or four dozen of fish on time.

In Remelton, County Donegal, I went to the big river to fish and saw a very big salmon in the shallow part of the river. Just up about where the salmon was there was a very deep hole. I knew if the salmon got into the hole I would never get him. I went back to the camp and I got four sacks. I put barbed wire around the mouth of the four sacks. This made the sacks the shape of catch nets. I got the four sacks near the hole so if the salmon took it in his mind to bolt he would have to go into one of the sacks before he got into the deep hole. I was seven years old at the time and the salmon still in the water was thirteen pounds in weight. The water he was in was about two foot deep. I walked into the river and to get where the salmon was I had to swim. If the salmon went down the river I would have no bother killing him. The river was at the mouth of the sea and it thinned out to about six inches of water. What was worrying me was the deep hole.

When I got about nearly three feet from the salmon I looked down at him. I had a long pointed stick in my hand. I made a jab with this stick at the salmon. I missed him and he very nearly broke my leg when he hit off me. He tumbled me upside down in the water. I got out of that bank and now up to the hole to where the sacks were set. I tried two of the sacks. The salmon was not there. But in the third sack he was inside in it as big as an ass.

As I pulled out the sack he gave a jump. He tumbled me head over heels again. I went into the hole. I very nearly had been drowned.

The salmon went down the river, still in the sack it was. Somehow I managed to get out of the deep hole after swallowing about a gallon of water. I took up the other three sacks to get them in the right places and there was about nine or ten big trout in them. I broke the trouts' necks by putting my thumb in their mouth and I pulled their heads back towards me. I threw them onto the bank. I got the sacks again and I went down the river looking for Sambo. Sambo, I called that salmon when I first saw him, and my full intention was to get Sambo.

When I saw Sambo, he was out of the sack and he was in the deep part of the river. He bolted when he saw me and he swam towards the hole this time. I saw him going into the middle sack and I got a rock in my hand. I put my foot on the mouth of the sack and I let the rock fall down on top of Sambo. He gave a jump inside of the sack. I hit him again and again. He lay still in the sack and I dragged the sack and Sambo out on to dry ground.

The greasy blood was falling down Sambo's belly from a wound on the back of his head, caused by the blow from the rock. What a beautiful fish he was. When I took him out of the sack he lay as still as the stones he was lying on. Not a move out of his body. He was like a large ingot of silver as still and pure as his weight. I felt like a hero now, and again I would look at Sambo. And I was sorry for him. I was sorry for killing him. He was a very game fish. But we did not feel sorry for him when I brought him back to the camp. Instead I was glad of him when my mother handed me over a big steak of him. It was well cooked in butter fat, with vinegar and lemon-juice. The only swimming he was going to do was in my belly. So Sambo found his way into eighteen little tummies.

That year I got a stroke. I lost the power of my legs and I had no power whatsoever in my back. The doctors said I was spending too much time in the water. The reflections of the sun and water were affecting me and he said I would never walk again. How wrong they were. For two years I was a cripple. I could not even stand up and I was fed up with everybody. One day a priest came down the road.

'Hello, my child,' cried the priest.

'Not too bad, Father,' says I.

My Mammy asked the priest to bless and consecrate the new wagon my Daddy was after building.

'I will to be sure,' said the priest. 'Have you any Holy Water?' said the priest.

'No, Father,' said my Mammy. 'I forgot getting it at Mass last Sunday.'

'Well have you got a cup of any class of water?'

'No, Father. The children did not go for the water yet.'

The priest took a cup out of the dish. 'Here, son, go down to that river and get me a cup full of water.'

I took the cup from the priest. 'Father,' I said, 'I can't walk.'

'Get up you lazy little boy and run down to that river when I tell you.'

'Father,' I said, 'I am a cripple. I can't even stand up. I wish to God I could run down to the river for you.'

The tears fell down the priest's face. 'I am sorry my child.'

Then one of the other children took the cup from him and got the water. The priest then asked my Mammy for salt and my Mammy gave the priest the salt. He took a stole out of his pocket, kissed the cross on it and he prayed over the water and the salt; now and again he would put a pinch of salt into the water. He then blessed me and the wagon. He told me to keep the water and I would get stronger.

That night I wanted to go to the toilet. I crept out of bed and I fell over the wagon. I tried to catch the shafts so as I could get up again into the wagon. The shafts fell down on top of me and I caught hold of the shafts so as I could drag myself back into the wagon.

Somehow I managed better than any other time and I was glad when I got back into the bed. I fell asleep, smiling. 'Thank God,' I said. 'Thank God.'

About three weeks after I could sit up and in a few days from that I was standing up. Then my Mammy brought me to a doctor in Dublin. He took the fluid from my knees and he told me to do as much exercises as possible. But he could not guarantee my walking again. He was also wrong. For exercises I tried dancing, and in two months' time I was, and still am, a very good dancer. And I have won prizes for dancing.

I was walking again, thank God. I have never been sick since and I hope to God I won't. I have never seen the priest since or before. I hope he is in good health wherever he is.

Every day I went out hawking with my Daddy, selling tinware and collecting rags and scrap, swapping ponies and donkeys, etc.

And I was a very happy young boy again. In the night-times I would go to sing old ballads and folk-songs at public houses. And at a horse or cattle fair I would sing for money in the hotels and public houses and I would come home to the camp with my pockets full of money.

I was always in my bare feet. I still did not give up my fishing though. One Sunday I was coming back from Chualin, near Boyle, County Sligo, and I saw a river and I went into it. I caught a good few trout. Just as I was coming out of the river, an English gentleman and lady pulled up their car beside me.

'Good afternoon, sonny. Can you please tell me how I can get to Waterford?' said the gentleman.

'Oh yes, sir,' I said. 'I can. But you have a long road in front of you.'

'How far is it, sonny?'

'Oh, about a hundred and twenty miles from here,' I said.

'Good heavens, is it that far?' said the gentleman.

'Yes sir,' I said. 'And I can't make it any shorter for you.'

'Indeed you can, sonny. Just tell me how I get there.'

'First of all,' I said, 'you may turn your motor-car around.'

'Good heavens, I have just come fifty miles along that road.'

'Well,' I said, 'that's not my fault.'

'Of course not, sonny,' said the gentleman.

'Well,' I said, 'go back to Sligo. When you get into Sligo, follow the signpost that says Athlone. Then ask for Kilkerry and from Kilkerry to Waterford. Kilkerry is about fifteen miles from Waterford. As a matter of fact,' I said, 'County Kilkerry is bordering on Waterford.'

'Can you please show me on the map the road to take, sonny?'

'Oh, I am sorry, sir,' I said, 'I can't read.'

'Well, how do you know, sonny, where these places are if you can't read?'

'Oh,' I said, 'we are Travellers. And we have travelled all Ireland.'

'Well, well, well,' said the gentleman. 'What have you got there?'

'Oh these are fish, sir, I caught in the river.'

'What kind of fish are they?' said the gentleman.

I looked at him very puzzled before I answered him. 'Water fish they are, sir,' I said, 'and we call them trout.'

He started to laugh. 'What do you do with them, sonny?'

'Oh, we eat them when we cook them,' I said.

He laughed again. 'Will you sell me a few?' said the gentleman.

'Yes, sir,' I said. 'I will. How many do you want?'

'The lot. I will buy the lot.'

'How much will you give me for the lot?' I said.

'Well, let me see now. I would say there is ten pound of trout there,' said the gentleman.

'You're wrong,' I said. 'There is about fifteen or sixteen pounds of trout there.'

'How do you know, sonny?'

'Well,' I said, 'I have caught fish since I was five years old.'

'Well, sonny, if you say there is fifteen or sixteen pounds' weight of fish there I won't argue with you. I will give you two pounds for them.'

'It's a deal, sir,' I said. 'You can have them.'

He gave me the two single pound notes and he put the fish in the boot of the car. In the boot he had all classes of fishing tackle.

'Well, I must say, sonny, I never did see a better fisherman. I watched you catch those fish. You are a proper artist at tickling fish. I also took the liberty of photographing you fishing.'

'I knew, sir,' I said, 'there was something catchy about you.'

The lady got out of the car. She had a camera in her hand and she took several pictures of me with the gentleman. They gave me a box of candy, and said, 'Bye bye, sonny.'

'God be with you,' I said.

Travellers never say 'Good-bye'. Good-bye is for ever. We always wish our company on parting a safe or holy wish like, 'God be with you,' or, 'God send you good luck. God keep you safe.'

When I was nine years old we were travelling the Counties Kerry, Cork, Clare and Galway, meeting other Travellers on our travels at fairs, and especially at Ballinasloe Fair. Hundreds of Travellers come to that fair, selling horses, donkeys, wagons, carts, swapping and dealing, telling fortunes, playing musical instruments. For a full week the fair would be on. Spangel Hill Fair in the County Clare is a very big fair, and then of course there is Puck Fair, County Kerry. In Puck Fair all the wagons are camped on the roadside. Hardly any of the Travellers go to bed during the fair. The Travellers have been attending these fairs for hundreds of years. And there are great legends about them:

> The hand that kills King Puck
> Will wither like the dew.
> The blade that cuts his whiskers
> Will pierce your heart too.
> The rope that hangs old Puck,
> Will execute its maker...

Old King Puck is a goat and he'd be crowned King Puck during the fair. It is also said that the single girl that goes to Puck Fair will leave it doubled.

In the night around the camp fires you would hear some of the best Irish traditional music that ever was played; reels, jigs, hornpipes, airs, marches, and old Irish waltzes – 'The Galway Snare', 'Father Murphy', 'Sullivan John', 'The Jolly Tinker', 'The Catcherman', 'Ellen Brown', 'Banclothy', 'The Maid in the Garret', 'Seven Drunken Nights', 'Heather Ale', 'Flower of Sweet Strabone', 'Lalley Mountain', 'The Beggar Man', 'John Mitchell', and many more different names of songs: 'The Maid of Mount Scisco', 'The Sligo Maid', 'The Maid behind the Bar', 'Rakish Paddy', 'Georgie Whites', 'The Washer Woman', 'Pigeon on the Gate', 'Down the Broom', 'Battering Ram', and 'Sally Gardens', 'Hornpipes', 'The Black Bird', 'The Cork Hornpipe', 'The Dawn of the Day', 'Wearing of the Green', 'Kelly from Killarney', and many more.

We are history that has never been challenged. English scholars could not make head or tail of Cant, or for that matter Irish scholars. So when they knew they were beaten because none would translate it for them, the English scholars put 'Cant' in their dictionaries as hypocritical talk, odd talk or peculiar talk.

The word for Cant in our language is Shelta. A Tinker was asked to translate Shelta to the tyrant Cromwell. 'I can't,' said the Tinker. And Cant it remained since, and Cromwell was none the wiser.

My Daddy got very sick in 1946. A bus ran into him at Harold's Cross, Dublin. Nearly every bone in his body was broken. His legs, arms and collar-bone and jaw-bone were broken. His eye was shattered and he was in a coma for seven weeks. And two of the horses was killed as well in the crash.

Well, for months my Daddy could not work. When he got better it was the world's worst winter, 1947. We had to sell the wagon and all our horses except one pony which we kept to pull the bad cart along the road and the bit of green canvas.

Never in the world have people suffered more than we did that winter. What I am writing, when the reader reads it, he will say to himself, or herself, it was impossible to survive. No, it was not impossible to survive. It was a miracle because I witnessed it and so did my little brothers and sisters, and my poor mother and father and our misfortunate animals.

A few days before the big snow of 1947 the weather was very bad. We were after coming from the Twin Towers in County Donegal. We were crossing Branards Cap and we were forced to turn back with the blizzards. Some of us was in our bare feet walking behind the pony and cart.

That evening we camped near a crossroads at a sheltering hedge. My father made the tent and my mother went hawking to the nearby houses to get the makings for our supper. The icy wind was cutting our skin on our hands and faces, and my little sister in my mother's shawl, only three weeks old she was, was crying with the bitter cold and at that same time my mother was very ill. She looked very pale, worn out and tired. The snow was blowing through her hair, and when a gust of wind blew, the half-melted snow would drop from my mother's brow on to my sister's face in my mother's arms, and when this happened we could hear a very delicate and innocent cry from the child in the wet frosty shawl.

Our blankets were in the cart and the snow water was falling out of them as my Daddy took them from the cart to put in the tent. When this was done all the children got into the tent, a frosty snot hanging from each one of their noses, their little faces red and blue with cold, and our little hands and feet swollen with the angry bitter weather. Our little terrier bitch, named Nell, keening with pain from the cold, came into the tent for shelter from the icy wind and snow.

My Daddy went to the wood for sticks to light the fire, and he himself was hardly able to walk. The frost was taking advantage of his broken and half-set bones. The poor pony outside trying to put her head into the door of the tent, the snow was cutting the eyes out of her and she was trembling with the cold.

My Daddy got back with the sticks, an armful of old twigs, and he dropped them from his arms on to the ground with weakness. He fell on top of the sticks and he looked up at the sky and said in a pitiful voice, 'God, look down on us.'

My Daddy managed to light the fire somehow.

And in about ten minutes the fire was blazing. When the pony felt the heat behind her she started whinnying slowly as if to say she was grateful. She pulled her head from the door of the tent and walked over beside the hedge. The smoke from the fire and sparks were blinding her but she was quite contented. And little Nell went to the fire and sat down on her behind and stared into the fire puzzled and amazed. The children came out of the tent and sat on bundles of straw. The steam was rising from their wet clothes and melting the falling snow in the frosty air.

The kettles were filled and put on the fire to boil, and my Daddy took the wet blankets from the tent and in turn dried them over the fire. Then my mother came back with some dry clothes and food the people in the nearby houses gave her. She also got some flaked meal and my Daddy put some of it into a dish and threw boiling water over it and gave it as a hot gruel to the pony. And poor Queenie was so glad to get it she nearly said thanks to my Daddy. And when she ate it she trotted up and down the road to keep herself warm.

Soon we had our food, and with every bite we took from the bread, lots of snowflakes we would have in our mouths. It was making the bread soggy. My mother was barely able to serve us all with our food, she was that ill with after-birth pains and pneumonia and bronchitis, and the snow at the same time was dropping down on her black hair and on her innocent face that was as pale as the smoky snow around her.

My Daddy and my brother Jimmy, after their tea, went to the houses for straw. My Mammy said to me, 'Do you want more bread, Johnny, son?'

'No, Mammy,' I said. 'I am too full now, thank God. Mammy,' I said, 'you are sick. You should lie down in the tent for a while.'

She looked at me with tears in her wet eyes, and her wet hair blowing with the wind around her pale face. She kissed me and put her two hands on my knees. 'Why do you worry about me so much, Johnny?'

'You're my Mammy,' I said. 'That is why.'

She tried to be cheerful. 'No, Johnny, I am not sick. I am just tired and fed up with this weather.'

'You are sick, Mammy,' I said, 'and very sick. I will make the bottle for the child. You go into the tent and lie down.'

'No, son. I am all right. When your Daddy comes back, don't say to him I am sick. Because I don't want him to know I am sick. If your Daddy knew I was sick I would have to go to hospital. And there would be no one to look after yous. So don't tell your Daddy.'

'All right,' I said. 'I won't.'

She pulled my nose gently, 'I will be all right, Johnny, son.'

It was nearly dark when my Daddy and Jimmy came back with two large bundles of straw on their backs, and one of the bundles they strewed and spread around the tent. Jimmy made a little shelter for the little terrier bitch with some of the straw, and the rest he gave to Queenie to eat.

We all went to bed at this time – there was about a foot of snow outside on the ground.

The next morning I was the first to waking, and the sweat was falling down off me with the heat. It was so close I could hardly breathe. The snow was covering the tent. Six foot of it over the tent. Not a sound could be heard.

'We are finished,' said my Daddy.

Then after a while we could barely hear muffled voices outside saying, 'They must be dead.'

It was a lot of farmers digging away the snow to get down to us. They managed to get down to us after some time. Then we were all pulled out, one by one. Then Jimmy started to dig for Nell. He found her. She was after having pups. Nell was dead and all the pups, except one was barely alive. And my sister put him in her bosom to get the life back in him. Most probably he was the first puppy and he was more strong than the others. We called him Spring.

The farmers brought us to the farmhouse and we all had a good meal and a good heat at the inside fire.

Queenie was all right. She found herself a stable during the night with a lot of sheep.

My Mammy gave my sister Mary one of the teats belonging to the child to feed the little pup with and Mary would not let that pup die. She blew down his neck. She rubbed him and shook him till the life was back in his veins, and then drop by drop she patiently let the drops of milk drop into the few-hours-old pup's mouth. He lived and we called him Spring – and all through the bad snow the farmer gave us the use of a big warm hayshed. And at the door we had a great big fire, and the people from around the area brought us blankets and clothes and food and milk. And at the same time my Daddy and Jimmy was helping the farmers to dig out the sheep and cattle from the drifts of snow.

My Mammy went to hospital a few days later. And she signed herself out after a fortnight. Then the snow began to disintegrate into slush and the weather was getting better and Spring was yelping. His eyes was just after opening when the snow went.

Then my Daddy and Jimmy made dozens and dozens of tinware articles and then sold them at the shops and houses. And my Daddy built a new wagon. My Mammy was better and all the children had dry noses again. And within a few weeks my Daddy built another wagon.

Queenie gave birth to a lovely black and white foal, and we called her Taxi.

My Daddy and Jimmy bought a job lot of articles from a big Co-op Hardware Store and they sold them at the fairs at a big profit, until we came to have six horses and about twelve donkeys. And Spring was under one of the wagons chewing at a big bone. It was the month of June, and we were camped at Brockah Corner, near the railway bridge. Brockah is a little mountain-town on the side of a valley, and just down below Brockah there is a wood and across from Brockah one could see little golden-coloured roofs of the white thatched cottages and the salmon jumping in the river below in the valley.

We left Brockah and pulled into Ballybokay. We met other Travellers, including Johnnie Doran and his family. Johnnie Doran was the best ulean piper in the world. He was buskering the fair and the whole fair stood to listen to him play his favourite reel 'Rakish Paddy'. When he played this reel he bought two fine horses, so a deal and a reel was going on at the one time. That reel will never be played by no man the way Johnnie Doran played it. Johnnie, God rest him, was also a smart man with the horses. Johnnie was very seriously injured shortly after. A wall fell on him and broke his spine. He died two years later in Dublin. I shall never forget his music.

I left the fair and my sister and me went out to the quiet country road. As we turned up the side-road to the camp I could hear the uninterrupted sweet voice of a travelling woman echoing across the valleys and hills. 'Mary,' I said, 'don't make a sound. Listen to that complete yearning in that voice.'

'Ah, will you go away out of that,' said Mary, 'you're too fond of music.'

'Mary,' I said, 'nobody can be too fond of music. Music is nature and the one that is not fond of music is unlucky.'

'Ah well,' said Mary, 'you're too fond of music.'

As we got closer to the camp we could see it was a woman called Mary Calley. She was singing a lullaby to her baby. As the notes went low in her voice, the bees kept the drones and beat going with their humming and an odd blue-tit or wren filled in the background with their chirping and whistling. God Almighty, it was something to hear. It was nature and real unspoiled and clear.

The song Mary Calley was singing was called 'A Mother's Lament':

> A mother cried while tears were falling,
> Rolling down like a lonely stream.
> Although she cried while the tears were falling,
> There she wandered day by day.
> There she worried, growing fonder,
> Of the child that made her joy.
> But till the next she will stay
> Till she finds her angel boy.

The legend behind the song concerns a mother that lost her little child and, as the legend goes, the bad fairies took her little child away and they put an old bewitched and bewildered half-human child in the cradle and took her lovely babe away. The mother waited at the side of the stream for months and months to see would the bad lureacones (fairies) bring her child back to her. She died broken-hearted when she saw her child floating down the stream. The baby was dead.

We are the mysterious people in the world; history knows nothing about us. When the first Gypsies came to Ireland from Egypt, they brought with them Egypt ways of life and living. The English dictionary does contain some of our stolen words like fetich which, in our language, means curse. Monya fetich means good charm, good luck. A wise man, we call him, connich fein. Intercourse is feick. Feeck means take. What was beating good scholars at our language was the way Travellers pronounced the words. Then when they was asked to spell that word it was like asking a rock to talk. And the scholar had to abandon whatever he set out to do.

We left Donegal and we went to Derry. We camped at the old racecourse. We met a lot of other Travellers there. There was not much for me to do, as this was the time I was crippled. I felt very sorry for myself. I could not go to fish or play or sing. I was crippled and to make it worse I got a sunstroke. The only life I had in my body was my hands, neck and head, the rest, except my tongue and brain was paralysed.

Spring was now a good size. He would always come over and lie down beside me and lick my face. No one could come near me because Spring was willing to suffer his death over me. I got a rabbit skin one day and I shook it. Spring took it out of my hands with his mouth and tore it to pieces. Another day a policeman came to the camp. I was on my own, the rest of the children were sorting scrap and rags up the lane. Spring started to growl when he saw the policeman.

'How long have you been here?' said the policeman.

'We came here yesterday, sir,' I said.

'Get up when you talk to me,' said the policeman.

'I can't, sir,' I said.

'You cheeky little brat. Get up or I will kick you up.'

The policeman came towards me. Spring caught him and then he bit his leg. The policeman was screaming for mercy. The policeman got the kettle bar in his hand to hit Spring with it, but three or four lurchers came from the other caravans. I shouted at the policeman to drop the bar. He did drop it and the dogs came over to me when I called them in Shelta.

'I am going to get these dog shot,' said the policeman.

'It's your own fault,' I said. 'The dogs was only protecting me. You came here to bully people. But you got the worst of it yourself. Wait till my Daddy comes back and he will give you a worse beating.'

The policeman walked away with his clothes in rags and no seat in his pants, saying: 'I will have them mongrels shot.'

I shouted after him, 'You will have to shoot me first.'

The policeman never came back.

One day a very nice farmer was herding cattle up the camp and one of the cows came over to smell me as I was lying down in the grass. Spring made a spring for the cow's nose and he swung out of it. When the farmer saw what Spring done naturally he was angry. But when he saw that Spring was only protecting me from the cow's walking on top of me, he patted Spring on the head and said, 'Good boy, that's the good boy.' Spring was glad that the farmer showed admiration for him and he licked the farmer's hand. And soon as he done that he came over and lay down beside me.

Spring was the cutest, cunningest, loyalest dog that ever was pupped. In the mornings he would come into the wagon and pull the blankets off me and lick my face. I am sure Spring had some idea what was wrong with me in his own way. He definitely had pity for me. He knew and saw himself as my protector. I trained Spring to do all classes of tricks just by word of mouth. For two years Spring was my playmate. He was my amusement with his tricks. He was my pal and my protector. He would sometimes go into the nearby fields and kill a rabbit or hare and bring it back in his mouth and drop it beside me. Then he would look at me and lick my face as if to say, 'This is for you.' No matter what I told Spring to do he would do it straight away. When I would be eating my food I could leave the plate under Spring's nose and he would not touch one bit of it. But if another dog came over to the plate, Spring would warn him with a growl. If he did not take the warning he would feel the sharp teeth of Spring. Spring had a kind of reform code to the other animals and they obeyed him. After all Spring was a travelling dog, born in the snow an orphan, and he classed our family as his family. There never will be another dog like Spring.

After I got the power of my limbs back, Spring was as glad as I was because there was more exercise for both of us. Wherever Spring was I was. When I would go to church, Spring would come to await at the door of the chapel for me till Mass was over. If I went to the pictures, Spring was with me. One day a shepherd was driving sheep and the man was in a bad way because his dog was not with him and the sheep was running all over the place.

I offered the man help with the sheep and I said to Spring, 'Caush comra.' In no time Spring had the sheep rounded up.

'That's a very good dog you have,' said the man.

'Yes sir,' I said. 'He is the best dog in the world.'

'Would you sell him?' said the shepherd.

Spring growled at him as much as to say, 'I will do you a turn, but you won't buy me.'

'He knew what I said,' said the man.

'Oh yes, sir,' I said. 'He knows every word, don't you, Spring?' And Spring barked.

We left Derry and went towards Tyrone and then towards Antrim. What a grand county that is. Giant's Causeway on the Bray of Hill sloping to the sea and glens and valleys, dells, lakes, and clear river. And our bright coloured wagons passing through the glens and the sun reflecting the blue, red and yellow colouring of the wagons and carts. Ponies, donkeys, mules, dogs and goats, the children sitting in the doors of the wagons and more of them running behind.

We camped at Ranulestown that evening with other Travellers named Conners and Doran. That night most of the folk went to the local pub where they drink black, creamy pints of Guinness like fish. Guinness to a Traveller is a food, a strengthener, a tonic, a beverage and a health drink as well as a lively community drink. Somtimes we give it to the babies instead of milk.

No matter what way we mix it or take it, it still remains one of the greatest drinks that ever we have drunk. It has reared many a child to be a man and secrets we like to keep, some of them anyway. It's the secret, sacred drink the travelling people got from Arthur himself in 1758, the year before he made it.

The Guinness is the Travellers' doctor in many different ways. Suppose I had the 'flu, the only doctor I would see is a black bottle of Guinness and it would cure me using it my own way.

When the old people came back from the pub the dancing and singing started around the camp-fire. Songs, reels, jigs galore. What a great night that was. And I stole some of their bottles while they were dancing, and myself and a little girl went out in the field and we drank the porter. We got drunk, and we fell asleep. When I woke up my head was paining me. I had to shake the little girl, she was still drunk. And I was afraid I was going to be blamed for making myself and the little girl drunk. She was about my age, nine and a half years old. I went to the wagons, everyone was in bed. So I went to the press and I got three or four blankets and I brought them into the field and I spread them over the little girl and myself and then slept in the field till morning because I was afraid to leave the little girl by herself. I thought maybe Willy-the-Wist or Jack-the-Lantern or some wicked spirit might harm the little girl and I would get the blame.

The next morning a lot of the older people in the camp woke myself and the little girl. I had to tell what happened and my father was very angry with me over my stealing his Guinness.

That same morning the police came and told us that we would have to move. So after our breakfast we shifted and we came on to Newry where the Irish patriot John Mitchell, 1815–75, met his downfall. There is a great song about him, and the name of the song is 'John Mitchell':

> I am a true born Irishman,
> John Mitchell is my name,
> To free my own great country
> From Dungiven town I came.
>
> I struggled hard both night and day
> To free my native land
> And yet I was transported
> All to Van Diemen's land.
>
> When I first received my sentence
> In eighteen-forty-eight
> My loving wife came up to me
> And unto me did say,
>
> 'Oh John my love cheer up your heart
> And daunted do not be,
> It is better to die for old Ireland's rights
> Than to live in slavery.'

> When I first received my sentence
> On inland Ireland's ground
> Thousands of my countrymen
> Was standing all around.
>
> My liberty was offered me
> If I would forsake their cause,
> But I would rather die ten thousand deaths
> Than forsake my Irish boys.
>
> Fare you well my wife and children,
> In heaven I will wait for you.
> Goodbye all true born Irishmen
> And my old country too.
>
> There is one request I will ask from you,
> That's when I'm dead or gone,
> Remember poor John Mitchell, boys,
> That wore a convict's chain...

Ah, many's a folk club or public house or camp-fire I sung that song at. We did not stay long in Newry and a few days later my Daddy said he was going up the country that morning.

We were leaving the rest of the Travellers. Nearly all the people in the camp was crying. They were very sorry and lonesome to see us go. 'Well lads,' said my Daddy, 'God Almighty be with yous, and send yous all the height of good luck.'

So the lash of the whip fell on the mare that was under the shafts of the wagon and the mare put her chest to the collar and away she pulled with the wagon behind her. We were still waving to the rest of the Travellers as we turned the bend of the road.

It is a very lonesome time when we leave other Travellers and then pull up that night on the side of a lonely by-road, with just our own family to talk to. We were travelling every day for over a week. Just pulling in for one night and then moving on the next morning till we got to Mullingar, County Westmeath.

There was a very bad R.U.C. sergeant in that town one time. I think he was there during the rebellious times. He was a bastard of a pig dressed in uniform. My Daddy often told us about him. I believe he was the worst man that ever was born from a mother.

When Travellers would camp around Mullingar, this bulldog of a police sergeant would not let the Travellers stay and sometimes during the night himself and a lot of blackguards would go to a camp and pull the Travellers out of their beds and demolish their tents and destroy everything.

But he did it too often. John Donohue put a stop to his gallop. The sergeant came to John Donohue's camp, John was not there, but John's wife and children were. The sergeant jumped on top of the tent and he broke the tent to the ground. When John came back the next morning, his wife was crying and his children were shivering with the cold. John lit the fire for the children and then he went into the town looking for the sergeant, 'John Bull's Under Snot Watchdog' as he called him.

John met the sergeant in the main street. John had an ash plant in his hand and the sergeant had a revolver. John walked over to the sergeant. 'Good morning, Mr Bulldog,' said John to the sergeant, and before the sergeant had time to speak, John hit him along the side of the head with the ashplant. The sergeant fell to the ground.

'Get up,' said John, '*or* I will kick you up.'

The sergeant went for his gun and as soon as he did, John hit it out of his hand with the ashplant. John kicked the sergeant up and down the town till the sergeant looked like a hug-a-day (scarecrow) and John left the sergeant lying in the street.

There is a song about it:

>Oh the public houses was not closed
>Here and there my two eyes goes.
>And I up and I struck the sergeant
>Over the eyebrow at the bar.
>I knocked him down you might be sure
>I trampled upon him on the floor
>And I kicked him into ribbons
>Before I left Mullingar ...

That sergeant was like a saint ever after. He got his own medicine and he did not like its taste. He never troubled another Traveller and I believe he died happy an old man.

We left Mullingar and we came on to Athlone, the centre of Ireland. And we camped at the Radio Eireann Broadcasting Station. It's a little country woody road leading off the main road. There we met the McDonaghs (Wexford Connors), Delaneys and Walls and we were all very glad to be camping with company again.

During that time Travellers had a contract with a bottle, jar and glass firm, and we were collecting all classes of bottles and jars, thousands of gross each day we collected from farms, cottages, hotels, and dumps. But we were also collecting rags, scrap metal, feather beds and horse hair, and buying and selling donkeys, horses, and so on. In the winter months we pulled the sugar beet and made cans, buckets, pots, kettles, baths, and basins, as well as mending them. And an odd fortune would be told as well. And we attended all the fairs and marts.

We left Athlone along with a lot of fish I caught that morning and we headed for Tuam, County Galway. There was about twenty families of Travellers with us at this time and we camped outside of Tuam near the old monument. There we met the Dohertys, Wards, Cashes and Sahoes. They were waiting around Tuam for the Ballinasloe Fair which is one of the busiest fairs in Ireland. Thousands of Travellers attend that fair every year and have done for hundreds of years.

All that day and part of the night the travelling men were swapping and dealing their wagons or carts and ponies.

County Galway is a beautiful country and it's a country that I could live long in and die happy, although we never travelled the County Galway much. Galway is the home of the great pipers and fiddlers and singers. There is a song about Galway, and one evening I was coming back to the camp with a can of milk in my hand and I heard a young girl, about sixteen years of age, she was. She was singing to her little baby brother and when I heard her voice, a thrill of pleasantness crawled up my spine. The yawn of her voice had a culture of its own. The name of the song was 'The Galway Shawl':

> It's Aranmore in the County Galway
> One fine summer's morning in the month of May
> I overspied a handsome colleen
> She nearly stole my poor heart away.

She wore no paint nor she wore no powder
Nor costly diamonds she wore none at all.
But she wore a bonnet with a red rose on it,
And around her shoulders she wore a Galway shawl.

We kept a'talking to ourselves, were walking,
Till her father's cottage it came to view,
Will you come in till you see my father,
He will play for you, The Old Foggy Dew . . .

At this stage a lot of noisy children came running down the road and my enjoyment was spoiled and I walked over to the girl and I said, 'Miss, that was the grandest bit of a song I ever heard.'

'Ah will you go away out of that, I am hoarse as an old cuckoo.'

'No, miss,' I said, 'you have a voice as sweet as wild bee's honey.'

She laughed and she put her little baby brother in the tent to go asleep and I could see there was a smile of contentment on the sleeping baby's face as she lay him down on the patchwork quilt in the tent.

'You're a nice little boy,' she said. 'What's your name?'

'Oh, my name is Johnny Connors,' I said. 'What's your name?'

'My name is Mary Sahoe,' she said. This girl was a pure picture with long curly golden yellow hair. I thought to myself if I was her age I would be more bolder and I would ask her for a date. But that was out of the question. I was only ten years old at the time and I had to abandon my ideas. It was a kind of compulsory matter, I suppose. Anyway, one can't put an old head onto young shoulders. But at the time I wished it was possible, that was one time I would have loved to be older, at least for a day or so anyway.

'Well, miss,' I said, 'I must get back with the milk. God be with you.'

'You too,' she said, and I walked on down the road to our wagons.

My Mammy was a sort angry with me over me delaying so long with the milk.

'What in God's name kept you, Johnny, with the milk?' said my Mammy.

'Oh,' I said, 'I was listening to that grand girl down there in the tents, she was singing a fine song and I had to wait to listen to her.'

'Why don't you tell a lie sometime,' my Mammy said, 'you always have an excuse.'

'No,' I said, 'it's true. I was listening to the grand fine girl, singing a grand song.'

And my Mammy laughed at me. 'Johnny, son, you never tell a lie. Never mind what I said to you. Here's your supper.'

Spring was after finding himself a few bitches, and one of the bitches had a whole litter off Spring. For Spring, he was lying down in under the wagon, a proud father of his pups. He looked at me in a very happy mood as much as to say he was a good-looking dog and the bitches got attracted to him. I looked at him and he wagged his tail.

'Mammy,' I said, 'that Spring is a stupid fool of a dog.'

'Why?' said my Mammy.

'Well,' I said, 'he got married too young and he's never going to feed all them pups.'

My Mammy roared with laughter.

A few days after Ballinasloe Fair, we travelled on to Rosscommon and from that to Ballina, County Mayo. At the fair of Ballina we met a lot of my Daddy's people and that was the only time in my life that I ever saw eight hundred donkeys together in the one bunch. Johnny Connors (R.I.P.) had nearly three hundred donkeys including some ponies. Jerry Connors had about a hundred donkeys. John Boy Connors had a similar number of donkeys and we had about sixty donkeys. Donkeys was a very big trade. Most of them were shipped to Britain as pets. But a lot went to the Continent. In fact some of the donkeys went to all parts of Europe, even to the United States and Russia. People say that it was cheaper to have a live ornament in their garden than to have a big stupid stone. And big ranchers always count it lucky to have a donkey running with their cattle. If a cow or a horse fall in a bog or swamp, the donkey will roar for help and he will continue to do so till the animal is brought to safety. Also when a cow has calved or a mare has foaled, a donkey will protect the calf or foal from dogs and other animals. People use the word, as stupid as an ass. A donkey is an ass, but he is not stupid. He is a great, cunning pretender. If a donkey don't want you on his back, he will buck and jump and leap to get you off his back, and if that fails, he will give in or submit for the time being, till he comes to a ditch or a trench. And when you think you have him broken and he thinks that you think you have mastered him, he will stop in his tracks very suddenly and you will be dumped into the hedge or trench. He will stand there looking at you trying to get out of the trench or hedge. The donkey will always make a fool out of a human in his own space of time.

We travelled to all the fairs in Mayo and all the towns, Foxford, Westport, Ballyhaunis, Claremorris, Goodcady, Castlebar, Manerhamilton, Culshamock, Achill Island and The Sound. County Mayo is the nearest thing to heaven. I never saw heaven, but I would swear if our Lord and His angels and His saints was ever changing their address they would stay in Achill, County Mayo, for evermore. The only thing they would have to do is put a pair of golden gates on the approach to the island and they could call it the New Irish Heaven on Earth. And what a grand place it would be. The birds whistling and singing and the salmon and trout showing off jumping in the river. Along the side of the roads, a good tinsmith hammering out a grand lively beat on his iron stake or anvil and a good musician playing an Irish lament. That's what I would call heaven on earth:

> Boys get together
> In all kinds of weather,
> Never show the white feather
> Wherever you roam.
>
> Be like a brother
> And help one another
> Like the true hearted men
> From the County Mayo.

Yes, Mayo is heaven's pastures on Ireland's ground.

My Daddy made two wagons, one for Jim Delaney and the other for Johnny Connors, and two good barrel-top wagons they were. When he had them finished he left Mayo and on to the County Cavan we went.

Times was very good. My Daddy was dealing in everything and anything, and he made a lot of three-legged tables, and he sold them like hot cakes. At this time we were buying all kinds of poultry, and at times we had as much as three thousand birds. Ducks, turkeys, hens, guinea hens, and bantams and chickens. We had a contract for them with a poultry and feather farm in Dublin. Anything a farmer wanted or any job he wanted mended, we would mend it, such as mowing machines, ploughs, hay-rakes and all farm implements.

My Daddy is also a great vet, and he could attend to any animal. So we were the jack-of-all-trades. Any kind of a job in the country we could do. We were builders, carpenters, dealers and iron workers, tinsmiths and horse dealers and breeders. We had the gift of the gum sha lack unick. Gum sha lack unick is an etc. etc. etc. Cross between a genius thing and a miracle. There is a song about the gum sha lack that I have written,

GUM SHA LACK

We are the travelling people like the Picts or beaker folk.
The men in Whitehall thinks we are parasites, but Tinker is the word,

> *With our Gum Sha Lack alayro,*
> *Move us on you boyos.*

All the jobs in the world we have done from making Pharaoh's coffins,
To building Birmingham,

> *With our Gum Sha Lack alayro,*
> *Wallop it out me heroes.*

We have mended pots and kettles and buckets for Lord Cornwall.
But before we could leave the house, me lads, we would mind the women and all,

> *With our Gum Sha Lack alayro.*
> *Wallop it out me hero.*

Well I have a little woman, a mother she is to be,
She gets her basket on her arm and mooches the hills for me,

> *With our Gum Sha Lack alayro.*
> *Wallop it out me hero.*

We have fought the Romans, the Spanish and the Danes,
We fought against the dirty Black and Tans and knocked Cromwell to his knees,

> *With our Gum Sha Lack alayro,*
> *Wallop it out me heroes.*

Well we are married this twenty years, nineteen children we have got,
One is hardly walking when there's another one in the cot,

> *Over our Gum Sha Lack alayro,*
> *Get out of that you boyos.*

We have made cannon guns in Hungary, bronze cauldrons in the year BC,
We have fought and died for Ireland to make sure she was free,

> *With our Gum Sha Lack alayro,*
> *Wallop it out me heroes.*

We can sing a song or dance a reel, no matter where we roam,
We have learned the Roman Nero how to play the pipes way back in time of Rome,

> *With our Gum Sha Lack alayro,*
> *Whack it if you can me boyos.*

A well-known man said to me one day, 'John, son, if you ever had to go to school just for a few years, there would be no man to touch you, you are a genius of your people.'

'Sir,' I said, 'if I had to go to school, I would like it very much, but if I did, I would not know my people.'

We left Cavan and we came on to my own home town, Dublin. Dublin the city of great fame. We camped at Dolkins Bran beside the canal, and there we met old McCann, Johnny Murphy, and the Camer Murphys. The Camer Murphys are my old Mammy's people. We never call our grandmothers 'grandmother'. We call them 'old Mammy' and our grandfathers 'old Daddy'. The Murphys are great poets and ballad makers, and the McCanns are good music makers and they were also great leather makers. They made boots, shoes, harness, and all classes of leather goods. And they were good in the boxing booths and rings. They were real professional boxers. They also made iron and tinware and collected metal and smelted the metal at the roadsides in makeshift furnaces.

Well, my mother was expecting my sister Catherine at the time and the very day and hour my sister Catherine was born my little sister Barbara died, God rest her little soul. This was a terrible shock to us all. And I will never forget that time, it very nearly killed my Mammy. She cried for a whole week till there was not a tear left in her body. Yes, my Mammy took it very bad.

The travelling children in my country could not read or write because the wobs and nese stach mon'ya feins would evict us night and day. We would be shirted night and day along the roads so we could not go to school.

My mother was crying and she was really sad and lonely. The tears were falling from her eyes.

She called me, 'Come here, Johnny, son.'

'What do you want, Mammy?' I said.

'Will you go down to the Convent, son, and ask the Nuns for a loan of a crucifix to put in the wagon. Because we are going to wake your little sister in the wagon.'

So I told my mother I would go to the Convent. My mother gave me two pennies for the bus fare.

At that time I was a little boy and I was in my bare feet. I had a very big rip in the seat of my pants and the tail of my shirt was hanging and waggling from the hole in my pants. Like a tail it was. I was like a clown.

Galune [Good God], I said to myself, I'll be saulked [arrested]. But, somehow I was not arrested and I came to the door of the Convent.

I knocked on the door and I could hear footsteps coming towards the door. The door was opened by a little Nun. She was dressed in black robes with a white front on them. She had a beautiful and pitiful warm smile on her face.

'God bless you, Sister,' I said.

'You too,' said the little Nun.

'My mother sent me down to ask you for a crucifix,' says I. So I told the Nun the whole story of how my little sister had died with pneumonia. The little Nun said she was sorry to hear that. She was really sorry because I could see the pitiful expression on her face. Then the little Nun asked me to come in.

'Thank you, Sister,' I said.

As I walked down the big, long hallway the noise of my two bare feet was echoing all over the place. It was like the noise of a big heavy duck walking: clap, clap, clap, slap. Finally we came to a big room and the little Nun opened the two big swinging doors and straight in front of us in the room was a lot of Nuns sitting around a big Jacobite table. They all stared at me for a good while.

'How the devil are you?' says I.

They all blessed themselves. I knew I was after saying the wrong words, but there was nothing I could do about it. I tried to change the words to 'God bless you, Sisters' but I was too embarrassed. I am sure you could boil a kettle on my face it was that red with shame.

'It's a grand morning,' says I. In fact it was evening. I was all mixed up with shame.

The Reverend Mother got up from the table and she walked towards me. 'What is your name?' she said.

'Oh, my name is John Connors,' says I.

'Where do you live?' said the Reverend Mother.

'I live in a caravan, Sister.'

'What age are you, John?'

'By Jaysus, to tell you the truth, Sister, I don't know. I know one thing, Sister, I lost my teeth about eleven months ago.'

'Can you read, John?'

'No, Sister, I can't.'

'Do you know any letters, John?'

'No, Sister.'

'Do you know your prayers, John'

'Yes, Sister.'

'What prayers do you know, John?'

'I know about that many.' I put up all my fingers.

'So you know ten prayers, John.'

'Yes, Sister.'

Then the other little Nun that opened the hall door for me came in and gave me a big mug of hot milk. The rest of the Nuns asked me questions. One Nun asked me, 'How many horses have you got, John?'

'We have a good few, Sister. We have the world of donkeys, and two caravans.'

Then another one of the Nuns asked me what I thought of Northern Ireland.

'It's a grand country, Sister,' says I.

'I am from Northern Ireland,' said the Nun.

'Yes, I know that, Sister. You are from Derry.'

The Nun was amazed. 'How do you know that, John?'

'Oh, I can tell by your accent,' says I.

'Where am I from, John?'

'You are from County Cavan, Sister.'

The little Nun that opened the door for me was watching me the whole time, and she just asked me one question, 'Have you ever been to school, John?'

'No, Sister, I never went to school. But I would like to go to school only the police and corporation men won't let us stay for long.'

'Well, I will teach you, John. You come here next Monday week at seven o'clock in the evening and I will see to it that you will know all your letters,' said the little Nun.

'Yes, Sister, I will come.'

It was time for me to go, and all the Nuns said good-bye to me.

'Yous need not say good-bye to me. I will be back next Monday week.'

As I walked to the door I looked back at the rest of the Nuns and I said, 'Good luck to you all, Sisters.'

As I was going out the door I said, 'Tell me, Sister, when will I know it's seven o'clock? I can't read or spell the time.'

'Ask somebody the time and they will tell you,' said the Nun.

I got on the bus and I went back with the crucifix. My mother was still crying when I arrived at the wagons. I handed the crucifix to my mother and she said, 'God bless you, son.'

The next day my little sister Barbara was buried. We were all very sad to see the little coffin going into the grave. Hundreds of Travellers were at the graveside – Johnny Clark and Izer Price, Willy Loveridge and some of the Grays were at the funeral, and a lot of Irish Travellers. They had come to the funeral in lorries and motor vans, ponies and carts and so on.

On the following Monday morning I awoke and I was in an awful hurry trying to get on my clothes. At this time I was well dressed.

My shoes were polished and I put on my good pants and coat and shirt.

I rushed out of the wagon. There was an old conishfein [gentleman] passing. 'What time is it, sir, please?' said I.

'It's half past,' said the old conishfein.

'Half past what, sir?'

'Half past eight,' said the old conishfein.

'When will it be full past, sir?'

The old conishfein looked at me. He got very upset and angry.

'Listen, young man, what damn time do you want it to be?'

'I would like it if it was seven o'clock,' said I.

'Well, do you want it to be seven o'clock in the morning or seven o'clock in the evening?'

'Dark time,' said I.

The old conishfein started to laugh. 'You are a comical little boy,' said he. 'You have ten-and-a-half hours to wait for seven dark time, as you call it.'

'Thank you, sir, and good luck to you,' said I.

'Dark time indeed. Ho, ho,' said the old conishfein.

As I walked away I looked back at him and I said to myself, a ruileahfein [madman].

All day I was asking the time. I did not want to be late for school at the Convent. Then I got my other sister, Maggie, to ask the time. A woman was passing and Maggie asked the old ladog [lady],

'What time is it, Mrs, please?'

The old ladog said it was twenty to six.

'What time did the woman say it was Maggie?' said I.

Maggie replied a whole load of minutes and a six.

My Daddy told me it was half past six. So I washed myself and I got on the bus.

The conducter said, 'Fares please.'

I gave him my penny. 'What time is it, conductor, please?'

'Twenty to seven,' said the conductor.

'When will it be seven o'clock?' said I.

Just then a gentleman got on the bus.

'What time is it, sir?'

'Wait a minute, sonny, and I will tell you.'

The gentleman took out a gold pocket-watch, 'It's ten minutes to seven o'clock,' said the gentleman.

'It is not,' said the conductor, 'it's just turned twenty to seven.'

'How dare you make so little of my watch,' said the gentleman to the conductor.

The two of them were still arguing when I got off the bus. (The times given by the conductor or the gentleman I can't be sure of, so the times I have stated are approximate.) I knocked at the door of the Convent and the little Nun opened the door.

'Come in, John.'

And that was the first time I ever was at school.*

About four weeks had passed and I could write my name JOHN. And nearly every minute during the day I would be saying, 'ZABQAZXOUWZ. ACB792Y14MN2Q,' and so on.

I would sing it all day, 'ABCDEFG HIJKLMNO PQRST UVWXYZ.'

Six weeks had passed and I could tell the time of the clock myself.

That was six weeks at night-school. Then the Nun asked me, would I like to go to a real classroom with little girls, because it was a girls' school. I said I would, so the next day for the first time in my life I was in a classroom. When the girls of the class saw me I could hear them whispering to one another, 'He is a gyppo.'

I was nearly mad. I shouted, 'Ah, shut up your big mouths.' I know it was wrong of me to treat young ladies that way, but they had started it.

After a while that day I got settled down to the class. And then I asked the teacher, 'Could I go to the toilet?'

'Yes, John, go right ahead out to the yard.'

I went into the toilet and I bolted one of the doors, and two girls came in.

It was a girls' toilet I was in.

'Hurry on, Mary, and pull your bloomers up when you leave.'

I made a burst for the door and my trousers tripped me up. I ran out the gate of the school. As I was going out I met the Reverend Mother.

---

* One thing is sure, that one can teach oneself how to read but one cannot teach oneself how to write properly. I have never been to school since. But I can claim to be an overgraduate from Oxford, because I went to night-school at Oxford for eight hours. So, to be precise, I had seven weeks, eight hours at schooling in my whole lifetime.

'What's wrong, John?' said the Reverend Mother.

'Those girls followed me into the toilet, the dirty things. They should be ashamed of themselves.'

I could see a smile on the Reverend Mother's face.

'You go back to your class, John, and I will sort it all out.'

I was ashamed of my life. Then it was playtime and the girls became to like me. I would skip with them, play ball with them. They became great pals of mine. The big bully girls were afraid of me, because when the big bully girls would bully the little girls I would stop them.

There was one big girl: I christened her, Young Elephant. She was a very fat girl and she would bump into the little girls and the little girls would fall flat on their faces. So one day she was bullying all the other little girls. 'Hold on there, you overgrown young elephant, don't be pushing any of the little girls.' So from that day onwards she never pushed any of the little girls, and if she tried to the little girls would say, 'I will get John to call you more names.'

I really enjoyed being at school. But the police and corporation gave my Daddy three days' notice and I had to leave school.

That night when I came back to the wagon, my Daddy said, 'Johnny, tomorrow is your last day at school.'

'What?' I said, 'I am not going to stop going to school.'

'Well, if you don't you will have to follow the wagons a very long road.

'Why?' I said.

'Because we are being shifted on Saturday.'

I could not sleep that night, I was fed up.

The next morning I went to school, and I told the teacher that this was my last day at school. She was very upset.

'Why must you stop going to school, John?' said the teacher.

'Because we are getting shifted.'

'Oh, I am sorry to hear that, John.'

At playtime all the girls gathered round me, 'Please don't leave, John.' Some of them was crying.

That evening I was forced to say good luck to all.

I was a very happy little boy and I wanted to go to school and I would not be able to go to school. So I said to myself, 'I will learn myself how to read proper.' Every sweet-paper with writing on it I would collect them all day. Tea bags, sugar bags and butter wrappers.

I would stay at shop windows reading everything that was in the windows. And big words like 'Palmolive', I would split them up, Pal-mo-live. And 'Corporation', Cor-por-ation. The only words that had me beat were medical words. 'Physician' was a killer. I did really lose my temper with that word PHYSICIAN. What really was making me angry was that words like PHYSICIAN, LAMB or KNIFE had silent letter words, and I would say to myself, the man that spelt KNIFE was a fool.

When I would be sent to the shops on errands, I would be hours reading everything in the shop. My Mammy often told me to get Lyons' tea. Instead I would get some other strange brand of tea so as I could read the strange words on the packet. Because I knew every word on the Lyons' tea packet.

The same way when my Daddy would send me for cigarettes. He would say to me, 'Make sure you get Woodbines,' and I would say, 'Maybe they have no Woodbines, what kind will I get if they have no Woodbines?' My Daddy would say, 'Get any kind.' I would get the strangest packet of cigarettes the shop had in stock so as I could read the writing on the packet. And if I was beaten at a word, I would go back into the shop and ask the person in the shop what the word meant. There were times people got angry with me over me asking so many questions. And they would simply say, 'Buzz off, you are a nuisance.'

Sweets with strange wrappings was the sweets I liked very much, even if they were horrible sweets. I don't think I ever enjoyed a sweet in them times, because I was not interested in the sweets, the wrapping was what I got more enjoyment out of. In other words, strange things were more helpful to me.

Also milestones, finger-posts, and most of all the rubbish-dumps were my teacher. When I would see a dump I would rather collect the old newspapers, comics and books out of the dump than go to the movies. Furthermore, I had been locked up on many occasions by the police and convicted for taking old books and papers and educational articles of my own choosing from dumps. So you could say I paid the hard way for the little bit of knowledge I have.

I have dined, wined and danced with many Heads of State and I have met Government officials from the ordinary local council men to the men in Whitehall, International Gypsy Committees and European organisations and officials of the European Commission, the

U.N.A., the Council of Europe and the National and International Councils for Civil Liberties, Conciliation Committees and the Race Relations Board, Lords and many statesmen.

I can thank only one person for that, and that person is the little Nun. She taught me how to defend the rights of the Travellers. Her work was not in vain. Strangely enough I never knew the little Nun's name. But their work is in the name of humanity, peace and understanding. They are miracle workers for the human race, and God bless them and their work.

After six weeks at school in the Convent, the little Nun said to me, 'John, I want you to be here at the Convent tomorrow morning at ten o'clock. You will be making your first Holy Communion in a couple of days. And I will have a surprise for you tomorrow morning.'

So that evening I was ready at last. Nearly six weeks of hard work had made me a scholar, and this meant a lot to me, and it also made a queen of the little Nun. She had mastered a completely illiterate boy within six weeks, and it made a man out of me.

Before I left the Convent that night all the Nuns gave me money and sweets. The money amounted to five shillings and most of it was in pennies, halfpennies and threepenny bits.

I went to a shop in Francis Street and there were a lot of one-arm bandits and slot machines in the shop. I put a penny in one of the slots and I won fourpence. I put another penny in the slot and I won the jackpot. I thought I was a millionaire. I had won eight shillings and fourpence. I changed the pennies with the woman behind the counter and she gave me silver money for the pennies. I then went across the road to the Tivoli Picture House. I paid the man at the door fourpence and I gave a penny for a big ice-cream.

I saw a great funny picture of Bud Abbot and Lou Costello. I like the Picture House, and I went on to a little shop. I bought two dozen of little holy pictures at one shilling and sixpence a dozen.

'How much do I owe you, Ma'am?'

'Three shillings, son,' said the old woman.

I gave her a half-crown and a sixpenny bit.

'Thank you, Ma'am.'

'Ah, you're all right, son. Watch yourself of the motor-cars!'

'I will, Ma'am.'

And off I went down along Merchant Quays in all the public houses, I sold my little holy pictures at fourpence a piece. I had about four little pictures left when I came to O'Connell's Bridge, and I went into a big hotel. I think it was the Gresham Hotel. I was only in there for a few minutes when a big gentleman called me over to his table. He was an American and his name was Roy Rogers, the film star.

'What are you selling, sonny?'
'I am selling holy pictures, sir.'
'How much do you sell them for?'
'Fourpence, sir.'
'Well now, I must buy one of those. Trigger would like one.'

I could see the manager of the hotel was not very pleased with me. He had a dry laugh on his face and by his looks he would rather see me gone. I suppose I can't blame him. But eventually he showed me to the door. He was very fair about it all and very polite.

When I got to the door, he said, 'Please don't come in again.'
'I won't, sir, and thank you very much.'
As I was walking away the manager called me back.
'Here, come here. I might as well buy one of your little holy pictures.'

He put his hand in his pocket and gave me a two shilling piece. 'And keep the change,' he said.

That was seven shillings I got, and so I walked away from the hotel. The second time the manager smiled at me and winked his eyes.

I had two Holy pictures left and I had a lucky night. I had about thirty shillings altogether in my pocket. It was 9.45 on the Lucky Coady clock facing the Bank of Ireland. I said to myself, 'I will sell these two pictures I have left.'

So round the corner in a pub, I asked a man would he buy a holy picture.

'How much are they?' said the man.
'Only fourpence, sir,' said I.
'Bedad, you are charging enough for them,' said the man.
'Oh, you bought a picture off me the other night, sir. And you were very drunk.'
'I suppose so, son,' said the man.
He bought the little picture. That man was the late Brendan

Behan, one of Ireland's greatest writers and play-writers, God rest his soul, Amen.

So I put the last picture in my pocket and I walked up to Christ Church, and at the corner of the Coombe and Patrick Street I got the last bus home to the barn. When I got to the wagon my Mammy said, 'Where were you, Johnny?'

I told her about the night I had and I gave her the money I had collected. She gave me my supper.

'Johnny, it would not surprise me if you will be a president when you grow up.'

I went to bed after my supper, and the next morning, about six o'clock, Spring came up in the wagon and he pulled the bedclothes off me, and he barked into my ears.

After my breakfast I harnessed the pony and yoked her under the first cart and I went out hawking, buying and collecting scrap metal. I bought a fair bit of scrap and rags and so on.

One gentleman said to me, 'What kind of scrap are you collecting?'

'All classes of scrap, sir. Such as old brass, copper, lead, batteries, machines and any class of scrap metal, or old, wet, dirty, dry or clean old rags. I would give you a good price for them.'

'If you say that again,' said the man, 'I will look about the place and any scrap that's here I will give to you.'

I did repeat the collecting words and the gentleman gave me a good pile of scrap and rags.

That evening I came back to camp and I sorted out the scrap and the rags and packed them, and I then went to the Convent.

On the way I thought to myself I should have been at the Convent that morning. I forgot blank about it. I said to myself, 'What am I going to tell the Nun?' I was going to make up an excuse, and then I thought it would not be lucky to tell the Nun a lie.

I knocked at the door of the Convent. The Nun came to the door. When she saw me she was not too pleased.

'John, you know you should have been here this morning.'

'Sister, I am very sorry, I forgot all about it till a few minutes ago. I am really sorry, Sister, and please forgive me. I know, Sister, what a disappointment it must have been for you. But honestly, Sister, I did forget.'

She smiled and said, 'Well, I will forgive you for this time. But make sure you are here tomorrow morning.'

'Yes, Sister, I will.'

The next morning I did go to the Convent, and I got my breakfast from the Nun.

After my breakfast, myself and the little Nun went down the city to a big shop that sold all classes of clothes and she bought me a suit and a full rig-out of clothes. From there we went to Domicans of the Quays and the Nun bought me a Saint John Basco relic and a silver medallion. Myself and the Nun came back to the Convent and she told me to put the new clothes on to see how they fitted me. While I was fitting the clothes on me, the Nun went to the kitchen to make the tea. I was dressed when she saw me, she hardly could speak. She did not cry from her eyes, but in her heart she cried.

'John, John, you look marvellous.'

'Sister, if it was not for you I would not look marvellous.'

She pulled a hanky from the sleeve of her robe and she hurried out of the room.

The next morning I made my first Communion and, after, I received the sacrament. Myself and the Nuns left the chapel in Meath Street and we came back to the Convent.

My breakfast was laid out on the Jacobite table and myself and all the Nuns sat around it. There was all kinds of cakes and fruit and other different kinds of food on the table. It was a high-class reception I received. After myself and the Nuns got our breakfast the Reverend Mother asked me to sing a song.

'Of course I will, Sister,' I said. And the song I sang was 'The Green Shades of Yon':

>Come on me jolly young fellows
>A warning take by me.
>Don't you ever fall in love
>With any young girl you see.
>For they will leave you broken-hearted
>Around the green shades of Yon.

>Tomorrow is the Fair day,
>We will all go to town.
>There will be five and twenty kisses
>For my own darling John.
>I will be content for ever
>Round the green shades of Yon.

> Oh me Mammy, she told me to get married in time,
> Get some handsome young girl that will keep up
>   your prime.
> But I would rather have my own darling for her
>   own sport and play,
> Nor all the gold and silver came by land or by sea.
>
> It's now that we are married
> And settled down for life,
> With our old tents and wagons
> By the old roadside
> And our children playing their games
> Round the green shades of Yon.
>
> They would rather have their own Daddy and Mammy.
> For their old sport and play,
> 'Nor all the gold and silver
> Comes between land or by sea.'

'That was a lovely song, John,' all the Nuns said.

'Well, Sister, I must say one thing. That I am very grateful to yous all for what yous have done for me.'

It was coming into the spring of the year when we left County Dublin. That morning my Daddy said to me, 'Johnny, son, will you yoke Queenie under the benog [cart]?'

'I will, to be sure,' said I.

So I got the harness and I yoked Queenie. It was a grand sunny morning as we got prepared, and the sun was dancing on the green and red paint on the cart – it was as if the brasses on the harness was alive. The reflections of the highly polished brass would dance on the shamrocks by the road making them an emerald clear green, and at the same time the reflections from the harness would light up the copper and bronze and brass articles inside the wagon. It was really a grand sight to see the cherry blossoms on the wild cherry trees like healthy pink faces, the children blooming with nature, and the tom-tit and the blue-tit whistling to their heart's content while the blackbird and thrush showed off with their clear notes as they whistled in the blackthorn bush to find their partners. The wren (the little king of the birds) bobbed up and through the fir bushes as the smoke from our camp-fire threw a low cloud through the ferns. The small ponies, donkeys and foals, getting herded by my brother and the goats and their kids wandering all over the country road. My Mammy making a patchwork quilt and my Daddy singing 'The Flowers of Sweet Strabane' as my brother and sisters loaded the newly made tinware on to the carts.

Then my Daddy shouted, 'Are yous ready to move lads?'

We all shouted, 'Yes, Daddy.'

He blessed himself and my Mammy got a bottle of Lourdes Holy Water and she sprinkled it over the road that we were to take. My Daddy then let the lash of the whip fall gently on Tom's back. 'Away with you, Tom.' And Tom put his large chest to the collar and pulled our wagon on along the road. Tom was our Irish draft-horse – he would pull a house down he was that strong, but he was very gentle.

When the wagon was pulled out all the carts then followed and the lurcher dogs and terriers walking along under the wagons and carts.

As we crossed the bridge, my Daddy shouted at Tom, 'Go on out of that will you, Tom.'

Tom went into a nice steady jog as he lifted his heavy legs spring-like as a ram into the air, the double beat of his hoofs hitting the road, one could jig a reel to the steady beat of Tom's hoofs. Clip clop, clip a clip, clop clip clop.

At Leixslip we camped that night, and my Daddy told me to get the cans and go to the nearby house for water. Away I went swinging the two cans as I ran to the little farmhouse. In the yard of the farm was the farmer.

'Good evening, sir.'

He never answered me but he just stood there staring at me. I stared back at him, I could see he was not too pleased to see me.

'Away, away to the devil with you,' he said to me.

'Sir, I would be thankful to you, sir, if you could give me two cans of water to boil for us to make our tea,' said I.

'The devil a water I have for the likes of you,' said he.

'Ah don't be so hard as you are, sir. You will have luck if you give me a drop of water,' said I.

'The devil a drop will I give you,' said he.

This man had a nose on his face and it was crossed between a two-year-old onion and the top of an olden-times blunderbuss gun.

He had the biggest nose in the whole thirty-two counties of Ireland. I could not stop looking at his nose, it was unavoidable, it covered his whole face (God forgive the remark).

'Well sir,' said I, 'you have the best nose in Ireland.'

'The devil take you and my nose,' said he.

'Faith, you are wrong, sir,' said I. 'If the devil took me he would take me as I am, and I would be doing him a favour and furthermore my Daddy would not be too pleased with the devil. But if he took your nose he would be doing you a great favour,' said I.

'Bad cess to you and my nose and the devil. I will put this pitchfork through you if you don't get to blazes out of here,' said he.

'Well,' said I, 'your nose is big, sir, sure as there's a roof on that house of yours, and since you are a wicked bad cavil ill-inclined man, I hope that your nose will grow as big as the Wicklow Mountain, because before you die and when you die, the last thing you will ask for is a drink of water and even that – that – that,' I stuttered, 'large compulsory nose you have will not save you.'

As I walked away he called me back.

'Hi, young fellah, come here, come here.'

At this time I was half afraid of the man with the overgrown nose.

'No. No. You can keep your dirty water now. I would not count it lucky to take it from you because you have your heart stuck in it,' said I.

'Well, listen to me, young fellah, I have not my heart stuck in the water,' said he.

'Oh yes you have, Mr. Nose, indeed you have. You looks on that water as if it was gold. You are what I call a water miser,' said I.

'Damn my poor misfortunate soul, you can have the whole wellful if you want it, young fellah,' said he.

'Thanks very much, sir,' said I. 'I will take two cansful for the time being.'

I filled the two cans out of the well.

'Are you satisfied now?' said the man with the nose.

'Yes sir, I am thankful to you, and I hope you will have good luck, sir,' said I.

'Listen to me a minute, young fellah. If you can give me a cure for my nose, I would be very grateful to you,' said he.

'Well sir,' said I, 'why would you want a cure for that nose of yours. It is God's will that you have it and you should not fly in

God's face. And not only that, sir, but there is many's a fine woman would be glad to marry that nose of yours,' said I.

'Well, well, well, be the holy man that's the grandest few words I've ever heard said,' said he.

'Indeed if you were a kind of half sociable, sir,' said I, 'you and that nose would get on in this world.'

'Ah well, from now on I will be a lot sociabler to people,' said he.

'Yes sir, I think you are right, but that nose of yours is a bit uncommon and unusual,' said I.

'I suppose you are right, young fellah, but will you tell me one mortal thing and I will never forget you.'

'What do you want to know, sir?' said I.

'I would like to know what uncommon means,' said he.

In my own mind I said to myself, corbed [finished] if ever I was in a trap, I am trapped now, said I, in my own mind.

'Well sir, uncommon means something we don't see every day. We will say for instance a film-star; we don't meet film-stars every day,' said I.

At this the man started stroking the nose with his hand. There was times I wanted to burst out laughing, but I was afraid.

'Well, young fellah, you have made me grand and happy and I am grateful to you, God knows, I am grateful to you.'

He went into the house and he brought out a bucket full of eggs and about three pounds of home-churned butter and a large cake of home-made bread, and two big two-pound pots of home-made damson jam.

'Here,' said he, 'that's for your family.' He even carried the food for me down to the camp. As the two of us walked down the lane he kept muttering to himself, 'Uncommon, uncommon, be Jaysus, uncommon.'

Travellers are famous for their stories, among them Tom Murphy. I can picture Tom sitting at the fire with his ould clay pipe in his mouth. I have been often told one of his stories since, but not the way that Tom told it to me. If I was to travel the world, I will never find a better story-teller than Tom Murphy.

It was a grey autumn evening, the sky with patches of fast-moving cloud as dark as a sloe, now and again the clouds would cover the moon and depriving us of the only natural bit of light in the sky, and when this would happen the blazing light from the camp-fire would blaze up our faces and woods and plantations all around us.

It was the setting for the story, a natural background, and the owls and woodcocks, 'coo-coo' they were saying as they sat in the thick growth.

Here is the story:

One time in Ireland there was this ould travelling man and the settled community couldn't bear the sight of him camping around the area, and every time he was in the area he would bother the people in the houses for water, and to make it worse the poor ould fellow was deformed (God bless the mark). He had a hump on his back. Every time he would knock at a door, the people would say, 'Get away, you dirty humpy Tinker.' So that winter he was found dead in his tent.

And the local priest made a collection from the parishioners, but the collection only mounted to a few shillings. The people were glad to see the poor ould Traveller dead. A very bad made coffin they put the poor ould fellow in, and they had to pack the corpse down in the old box-like coffin. They had an awful time with the hump, and the body was frozen stiff.

So they walked him in the chapel, and a very bad rainy night it was. The priest got into the pulpit to give a sermon about the poor ould fellow. 'Well, my dear brethren, we are gathered here tonight to show our last respects to this poor misfortunate poor soul and, mind you, you were very bad to this poor man when he was alive. I know some people in this chapel right now that called him humpy Tinker, humpy so-and-so, and so on. Well brethren in the face of God this was a very un-Christian thing to do.'

Just then, lightning struck the chapel again, and with the vibration the badly made coffin burst open and the priest ran for his life down along the aisle of the chapel, as he ran his cloak very near tripping him up.

As he was going out the door the strong wind closed the door on his cloak, and he screamed, 'Let me go, you humpy Tinker, let me go. I never done nothing to you.'

Camp-fire stories like this often made me jump when I was a child.

Approximately in 1920, my grandfather, my wife's two grandfathers, and their wives, were at a fair in Aucrim. Five small children came running into the fair crying, 'Mammy, Daddy, Mammy, Daddy, the police is after burning the tents and the rest of the yolks [things].'

My grandmother, Mary Anne, was expecting my aunt Barbara at the time.

A sergeant came over to the women and he hit my grandmother a punch.

My grandmother was drinking a bottle of Guinness – as soon as the sergeant hit her, she hit him with the Guinness bottle. He fell to the ground and then he went for his gun.

The swiftness of the ashplant in my wife's grandmother's hand knocked him kicking. Five policemen came and they were hit to the ground like hailstones. A battalion of policemen came. By this time the travelling men had joined the women, the battle was started, and the travelling men charged the battalion of police.

There were fifteen Gypsy men and ten women against one hundred police. Within thirty minutes, one hundred and six police were left out to dry in the streets of Aucrim.

Night rolled on and the Travellers had no place to sleep as everything was destroyed by the police. So what ran into the Travellers' minds was that the police had destroyed their home, so they were going to destroy the police station. They went into the police station and they broke up all the furniture and they slept in the policemen's beds and cooked and ate their food. One mistake the Travellers made and that was to take the Crown sign down, and they burned it. The next morning, all the men went to the pub. These fifteen travelling men had fought for Britain and some of them had been decorated for valour in the 1914–18 war by the King himself.

Squads of police and Black and Tans moved into the town with full battledress that morning. The travelling men were stupid drunk at this time, but they fought with ashplants till my grandfather fell very seriously injured. Six of the men were arrested, they were tried the next morning. The judge dropped all the charges except one, and that was destroying the Crown of His Majesty. The judge sentenced them to from one month hard labour to three months hard labour.

Now let me speak of how British justice works with reference to the Gypsy.

At one stage of a case I was put out of court. I shouted that there was no justice in the court. That it was more like an auction room than a court of law. This was the time that a police witness said he saw a Gypsy's lurcher dog taking bottles of milk from the doors.

Another policeman said he saw a travelling woman throwing out tea-leaves and he charged her with a litter offence. But, at that very same time, demolition workers were knocking down old buildings nearby, the dust and rubble was falling from the old buildings – a greater mess than the tea-leaves.

When three little travelling children were burned to death during police harassment in the Midlands, the police told newspapers that the mother and father had been in the pub. This was just propaganda. In fact, the parents were locked up in Walsall police station when their children were burned to death.

The police were summoning the Travellers and trying to move their caravans off the magistrates' car park.

This is the truth at last, because there never was a policeman who can tell the truth.

Once, when I was tried, the judge said to me as he sentenced me, 'Mr Connors, the police must be protected from men like you.' This was the time when I had been protecting my wife and children from police officers who attacked us in the middle of the night. One of the policeman who attacked my family was on trial in the same court. I saw him in the police cells. He was charged with sexually assaulting an innocent child, for which he was fined a small fine.

I have respect for policemen who respect their uniform, and I think everyone has. But I cannot respect a man that nearly kills my little son through prejudice and kicks my wife unconscious a few hours before her child is born, and breaks my caravan and beats me stupid.

As my father would say, the worst mistakes are made in bed; how right he is, but prejudice is not a mistake, it is an evil.

On 4 June 1969, I was escorted from Birmingham prison to London where I met Marc Sand, the Secretary of the Social Commission of the Council of Europe, and another member of the Social Commission, Mr Wiklund, a Swedish M.P., and many others.

On 5 May 1969, I sent a forty-one page statement to the European Commission of Human Rights in Strasbourg and on 16 May 1969, I received a reply from Strasbourg. They wanted details of all the cases of brutal treatment that the travelling people had suffered in

Britain, as they wanted this information to use at the Oslo Conference in July.

My wife and children went to the House of Commons and parked their caravan at the steps. She was expecting her sixth child, she was also suffering ill-health, she had T.B. and thrombosis. She was fed up; I was in prison, and she was getting shifted every day by the police. Later my wife gave birth to our son, Grattan Joseph Patrick.

So, what must we suffer to prove we are human? What must we do to prove that authority is wrong? What must we suffer to prove we are not getting justice?

And what pain must our women suffer when we are not with them? Just because prejudice minded people are against us? Let's hope it will change.

My grandfather and his father and father before him were great musicians, story-tellers, singers and dancers. On a fair-day they would go to the town and busker the fairs till evening playing fiddles and the ulean pipes, and now and again they would swap or buy a pony or a donkey in between playing their instruments.

I often saw a travelling piper playing the reel 'The Maid Behind the Bar', or 'The Maid of Mount Sisco', while one hand would be on the chanter, the other hand would slap some other hand, and a jig and a reel would be going on at the same time.

One of the nicest and sweetest things to hear and see is to leave a noisy fair and to walk out along a quiet country road to a camp and find a travelling woman singing to a child and the birds whistling and the bees humming at the one time, it is pure heaven on earth.

The sweet echoing voice of a loving mother pleasing the child and pleasing herself and the nature all around her. One favourite song of the travelling people is a mother's lament; it is a cradle song, it has a very low air and it is a song about a child that was taken away by the bad fairies, and the mother died broken-hearted when she saw her child after two long years floating down the stream with the floods. When a travelling woman would come to that part of the song the tears would fall down along her red cheeks and on to the face of her own child in her arms, while a feeling of nature would crawl up the listener's spine...

I believe the reason why a Traveller is persecuted so much of the time by the police and local authorities is because the Traveller is full of nature and tradition. Tradition is a Traveller's way of life. Nature is himself. He has great time for people that have time for him. A settled community person who respects a Traveller, the Traveller respects him, and the Traveller will wish them all good luck in the world. But if a settled community person, such as the police, local authorities or a bad farmer do harm to the travelling community then the Traveller will curse that person and strongly invoke that that curse will meet that person.

I have had personal experience of a broken-hearted travelling person's curse; it is the only weapon they have against their harasser.

There is no fair play for a Traveller in a court of law. The police, when they harass Travellers, they are armed with a uniform. Some police and councillors are proper gentlemen and very good natured, but often we meet dirty blackguards, like the policeman who nearly killed me in a police cell. He met my curse a few days later – he was convicted of a charge of sexual assault on a young child.

'The public must be protected,' as a judge said to me when a policeman kicked my wife stupid three days before her baby was born. I hit the policeman because I would want to be a mongrel dog to see two police kicking my wife, and I not protect her. The judge will meet his downfall yet. The wrath of the seven angry deaths will meet him sooner or later, and sooner, I hope.

A Traveller's curse is fatal at times.

In Dublin, one morning, a certain travelling woman was after giving birth to a baby, and the mother of the baby has an abscess on each of her breasts. The mother could not feed her week-old baby from her breasts and the baby was crying for a drink.

Just then, a man came along the road with a ten-gallon churn can of milk on the front carrier of a carrier's bike. The mother of the child asked the man to sell her a bottle or a cupful of milk as the baby was badly in need of a drink.

The man replied, 'That is your problem, not mine.'

'For God's sake, sir,' said the woman, 'sell me a couple of spoonfuls of milk for the baby.'

'Not for you, or any baby's sake will I give you one drop of it,' said the man.

The man got on his bike, the woman cursed him, he looked round and fell off his bike. He broke his two legs and his arms; all the milk was spilled out on to the road, except for the fill of the lid. That man crawled back about ten yards with the lid full of milk, handed it up to the woman saying, 'I am sorry, missus, God forgive me, here is the milk.'

On another occasion I saw a fine healthy policeman telling lies in a courthouse against a travelling woman. At a split second's notice, in a low voice, that woman said, 'May he fall out of the witness box.'

Before she had the words out of her mouth, the policeman fell out the witness box like a parachutist out of a plane.

A very bad and inclined magistrate that was prejudiced against Travellers fined a Traveller for camping and while he was summing up, he said to the Traveller, 'We don't want to see you around here any more.'

'You won't see me any more, sir,' said the Traveller.

In fact, he did not see anyone let alone a Traveller – the magistrate took a heart attack and died.

On another occasion in Birmingham, a very old travelling woman walked into a pub where I was.

'Sorry, missus,' said the bartender, 'we don't serve your people here.'

'For God's sake, son, sell me a half-glass of whisky, I am very cold and I am not too well.'

'No,' said the bartender, 'I will sell you nothing and get out.'

'Well,' said the old travelling woman, 'I am afraid again the day is over, you will have to go some place yourself.'

The old woman walked out of the door. It was snowing at the time. Just as she put her foot on the path, the pub went on fire. She got her bottle of Guinness and her half-glass of whisky across the road in another pub.

Another time in Ireland, I was about nine years old at the time, we were camped near Antrim town, and a travelling woman said to the farmer that was going into his field, 'A good morning, boss.'

'The devil a good morning it is when you are camped here,' said the farmer.

'Don't bite me, like a good man, sure I only said good morning to you,' said the woman.

'Well I don't want to see your horses in my field,' said the farmer, 'you're nothing but trouble, I don't want you around here.'

'God save us, sir, you are a bad man,' replied the woman.

The farmer was going to hit the woman – 'Get away, God's curse to you, you should be ashamed of yourself,' said the woman.

The farmer simmered down and he got ashamed of himself.

'I am sorry, missus, I did not mean any harm.'

He opened the gate of his field and into the field he went driving his tractor. As he was going through a gap in the hedge, a stick or a bit of a bush caught in his coat; he fell off the tractor, and the back wheel of the tractor went over his leg, and it done a terrible lot of damage to his leg.

No getting away from it, the Travellers did often put their horses into a farmer's field at night and many's a Traveller was murdered by the farmer over it. Well, after all, you can't see a horse go hungry. Travellers are very fond and good to animals. Travellers do not think any harm out of putting their animals into private land; they say that grass was there before there ever was a farmer. God did not put the grass there for any one man. And grass will be growing over us all some day.

The travelling children did not have much chance to go to school. We were never allowed to camp for long in the one place. I can still picture the big old fat guard on an upstairs model bike, like a fat tomcat on a pair of scissors. Before he could get down off his bike, he would be out of breath.

'Well, I am afraid you will have to move, the neighbours are sending in complaints.' It would not be the neighbours who were sending in complaints, it was himself. He would use discriminating words against us to the neighbours. After all, there is no crime in the country parts of Ireland and the law must see that he do his job, or not he would get twice as fat, and he would not be able to get up on the bike, never mind to get down off it.

Fairly speaking, the police were not too bad in Ireland against the Travellers, but believe me, there were some self-made bastards among the guarda. I never will forget a sergeant in Milford, County Donegal; I was just nine years old and I was coming back from hand-fishing. I had a hank of trouts and eels in my hands. I was after tickling in the river; both of my hands were full of slippery trouts and eels.

As I was walking past a thatched cottage, a cat must have smelt the fish, and the cat came through the half-opened window. There was a big breeze out, and the cat must have hit the stick that was holding up the window. The window slammed down and it got broke.

I still carried on along the road, and an old man about seventy years old came out of the house; he blamed me for breaking his window.

'I swear to God, I never broke or even went near the window.'

The old man said to me, 'Is there anybody else with you?'

'No,' I said, 'there's not.'

'Well, you broke my window,' he said.

'How could I break your window,' I said, 'and you looking out of it.'

The old man brought me into a shed, he beat me black and blue with a broom. He locked me up in the shed, and he went for the sergeant. About an hour later, himself and the sergeant came to the shed, unlocked the door, and told me to come out.

'Well boy,' said the sergeant, 'who broke the window?'

'I don't know, sir,' I said, 'but it must have been the man himself, or the cat that knocked the piece of stick from the window.'

'You broke the window, didn't you?'

'I did not, sir,' I said.

The sergeant hit me a hard slap on the ear, I could hear bells ringing in my ears. 'You did break the window, come on, you were passing and you threw a stick at the cat.'

'I did not,' I said.

The sergeant hit me five or six slaps on my head and face. The blood spouted out of my nose.

'You did break that window, if you don't say you broke that window I am going to beat you and beat you till me arms get tired,' the sergeant said.

Just then my Daddy came down along the road. He saw my eyes swollen and the blood running down my face.

'What happened to you, Johnny?' my Daddy said. 'Did you get knocked down by a motor, or what?'

'No,' I said, 'the sergeant done it.'

My Daddy had a loaded butt whip in his hand which he always carried.

'Did you do that to my child, sergeant,' said my Daddy.

'He would not tell me who broke the window, and I lost my temper,' said the sergeant.

My Daddy turned around on one foot and he swung that whip, and it hit the sergeant along the side of the head. He hit the ground, the sergeant did. My Daddy unfurled the lash and he hit the old man a tip on the leg.

'The cat broke the window, the cat broke the window,' the old man said.

The sergeant got up from the ground, 'I am going to arrest you for assaulting me,' said he to my father.

'Not till I beat the — out of you,' said my father. My father left down the whip on the ground. 'Put your hands up to save yourself, you big stupid bastard,' said my father. My father and the sergeant got stuck into it. My Daddy won and myself and him walked away. There was never anything about it, and my Daddy was not arrested, but I was sore for a month after.

No getting away from it, I have seen manys a travelling child the condition they would be in after leaving a police station in Britain.

One thing I will never forget is the time outside Stockport, Cheshire, England. All our people were arrested, I think it was ten men and two girls. This was over a piece of copper pipe about one foot long that one of the Travellers was using for an earth rod on a radio. All the Travellers were lined up in court like cattle and the magistrate, the words came out of his mouth like bullets out of a machine-gun, 'Six months.' 'Six months.' 'Six months.' 'Six months.' 'Six months.' 'Six months,' and Borstal training for the two young innocent girls, they did not steal anything.

I suppose that magistrate was so proud of himself that he must have pissed in his trousers. If I had been two years older, I would have been arrested and jailed the same as the rest.

Oh God, what the wives of them poor innocent men went through for four hard months, God only knows. Shifted night, noon, day and morning, sometimes without their breakfast, and those women had to provide for their children.

The poor women, some of them pregnant, had to yoke up the wagons in the spilling rain and snow and go out and collect the price of the children's food, as well as being shifted.

The life a Traveller leads is an up and down life. There are some good jolly times with the police and Travellers. I remember one policeman near Bristol, he would come up to the fire and he would sing folk songs for us, and we would sing a few songs for him. He was a great man and he was very fond of me.

Myself and him, when he would be off duty, would go to a pub and drink like fish till closing time. Then sometimes I would go to his house and both himself and his wife would treat me like a gentleman and I must say his wife was a pure picture. She was a fine, good-looking woman, God bless her and save her.

One day, I think it was a Sunday, the policeman pulled up and asked me would I go over to his house with him, he said he had a surprise for me. I did, I went with him. As we pulled up at the house I could hear the banjos, guitars and fiddles playing 'The Beggar Man', and fair play they could play.

When we went into the house there was a small open-top oak barrel on the middle of the floor. The barrel was full to the neck with real good rough cider.

I know, before I left the party, most of the cider was inside me. There was a young girl there, she was a really good singer. She sang 'The Rocks of Baun', and fair play she sang it well.

Then I remember one time in Manchester, I was after drinking very heavily during the winter and I was nearly on the rocks, and my lorry was not taxed. I had about £4 in my pocket and I was hawking a range of houses for scrap. I was getting a good bit of scrap in the houses, when I looked and I saw a policeman at the lorry.

I don't think he looked at the window-screen of the lorry, but I did not go back to the lorry, as I thought he was going to summons me for no road-fund licence. He walked away from the lorry and as soon as he did, I went back to the lorry and drove it on.

He followed me up streets and down streets in his car, so I pulled up. 'Well,' said he, getting out of his car, 'I have been following you for over an hour.'

'What for, sir?' I said.

'Well,' said he, 'my father has a lot of scrap and he wants to get rid of it; you can go to this address, tell him I sent you.'

I went to the address the policeman gave me and I got £22 worth of scrap from his father and a good dinner as well. I did not pay his father any money for the scrap, but I shifted the fill of the lorry of old bricks and rubble, in lieu of money, or as the Traveller says, for other services rendered . . .

One week in Walsall Town Hall, a meeting took place between the police chiefs and head councillors. The press was barred from this meeting, and so was myself because it was a secret meeting. I don't know what was said against the Travellers in the meeting, but one thing I do know, the police and council members talked of a plot to get rid of the Travellers.

The police told the council to tow us from the council owned land, as they themselves could not tow us from the land. Once the caravans were on the road the police would summons us then would charge us with all kinds of offences. The police were giving false statements to the press to be used against us or to make the settled community turn against us.

The next morning some of the Travellers were arrested and charged with being Gypsies camping on the highway, stealing, assault, breaking and entering, failing to give their names to the police, dropping litter, camping within a distance from a dwelling-house, spitting in the street, no lights, obstruction, using indecent language, failing to show their driving documents.

Twenty-eight times that day I produced my driving licence and insurance. The first day's summonses totalled sixty-two and the full total was three hundred. Every two minutes of the day we were summonsed for an offence. The persecution went on and on, night, noon and day. The police thought we would move away from the Midlands, but what a terrible shock they got when we turned up at court.

A lot of the charges were dropped but the magistrates were throwing out the fish to get the salmon. We appealed to the Quarter Sessions, we won some of the cases, but the judge was more like Hitler than the magistrates. He proved that he was prejudiced. He said in his summing up, 'I am going to drop the fine, but any Traveller that comes in front of me again, and any Traveller refusing to move their caravans, I will not be so lenient with them.'

But the question was where could we move to? All camping sites were banked up with piles of earth, and trenches were dug across all open land to prevent us from camping on them. I am sure if one of those so-called policemen, councillors, or the judge was in a higher authority's chair, they would have had us put into gas chambers, every single one of us.

Then with the brutality the police used towards the Travellers it makes one think if those detonators were planted on the site by the authorities, and if there was any truth in this!

What is the Irish government, the British Government and the U.N. Commission on Human Rights going to do about these things?

A harmless young child blown to bits at the hands of the local authorities; Ann Hanrahan, two and a half years old, crushed to death during an eviction near Dudley, two miles from Walsall.

My own little son very badly injured and my caravan smashed to pieces (and I asked the police to give me time to take the child to hospital, and him bleeding in my arms and in agony with pain – 'No,' was the answer).

About nine miles from Walsall, Birmingham, twenty-eight Travellers arrested from their beds in the night, the charges being drunk and disorderly.

Walsall – during an eviction, three little girls burned to death.

Walsall – my wife kicked black and blue by the police in her own caravan three days before her baby was born.

Walsall – I was kicked unconscious.

Walsall – a sister at Walsall Hospital refused to treat us. Walsall councillors said, 'Kick them out at all costs.'

Walsall – that my heavy curse may fall on your jackboot mob and every magistrate in it, and that the suffering my people have suffered may fall back on the authorities of Walsall.

I was always fond of good-looking girls. The first time I ever fell in love was with a girl that I worshipped the ground she walked on. Although I never spoke to her till one day I was swimming in a river near Appleby, and I felt a lot of pebbles hitting me on the back.

I got out of the water to find who was firing the pebbles at me and there behind the bank was this girl. God made her to be loved and love her I did.

In about five minutes' time, the sun was shining on my back and the shade was shading her. When I got up my face was as red as a turkey-cock's. But whatever happened, I never enjoyed anything better.

The Travellers' love affairs are something of a wondrous nature. A little boy and girl, seven or eight years old, may play together at that age as all children do. The family may split up and that little boy or girl may never see each other again for maybe ten years or more. When they meet again in their teens, they might start courting and maybe the family would split up again.

No matter how long it will be, that boy and girl will still love each other; the girl would keep in touch with him through other girls, and the boy would keep in touch with her through other boys, although none of the girls would try to go with that boy, and none of the boys would try to go with that girl.

Although they may be hundreds of miles apart from each other, the message would be brought by word of mouth. Then when they would meet, they may ask their fathers and mothers for permission to get married, but if the fathers and mothers don't want to lose the only big boy or girl they have, the boy and girl would run away to other Travellers up and down the country and the next day they would be brought to the priest, and their names given to get married.

The Travellers that the boy and girl run to would make sure that that boy and girl had kept apart till they got married. But I suppose the damage would be already done on the run, or on some lonesome road or haystack or barn. Nobody can stop nature, I suppose, and that would be it.

Ninety-nine per cent of all travelling girls are virgins till marriage, they do not believe in intercourse before marriage.

How I met my wife, I was five years old, and she was about five years old. My mother bought me a pair of Wellington boots and myself and my wife scratched each other's faces, she wanted my new boots and I would not give them to her. That was only for about a half an hour and I never saw her again for fourteen years. I can tell you when I met her again then I had no intention of scrabbing her face because it was beautiful, but she did not know me, nor I know her. She thought I was a settled community boy and she asked me for a match.

'Have you got a match please, conya?'

'Yes, I have, nupe,' I said.

She got very embarrassed, she very near died of shame.

'I am sorry,' she said, 'I did not know you were a pav.'

I talked to her for about five minutes. She asked me where I was going, I told her I was going to the dance. I asked her if she went to dances, and she said, 'My Daddy would kill me if he knew I went to dances.'

I made a date with her for the next night. The next night she turned up at the dance and I popped the question to her and we ran away, and it would not be fair to tell what happened that night or early next morning, but whatever happened, it was old nature himself trying to please himself, and any cat will drink milk if it is put in front of it.

I can assure you I found out what I wanted to find out; I was the first and last, I can assure you. And we lived happily ever after.

What kind of dog does a Traveller have? Well, they breed their own breed of dog, and one breed is a lurcher. The lurcher is a very hardy and cunning dog. He is bred between a collie and a greyhound. The mother of the pup would be a greyhound, and the father would be a collie, and when the pup would be about six months old, they would be brought out in the land to chase a hare or a rabbit, then at about fourteen months, they would hit the daisies after a hare; it is not many hares that get away with their lives from any one of the lurchers.

Then the terrier is bred between a Manchester terrier and a wirehaired fox terrier. This breed would follow a rabbit or a fox or badger no matter where them rabbits, foxes or badgers went, and there would always be a kill.

The Travellers' dogs will not let any man or dog from the houses come near the camp. Most of the Travellers' dogs know Shelta or Gammon, and some Travellers call their dogs in Gammon, Romany and Shelta.

What kind of food do the Travellers eat and cook, apart from tinned food?

A meat stew or rabbit stew is to get a rabbit, skin him and dress him, cut the rabbit into small chunks, put the pieces in a pot or saucepan, half fill the saucepan or pot with water, get a lemon and cut the lemon into four quarters and put the lemon in the pot with the rabbit and add a small spoonful of salt.

Boil for about ten minutes, remove the four parts of the lemon from the pot, add about four pounds of potatoes, each cut in two halves. Mix about three tablespoonfuls of cornflour with water in a cup, make sure there are no lumps in it, stir the cornflour into the pot; then get a good size parsnip, cut it small and also get a few young carrots, or a couple of big red ones, and cut them small; get a half cupful of pearl barley, a small bit of thyme and about a quarter of a pound of cabbage; cut the cabbage very small, get a turnip and cut that into small chunks, and get about fifteen leaves of nettles (the nettles won't sting you if you put it in a bowl and pour hot water over it), then cut the nettle leaves very very small and add to the boiling pot.

Don't forget that pearl barley will burn and taste the stew and ruin your pot if you don't stir the pot now and then.

Greasy water stew is different. Get a piece of bacon weighing about one and a half pounds, put the one piece of bacon into the pot and boil for twenty minutes – the leaner the bacon, the better.

Then put in three or four pounds of potatoes in the pot, don't cut the potatoes, put them in whole, then get a good head of cabbage weighing about two pounds, strip the leaves from the head of the cabbage and put in whole (cut any big stalks off the leaves, of course), then add two teaspoonfuls of baking powder, stir the pot once and take out the bacon; put it on a plate to cool and let the remainder boil till the potatoes are cooked, and the cabbage is well softened.

The greasy water is good tasting soup, if you add colouring and flavouring. Take your potatoes up with a ladle and put them on plates to serve with the cabbage; then cut your bacon into small slices. Any good fruit sauce is very pleasant and nice on the bacon.

Hedgehog stew is the same way: cook as the rabbit or meat stew, but it is not often Irish Travellers eat hedgehog.

I have eaten hedgehog, it is the nicest meat I have ever tasted, it is a sweet delicate pork taste. With the hedgehog it is best to kill it fast, I would not kill a hedgehog slow and I never have. He is too harmless looking, but when he is cooked, boy he tastes good.

Get a hedgehog and roll him in clay, put him into an open fire till he is baked, break the clay, leaving you with succulent sweet pork.

How do you cook a hare?

Cut the hare in about six or seven pieces; after skinning and dressing, boil the hare with two lemons cut in half; when the hare is half cooked, we fry it in a pan full of fat or butter till the meat is golden brown. We serve with roast potatoes and boiled mashed turnips and carrots.

Call Cannon is well-boiled potatoes boiled in milk and water, mashed, and spring onions cut into pieces and thrown in when the potatoes are being mashed. We serve with trout and white sauce.

Apart from catching trout, we cook the trout in butter fat until it is golden brown, and we sprinkle it with lemon juice and white vinegar mixed fresh.

Snipe, pheasant, moorhen, partridge and wild duck we roast on a spit on an outside open fire.

How do we bake bread? Four pounds of S.R. flour, or ordinary flour, mixed with butter, milk and cream of tartar. Or, four eggs, four pounds of S.R. flour, six spoonfuls of sugar, one spoonful of salt, one packet of custard powder; mix eggs, sugar, salt, and custard in a bowl with a good helping of butter and beat well. Put the dry flour in a bowl and mix all the ingredients together into a thick paste and bake in separate baking dishes.

Honey balls are little round cakes about half the size of a hen egg. Get two or three large spoonfuls of honey and mix them with flour and well stewed apple and a well beaten egg. Make into little balls, put them in a pan of butter fat and cook till they are done. Remove them to cool and serve with cornflour or custard.

Potato cakes: get four or five cold boiled potatoes and about two pounds of S.R. flour. Mash and mix well together. Roll out the paste, add a shake of pepper and cook on a flat shallow pan.

Travellers believe in poltergeists and ghost stories, superstitions and happenings.

If a Traveller sees one magpie on the road or in a field we count it as bad luck. If that magpie hops along the road in front of us, we will turn around and wait till the next day before we pass that spot. Two magpies are for good luck, three magpies are for a wedding, four magpies are for a death, five or six are for money, seven represent some story that will never be told.

A dog howling with his head towards the sky is counted as pining some human life away.

A four-leaf shamrock or clover is very lucky to find.

A badly rusted horseshoe found in a stubble field is very lucky to find.

A rabbit's foot is a lucky thing to have, but the rabbit must be a doe in young that was killed by mistake.

To argue in the morning is counted as very unlucky.

To miss going to church at your own fault is very devilish, and unlucky.

The banshee is a ghost of a young woman with very long hair which she always combs at night when she appears with the comb in her hand. There is nothing to fear from her, but when she appears without the comb, there is trouble in the wind.

I have never seen a banshee, but I know lots of young and old Travellers who have seen her. She appears as a token of bad news to people with 'O' in their surnames.

As I say, I have never seen the banshee, but I heard her. It is the most frightening roar that ever could be heard. When she roars, the echo of her voice vibrates you and anything that is around you.

I will never forget that night a friend of my Daddy and Mammy was in hospital in Dublin and we were camping near Coleraine in the North of Ireland. There were five other families camping with us at the time. There were about thirty people there altogether, and we were all in bed about twelve o'clock, and on she comes.

When she starts to roar it is real low at first, and all of a sudden – WHA, WHA, WHA.

My Daddy got up out of bed after saying a few prayers and he walked outside into the dark night with Holy Water in his hand. He threw the Holy Water into the road and around the shafts of the wagon saying, 'God give you rest.'

You could hear all the rest of the Travellers saying to my Daddy, 'Did you hear her, Mick?'

'I did,' my Daddy said, 'I did. There is something wrong with some of the lads.'

Two or three of the men went with my Daddy to the phone box, my Daddy phoned the hospital in Dublin.

'Hello,' he said, 'can you let me know how Mr Peter McCann is, please?'

'Who is calling please?'

'Mr Michael Connors,' said my father.

'Well, Mr Connors, I am sorry, Mr McCann died fifteen minutes ago.'

'God rest his soul,' said my Daddy, 'I knew when she came there was something wrong.'

Strange, but true, I can't explain it. I hope someone will, but I swear to God and all belonging to me that is dead, I heard the banshee that night with the rest of the Travellers.

Some people would laugh at a person when he would tell things like that, maybe that person doesn't know what will happen to himself, and anybody is entitled to not believe, or believe.

There is a road that leads out of Newry, not the Warrenpoint Road, but the road the hospital is on. Well, that road is badly haunted up at the crossroads near the little stream. Travellers have camped there, and many's a bad fright they got from a ghost. Here is one fright a Traveller got.

We were camped there with about twenty families and this woman; it was a moonlight night and there were a good few of the men at the fire when we heard a scream, 'My child, my child, my child.'

Something came into the caravan and took the child from the mother's arms who was sleeping in bed. Whatever or whoever it was had to climb up the steps of the wagon, past the men at the fire, open three bolts and take the child from the mother's arms and walk down the ladder past the men at the fire and leave the child on the middle of the road.

For a start, it is impossible to open bolts from inside a caravan door when you are outside. When I say it's impossible, I mean it is impossible to open them without making a noise or breaking the windows or doors. There were five or six men, three or four yards away from the door and they say they saw nobody go in, and nobody come out of the caravan. Yet the child was on the middle of the road, and the doors are still bolted.

Now suppose the child fell out of the back window, he would have about seven feet to drop on to rough gravel. He would no doubt be scratched. Then the question is, how did he get into the road? Crawl? No, he was only three weeks old. But the child was not harmed in any way. That child is a married man now, and he has children of his own.

Another time we were camping at Brocke near the Realing Bridge, Co. Donegal. There is a good rebel song about the same place called 'Johnston's Motor-car'. Well, we were camping near the wood and it was the first time we were ever camped there, and it will be the last, on that part of the road anyway.

At about twelve or one o'clock, we heard noises and there was nobody outside, all the children were in bed and so were the adults. The pots and kettles and cups were thrown on to the road and large stones were thrown for about ten minutes. The horses were galloping up and down the road, and yet there was nobody leading them. The dogs were afraid of their lives an they were yelping as though someone was hitting them. Whatever it was that was breaking the things outside, it was frightening the lights out of our dogs and horses.

When all the lads got up, there was no one outside. Whatever kind of a ghost or spirit it was, he did not want anyone there.

We met other Travellers a few months after and they told us the same thing happened to them in that same place, thirty years previous to our happening.

There are thousands of stories like this. But why I mentioned these three is, I was present when they happened.

One story I heard and I checked was that of Willy Loveridge. This happening happened in the middle of a bright summer's day near Blackwater.

Willy was camped near the river; a man with a raincoat came down the road, he was well dressed but what made him look odd was the raincoat in the middle of the summer, and the sun was splitting the trees.

'Good day, sir,' said Willy.

'Yes, it is,' said the man.

'Tell me,' said Willy, 'would you be buying something out of the basket off me?'

Willy went up in the wagon and he brought out the basket. When the man saw what was in the basket, he turned into a whole lot of colours and he disappeared. He just vanished into thin air.

What was in the basket to frighten him, or what article in the basket made him vanish? Well, when I asked Willy and his four sons about it, they told me the exact same story as their father and mother did, and it was a story that was told to me years after it happened and I checked the story many's a time with the same people. The articles the basket contained were shirt studs, tie-pins, laces, nail and clothes brushes, razors, razor blades, elastic, snow storms in a little glass, articles which are filled with water and a religious figure inside, holy pictures, Holy Water fonts, combs, fine combs, tooth brushes, and small mirror glasses and religious crosses.

One of those articles in that basket made that man disintegrate, whichever one it was, I would like to know.

What kind of drink do the Travellers drink?

Well, for the last two hundred years or more they have been

drinking Guinness mostly; poteen and whisky are their next favourites. But Guinness has often reared a child. If the child started crying in the night, and there was no milk handy, a travelling woman often opened a bottle of Guinness, put a teat on it and gave it to the child to drink. It's a matter of fact, I have often done the same to my own children and every day I buy a couple of bottles of Guinness for my children to drink.

What kind of transport did the Travellers have through the ages?

Well, the earliest form was walking with the knapsack on the shoulder or the bag on the back, then they would cut a branch from a big bush or tree and they would put all their belongings and small children on it and drag it manly across valleys and dells.

Then the common cart, and from the common cart to the barrel cart and round-back, or back to back trap cart. From the trap cart to the four-wheeler, and turntable and from that to the Ford five cwt. motor-van or car, and now the present day heavy motor-lorry.

What kind of sleeping accommodation through the ages?

The earliest form was a manger or cow-shed or stable, from that to the wattle tent, then the shelter tent, then the horse-drawn wagon and the luxurious new trailer of the present day. There are still Travellers living in wattle tents in Scotland and Ireland.

What kind of sport do Travellers have apart from boxing and hunting and fishing?

The Traveller is a good card-player, and then there is the game of horseshoes, and quoits; jumping, running, hurling, handball, skittles, side-kicking. Side-kicking is a game with two people kicking one another sideways, and none of them can kick the other frontways or backways, whoever does will lose the game.

The work the Travellers have been engaged in: the first employment was from coffin-makers, before Christ, as well as metal running, from smiths in metal of all known kinds, tinsmiths, dealers, horse-dealers, farm-workers, scrap collecting, road making and property repairs.

More recently the Travellers are buying and selling antique furniture, and tarmacadaming private drives, demolishing and rebuilding. The scrap collecting is still going strong.

But all through the ages the Traveller has been, and still is, and always will be entertainer in traditional Celtic folk song and music.

I am writing this part of my memories in a prison cell, and as I think back now to my childhood days as I sit in this ould lonesome cell, it makes a young chap of me again.

Ah faith, what would I give, this very tormenting minute, to be able to sit and have my natural freedom like the fox, badger, and partridge. I can only just memorise what it was like to have the ould barrel-top wagon pulled by the side of a grassy road and a clear spring river running like quicksilver along by the side of the ditch, and the rainbow and brown trout showing off, jumping out of the river as if they had not enough freedom in it.

And at that time, like an artist, I would be catching them with my own two hands that God gave me. Ah, what makes a man? Only his mother and a little tough blessing from the man above her. Misfortune hits the best of us at times, as I often said to myself when I would be after taking the freedom from the hare or the rabbit for to cook them over the open stick fire. Ah, and the grand few trouts, and my mother dressing them in all kinds of herbs ready to meet their doom; and the lurchers and terriers having a feast for themselves out of what would not be fit to eat for human consumption.

God be with those days, 'cause they were the days of freedom, the days of the barrel-top wagon.

My great, great, great, great-grandfather and my father and my mother and myself had wagons as our home for many's a year, and we still do today. Is it not a pity that some asses fool made the motor-car?

It's many a slice of begged bread I ate in the barrel-top wagon. It's many a rabbit or hare or deer I've cooked on the stove. It's many a hard time I've had and manys a rousing time I've had in the barrel-top wagon, or bender tent. It's many a time we were shifted by a big fat guarda or policeman, he would come up to the camp on an upstairs model bicycle and him like a tomcat riding a pair of scissors. He would say, 'You will have to move now.'

Of course he had to do his job, if he did not do his job, he might get too fat and he would not be able to get down off the bike, never mind get up on it again.

'Tis many a time I danced a good reel on the floor of a wagon when a good ulean piper would be playing the tune 'Down the Broom', the notes would be flying out of the chanter like doves out of a nest. Ah, how peaceful it would be, how comfortable it would be to witness this once more with my own two eyes and ears.

I can well remember the beat of the horse's feet as he pulled the wagon along the twisted lanes, across valleys and dells, at the same time the bright sun dancing on the red and blue paint on the wagons, as the shade of the trees deprived the colour of its gloss when we would pass a woody road with our barrel-top.

Don't it make a man fret his heart out when he memorises all those things. Soon I pray I will be sitting beside my old open stick fire with my own true love sitting on my ould knee, like a wild Irish rose and, when there is no light left in the sky for that day, I will say to my true love, 'Come on my ould thrush, up in the wagon we will go to bed and pray and make a few natural mistakes.'

Ah, it's a terrible world, a compulsory world is that of the Gypsy in a bricked prison cell. One thing I am sure of, I cannot be stolen. But isn't it a terrible pity that they would not give me permission to do my time on the lawn of the prison with my old barrel-top and open stick fire.

Life is as strange as a wagon. 'Tis never here nor there. But there are a lot of morrows behind me now and compulsory matters won't let me be gone, 'tis a pity indeed. I suppose this ould world is not as bad as we make it. Human selfishness has destroyed it, and we will some day destroy the world ourselves for all.

Here is a little poem:

> The cell was never made for me
> Nor I was never bred for it.
> Nor was the little wren bird hatched
> To be put in a cage.

Part VII

Further Information – Some Notes on Britain's Gypsies

'Fifty years ago, when I was a child,' writes Marta Adler, 'Gypsies had no nationalities. They were the truly free people of the world, wandering wherever they wished, admitting allegiance to no government, though proud of a deep loyalty to all laws which they considered just. Then, after World War One, most of the nations of Europe decided that the Gypsies must be registered in the country where they lived, and from that time onwards wherever the Gypsy babies were born, that became their registered birthplace and country of origin.

'The result, of course, was that the Gypsies became subject to national laws and were expected to carry passports, although in fact few of them troubled to do so. There were always disputes about this lack of 'papers' after 1918. At the time when I first fell in love with the Romanies, no one expected or demanded to see them. The gayly decorated caravans drawn by their horses with gold and silver ornaments on the harness, which I saw in my childhood, used to travel on more or less annual routes which brought them at the beginning of each spring from one of the Balkan countries into Austria and then to Germany.'

It is no longer like that now.

Gypsies

How is the number of 50,000 Gypsies arrived at?

The Government Survey published in 1967 can be proved to be an underestimate (Gypsies are hard to find). The researchers found 15,000 Travellers on the road in England and Wales and said that they were increasing at the rate of about 1,000 a year, and that this was probably an underestimate.

Later surveys for Scotland and Northern Ireland give us another few thousand, and so we arrive at a figure for those now on the road in Britain as a whole at the present time of about 25,000.

This is defining Gypsies in the way that the law does – those who are living the Gypsy way of life. There are of course many sub-divisions among these Gypsies, those who are of racially purer stock, or richer, or English as opposed to Irish or Welsh, tending to look down on others, according to the usual vagaries of tribal or racial or class intolerance.

But besides these people there is this other group who have as great a right to call themselves Gypsies. These are those who for one reason or another have moved into houses.

They will tell you, when you knock on their door, with pride, that they are Gypsies. Not for them the uncertainties of some Gypsies on the road who will deny being Gypsies or ask you to refer to them by euphemisms. These people are Gypsies and proud of it. The reason for their being in houses, they will often say, is that the disadvantages of life on the road have come to be greater than the disadvantages of life in a house. How many in fact would return to the road if we ceased harassing them is a difficult question; but it is a fact that house-dwelling Gypsies are already moving onto local authority sites.

It's worth remembering that a quarter told the Government researchers that they had at some time lived in a house and were now back on the road. It is hard to know how many who moved into houses are at this moment teetering on the verge of returning to the road.

I asked those Gypsies to whom I spoke whether they had ever lived in a house. Usually the reply was that they had not. But I also became aware of another small group of people; those who, starting as Gorjios, had made the leap into Gypsydom by going on the road, thus forming a new generation of Gypsies.

'They say that we're dirty Gypsies'

The reader will have noticed how many Travellers I talked to spoke of the way that they felt society as a whole was prejudiced against them.

'They say we're dirty Gypsies, but we're not,' is a common remark made by Gypsies. Often this is made in a caravan which is spotless but which is surrounded by what Gorjios would call filth.

To a Gypsy, if he sees it as filth at all, it seems negligible compared to the ugliness which we Gorjios have made – our vast and hideous factories belching smoke into the air, our whole culture of cities with their tarmac, lamp-standards and slums, our motorways with their concrete ugly furniture, our poisoned rivers, the polluted sky.

Gypsies usually claim that they themselves are tidy, it's we others that are untidy. That we make more mess than them. But it is also true that many would like to surround their caravans with more tidiness than they do. They are almost always refused refuse collection by local authorities, hence it is hard for them.

The allegation that Gypsies make a mess was discussed in an article by John Seymour in the *Listener*: 'Gypsies allegedly make a mess. But who makes the greater mess – the Gypsy with his few old rags, scrapped motor-cars which were lying around before he got there anyway, and his broken prams, or the settled people with their deforestation, ribbon-development, vast hideous suburbs and their bulldozer attitude to the countryside? The real reason for the hatred of the nomad is that some people cannot stand anybody who is different from themselves.'

Thus Richard Wade: 'Has anyone ever tried to look at it from the other point of view? The Gypsies are accused of being thieves, for instance, but to the Gypsy mind we have stolen the countryside from him. He once had wide grass verges at the sides of the roads to camp on and nobody needed to interfere with him. There were enormous commons where he could lose himself and camp comfortable for the winter without being moved on. All these have been closed, taken away from him, by a land-hungry settled population which in its greed seems to want everything the good Lord made.

'Legislation has recently been passed to provide sites up and down the country where Gypsies can stay, and thereafter nobody will be allowed to camp by the road any more, not even for a day. But the Gypsies themselves (whom no one so far has bothered to consult) think that left alone they could solve their own problems. Adjust the planning laws so that, with certain safeguards, a man can buy a suitable field and live on it with his trailer caravans when he is not travelling, and the "Gypsy problem" will disappear.'

'They say that we are thieves'

Gypsies also often sadly remark, 'They say that we are thieves.' There are certainly thieves amongst Travellers, just as there are amongst the settled community.

We settled folk are not all discriminated against just because a few of us happen to be thieves. In the case of Gypsies, this does seem to happen.

In defence of those who are delinquent, it must be said that they have more justification for being so than have their Gorjio counterparts. For delinquency is almost always the product of a deprived upbringing and a man's sense of being discriminated against. How surprising it is, in a way, that the Gypsies are so honest.

Some of them have told me that the police, when searching their caravans for suspected stolen goods, have taken things away which they never returned. A very few, remembering the stones that break their windows, the constant harassing, the aggression of settled society, hit back by picking up something that belongs to somebody else. Have we a right to condemn them for doing this?

Let us give them a decent life – and then condemn the few who commit acts of aggression.

According to information provided by the chief constables of seventy police authorities who had 'Gypsies or other Travellers' in their areas, only twenty reported that they were suspected of criminal offences; in all these cases without exception, these were restricted to minor offences such as petty thefts and petty poaching. The remaining fifty police authorities did not suspect Travellers in their areas of any crime.

Value of the Gypsy culture

Most people who have actually got to know any of Britain's Gypsies personally will testify to the great enrichment of their own lives which has come about as a result of contact with the Gypsy culture.

Our word 'romantic' is used to describe these things which Gorjios throughout time have felt was most valuable from the Gypsy way of life – and 'romantic' is an important concept in our culture. This enrichment has recently taken tangible form in the caravan, in which some three million British Gorjios now take their holidays. A few hundred thousand Gorjios own caravans rather than rent them, and about two hundred thousand actually live in them.

In times past the Gypsies made great contributions to the birth of horse-racing. The origin of much that is good in our fairs and circuses can also be traced to them. Our word 'cushy' comes from their 'cushti', – and 'pal' comes from their 'pal'. And other words.

Their style of decoration contributed to that of both the public house and the fairgrounds.

Their belief and joy in the open-air life is now indulged in by more and more Gorjios, and from them we have taken medicinal remedies. From them comes the gift of fortune-telling and many is the fortune-teller who has invented Gypsy blood even if he doesn't have it.

Even the British Travel Association cashes in on them. In a recent *Coming Events in Britain*, they say: 'Despite the passing of some of the old ways, the Gypsies cling strongly to tradition and live, in many respects, much as their ancestors did. Because he spends his life in the open, the travelling Gypy is a born naturalist, and his knowledge of the habits of animals, especially of horses, is remarkably extensive. The women are practised in the use of wild plants and herbs, and they make herbal remedies from recipes handed down from generations past.

'The gathering and selling of wild flowers is often one of their principal means of earning a living, and for this purpose they will bring their baskets into town, returning to their caravans when they have sold the day's harvest.'

Coming Events in Britain actually showed pictures of Gypsy caravans. This cashing in on the Gypsy image is similar to the way that

America cashes in on its Indian image – or South Africa its 'native' image – while treating the actual people carrying on this life-style with contempt.

In all these as in many other ways the Gypsy has influenced us and will continue to influence us.

But perhaps even more important is a value that is less easily verbalised than this. Jan Yoors has written in his book *The Gypsies*: 'The Gypsies, seemingly immune to progress, live in an everlasting now, in a perpetual heroic present, as if they recognise only the slow pulse of eternity and are content to live in the margin of history. They are in constant motion, like the waving of the branches or the flowing of water. Their social organisation is forever fluid, yet has an internal vitality. The inner cohesion and solidarity of the Gypsy community lies in strong family ties which are their basic and only constant unit. The larger groups of family units, the horde, they call the kumpania. It remains highly mobile, constantly scattering and regrouping as old relationships and alliances shift, as new patterns of interest develop.'

A curious ignorance of even the basic principles of the nomadic way of life was recently shown by Birmingham's Alderman Frank Griffin who said of Birmingham's Gypsies, 'If they were people coming into the city with a view to settling down as ordinary citizens we could accept them in the normal way. But I do not think that this type of person intends to settle anywhere.

'Generally he does not pay taxes, he does not conform to normal behaviour and he is often lawless.

'I am inclined to side with the average citizen who does not feel that he should encourage people in this way of life, or that he is under any obligation to provide for them.'

One Gypsy commented on this, 'What a terrible day it is for Britain when people are discriminated against merely because they do not conform to normal behaviour.'

How much are the Gypsies persecuted?

The reader will have noticed the number of times those Gypsies I talked to in this book were harassed and persecuted. He will also have himself noticed reports of incidents of Gypsy persecution in the press. How common is all this?

I did not choose those I talked to because they had had a hard time. I chose them, as near as I could, at random. I found that almost everyone I spoke to had been harassed. And this is one of the strongest memories I have. I remember the exuberance and happiness and enrichment which the Travellers were able to transmit to me. But also, I think back with sorrow to how in almost every case those who I spoke to had been given a rough time by us, the Gorjios.

Even when the tragic side of a person's life was not at once apparent, it became so when I got to know them better.

In the course of editing *Romano Drom*, a newspaper provided as a service for Gypsies, I subscribed to a press-clipping agency who sent me every reference to Gypsies which appeared in the national and provincial press. I had to cancel my subscription after two months or so because of the sheer bulk of clippings that poured through my letter-box. It was overwhelming, both financially and emotionally.

The majority of the clippings fell into two categories. Either the residents of some area of Britain had objected to the establishment of a Gypsy site in their area and had managed to employ delaying mechanisms. Or, and this was the most common, it was the old tale of Gypsies being hounded (often with police support) from some particular area. For day after day, and in many cases with many on each day, these tragic clippings arrived. And it's important to realise that those who evict the Gypsies don't usually want publicity. They try not to let the local newspapers know. Those incidents that were reported in the press must be only a fraction of the total number happening today, now, tomorrow morning.

The story of Gypsy persecution goes on for ever.

The Cox Lane Gypsy site was where the Gypsy sequence in 'Cathy Come Home' was shot. The Gypsies living there were harassed to such an extent that they built a thirty-foot-high rocket, made from a telegraph pole and packing cases. Perhaps, they thought, there would be more space on the moon.

Mr Mingo Smith said, 'We can't stop here because they're summonsing us – even though it is our own land. If we go out on the road we'll be prosecuted for camping on the highway. There's only one thing we can do – take off.'

A horse was used as an excuse to harass Gypsies on a traditional stopping place at Colney Heath near Watford. It was said that householders had been embarrassed by a Gypsy stallion behaving as nature intended! A councillor, Mr Peter Reeves, said, 'We must press hard with the summonses, otherwise the common will be covered with horses.' Yet Gypsy horses have always grazed there.

Mr Thomas O'Doherty, a Gypsy Council spokesman for the North, says that in Halifax police moved on Gypsies before they even had time to stop – and then claimed that they had no Gypsy problem.

In Newcastle, he says, where Gypsies have been going for countless centuries, the police forcibly removed Gypsy children from school. This has also happened in Birmingham.

A blind Gypsy was trampled unconscious into the mud by police during an eviction from a field adjoining Hill Field Lane, South Bushey, Herts. The blind man, Albert Chapman, had a wheel brace in his hand with which he was going to wind up the jack of his caravan preparatory to moving it.

'At this point,' says someone who saw it, 'Albert was still carrying the wheel brace . . . as was known to many of the police from previous occasions, Albert was blind. He was wearing glasses. He walked towards the voices carrying the wheel brace in his hand and reached out towards them with his left hand.

'The Inspector then shouted, "Come on some of you boys." A number of the police charged into the field from the road and grabbed Brother Boy (the son of Albert). Albert continued to walk towards the noise, the police then went berserk. Albert then fell on to the ground under the weight of the police . . .'

Prior to the extermination of the German Gypsies, Gauleiter Portschy of Steiermark wrote to the minister responsible in 1938, 'For reasons of public health and particularly because the Gypsies have manifestly a heavily tainted heredity, and because they are inveterate criminals who constitute parasites in the bosom of our people, and cannot but produce immense injuries, subjecting to great peril the blood purity of the German frontiersmen peasantry, their way of life and laws, it is fitting in the first place to watch them closely, to prevent them from reproducing themselves, and to subject them to the obligation of forced labour in the labour-camps without, however, preventing them from choosing voluntary emigration abroad.

'... The arguments in favour of sterilising the Gypsies can in fact *a priori* be tacitly expanded to the point that it can be achieved, by the law alone of prophylaxis against progeniture which causes hereditary diseases ... we must make use of this law fearlessly and unreservedly.'

Why are they disliked? Is it that the rest of society envies them their freedom?

'Oh yes, we get a lot of Gypsies from those parts,' says a policeman derogatively, when stopping me as I am driving a decrepit car. 'Are you a Gyppo?'

He spits the word out as though it were a term of abuse like 'nigger'. His mistake gives me one of those rare opportunities to experience life as a Gypsy does.

One council actually advocated the use of dogs to chase them away. Another cut down the trees that surrounded their stopping place, so that the Gypsies were exposed to the winds.

When being towed away from a third site, illegally, children were left in a caravan. One boy fell from a bunk that disintegrated, cut open his foot, which later festered.

A deserted Gypsy woman was taken to prison in Ireland, leaving her nine children alone by night in a tent.

The H.M.S.O. booklet *Gypsies and Other Travellers* disclosed that, of Gypsies on unlicensed sites, three-quarters or more were liable to be moved on in many parts of Britain.

One local authority worker spoke of 'a merry-go-round, chasing them over our border and from site to site within our area'.

A member of the Simon Community has written as follows, 'The Gypsies finally moved out of Bootle on Saturday. They were hounded all day until they came to rest in Smith Street, Liverpool. On the Monday, Liverpool Corporation issued them with twenty-four hours eviction notices and tried to take them off on Tuesday. Several people turned out in support of the Gypsies and after appealing to the workmen and council officials the eviction was averted. However, the authorities were back the next day and the caravans towed off and left by the side of the road. Not wanting to be prosecuted for obstruction, the Gypsies pulled on to a large piece of waste-land just opposite us in Shaw Street. Here they have remained for over a week now. The Council made one attempt to evict them from here, but gave up their efforts after a person was injured. This man lay down in front of a lorry in protest, and the lorry was towed away over his leg. We are pleased to say he is all right, the leg was bruised and the bone chipped but not broken.

'We have been in touch with councillors and Town Hall officials, and have alerted the Gypsy council about the plight of these people who always end up on the wrong side of the law.'

And I think of the death of Linda Doyle, the first child of a young mother of eighteen.

This little girl died of exposure after the family had been forced to move their tent three times during the wet winter weather.

Here are two other recent cases. An old lady had her tent torn down shortly before Christmas leaving her exposed to the cold winter weather without any other form of shelter.

A mother was harassed and moved on by police despite the fact that her children were ill in hospital and she needed to go to see them.

The struggle for rights

To get their rights, Gypsies have been fighting increasingly steadfast battles. One of the first of these battles was at St Mary Cray where, after attempts to evict them, thirty families barricaded themselves in, defending themselves with five-foot railway lines embedded in concrete. There was much fighting and many attempts to harass them.

And the upshot? The local authority provided a site for them and has provided work – Gypsies have been given the job of collecting all the abandoned cars in the area.

Later the Police Federation urged that police should not be actively involved in these scenes, although this does still seem to happen.

The next council to provide a site was Havering. This was after another heroic stand by the Gypsies on Hornchurch Airfield.

A fine stand at Eastern Avenue, Redbridge, followed, so now a permanent site has been made at Forest road.

At Hillingdon the council was employing a full-time 'ranger' whose job it was to move on the Gypsies. It is said that the council was planning to take on a second ranger. There were about eighty families here. After being harassed by rangers, many families moved on to a site called Colne Park Caravan Site, West Drayton.

The response of the council was to send in towing vehicles, bulldozers, police. But the Travellers received a tip-off and barricaded the gate. The council got a bulldozer to smash down the gate. A caravan was brought up to the gate and set on fire. Behind this, a second caravan was filled with concrete and made immovable. Chaos followed and riot police were called. But the upshot was that Hillingdon also agreed to provide a site.

At Enfield there was always a stopping place. Recently the council decided to close it down. Fifteen families moved their caravans into Mollison Avenue.

The council arrived with towing vehicles, but the Gypsies talked to the workmen who said they were not happy about this and would refer it to their Union, the N.U.P. The Union said that no force must be used. So the Gypsy women roped themselves to the drawbar of their vehicles. The towing vehicle backed up to the caravans, the workmen refused to go further, the women clung to the tow bar ...

At this point a councillor announced that he would meet a delegation of families if they were prepared to leave voluntarily. The Gypsies agreed, and did leave.

Next day they asked to see the councillor, but he seemed to have changed his mind. 'No, I didn't mean leave the site, I meant leave the borough. Anyway, I don't speak with Gypsies.'

The families moved to Alma Road, from which they were also evicted, and went on again to some waste-land near Turkey Street. And it was at this point that this council, too, said it was considering giving the Gypsies a permanent site.

The need for organisation amongst Travellers was the subject of an address by Mr Gordon Boswell at the most important meeting place for Travellers – Appleby Fair.

Speaking from a loud-speaker van at this great gathering, he said, 'I'm not an educated man, but I'm a man of experience and I do know the way these things are done. Some of us have been talking this over – the travelling people who are on this ground – and we say and agree that we're willing to form this Travelling Traders' Association (suppose that will be the name). You may not see results right away, the first year ... but there's got to be a beginning for all things, and this would be a great opportunity. Because you are driven from pillar to post, out of one district to another and you have no rest on the road. There is a remedy for our people; we are British subjects, we are entitled to justice. Other minorities in this country, even those who come from abroad, are looked after and their human rights respected, but you've got nothing, or nobody to care, or no place to live, nor even to rest. You are technically a people "of no fixed abode" ... And what I would like to see is some camps up and down the country. I'd like to see three types: a permanent camp where old people can go and stop and rest and be left in peace; a transit camp where you can come from one town to another and pay to go in and travel the country from north to south if you wish, and camps where you can stop in decent comfortable conditions in the winter months ... I'm not thinking about you men, I'm thinking about your little children. The time has come when they should all be able to go to school and get some education.'

Organisations that help Travellers

In a world that is increasingly bent on depriving Travellers of their traditional ways of life, who is to stand up for them? Little seems to have resulted from Gordon Boswell's Travellers Trading Association. Besides this, there is the Gypsy Council (see addresses of these various organisations at the end of this book).

The Council has not got the confidence of all Travellers, but is none the less a group of Gypsies and their Gorjio helpers who have the ear of the Department for the Environment and many local authorities. Gypsies who have been prominent on the council are Mr Tom Lee, Mr Jimmy Penfold, Mr Tom O'Doherty, Mr Fred Wood, Mr Roy Wells and Mr Hughie Smith.

Grattan Puxon, the former Gorjio secretary, travelled constantly to support Gypsies in danger of eviction anywhere in Britain.

One member of the Gypsy Council who has worked tirelessly for the Travellers is George Marriott, an ex-soldier and prisoner of war who, paralysed in the course of military service, says, 'I got used to fighting the Gestapo in Germany. Now that I'm back here I find that the Gestapo is here as well in the form of the police who, acting under orders, harry Gypsies and move them on. I fight them.' Others who have worked hard are Dr Donald Kenrick and Dr Thomas Acton, and these provide what Acton has called a 'Gorjio Civil Service' for the Gypsy Council.

The Romany Guild is an all-Gypsy organisation which has been set up by Tom Lee.

The National Council for Civil Liberties has done useful work in fighting for Gypsies. So has the Minority Rights Group and the Institute of Race Relations.

Throughout Britain, Gypsy Liaison Groups have sprung up whose aim is to form a needed connection between Gypsy ways of thought and local authorities, and to help local authorities to set up sites that will be suitable to the Gypsies. There is still an urgent need for people to undertake this important work.

The Minister of Housing has, in a recent circular, suggested that liaison with Gypsy Liaison Groups by local authorities would be useful. You may get details of local groups from the Gypsy Council or the National Council for Civil Liberties.

What the Reader should do now

The following notes are based on a document drawn up by Brian Richardson for the N.C.C.L.:

1 Find out what proposals your local authority has for meeting Gypsies' needs, including its response to the Caravan Sites Act and its educational provision for Gypsies.
2 Establish contact with your local Travellers. Remember that their first reaction may be one of suspicion – they have probably had bad experience of Gorjios.
3 Discuss the local authority proposals with Gypsies to see if they seem satisfactory. If they seem non-satisfactory, give publicity to this fact. Create public discussion to spur the authority to greater action. Attend any public meetings called to discuss site proposals. Assist the Gypsies in putting their case. Watch and respond to news items and letters in the local press. Educate public opinion. Check the *quality* of the provision of sites being made or being proposed. Are the sites fit for Gypsies to live on? It is not just enough to say 'sites' and think they will automatically solve everything. A diverse range of accommodation is required. Check on the educational provision being made or proposed. These things may be all right on paper, but not in reality.
4 Have you a local Gypsy support group, or Gypsy Liaison Group? If you have, join it. If not, consider founding one.

5 Ensure that police attitudes and action do not conflict with any enlightened Government and local authority policy.

Martin Luther King has written of the steps an individual should take when he has located an injustice:

1 *Define the injustice exactly.*
2 *Negotiate* with the relevant authority. Only if the negotiation breaks down should you go on to the next step, which is
3 *Self purification.*
4 *Action.* This may be legal, semi-legal or illegal. Always keep the channels of communication open and, when your end has been achieved, move on to
5 *Reconciliation.* You have achieved an end to the injustice, so now make sure that goodwill reigns once more.

The Government should be encouraged to act. After all, it is Government action which has deprived Gypsies of their most obvious camping places of all – the grass verges of our roads. What new areas of ground have been made accessible through other Government action? The answer is: abandoned railways, the new lay-bys caused by road-straightening and the spaces under motorways. Therefore the Government should give camping rights in those places as a gesture of goodwill to the Gypsy people.

Here are some other things that I would like to see:

1 Discrimination the other way. The blatant anti-Gypsy discrimination in the Highways Act should now be turned into pro-Gypsy discrimination. If you are a Gypsy, you should be allowed to camp beside the highway. Various other Acts, especially the Town and Country Planning Act, should be amended in favour of the Gypsies.
2 All commons and all fairs where Gypsies have traditional rights should be registered by the Gypsy Council and kept accessible to the Gypsies for ever. Where such rights are denied, the Gypsy people should be compensated.
3 Most Gypsies like to settle down in the winter for a few months. It is during these months that their schooling must take place. Each local authority must provide a 'school' for the Travellers in

its area. During the summer months many Travellers will continue to want to travel, and this should be respected. Their children help them out in many things they do and thus gain education in the traditional sense – that is from close association with their parents so that, in many skills, Gypsy children are quicker than Gorjio children.

4 Local authority sites must be built to the number originally envisaged and must be made free from the sort of repressive regulations which so far have so upset many Gypsies who have used them.

5 Also a network of transit sites must be built, where these are not provided for by the existing network of commons on which Travellers have traditional rights.

6 Local authorities must look more kindly on the right of Gypsies to keep their trailers and live in their trailers on plots of land which they have bought. The senseless and bigoted refusal of such a thing, which finally led to the death of Mr George Finney, a much respected Midlands Traveller, must be brought to an end.

7 Gypsies must be allowed to camp on a farmer's land if he is prepared to let them. At the moment he faces prosecution and farmers have been obliged to prevent Gypsies whom they otherwise would have liked to have had staying there.

8 A larger place must be found on our housing lists for those Travellers who would like to move into houses.

9 The great days of scrap-dealing may be over. Gypsies report a falling off both in price and quantity of scrap available. New trades must be found for them suited to their nomadic but hard-working natures. They have no desire to go on Social Security, but that is where they will be if we are not careful.

10 As a new generation of literate Gypsies grows up, they will be able to speak for themselves. Committed Gorjios will then be able to retire from the field. From among these new literate Gypsies a special Gypsy representative must be elected who will look after Gypsy affairs from a permanent position in Whitehall.

There is no time to waste – everything that I advocate should have happened many years ago. Meanwhile, before our eyes, the fabric of a culture is being shattered. And, what is most terrible of all, as local authorities come to realise the implications of their statutory duties, the harassing of Gypsies is being intensified, in the hope that they will leave the area and the local authority can say they have no Gypsies. Many Gypsies are growing desperate.

A Midlands Councillor has spoken as follows about Gypsies in a Charles Parker programme on the B.B.C.:

'How far does it come in your mind before you say "I have done everything I possibly can and I will help the broad mass of these people, but there are some I can do nothing with whatever."

'Then doesn't the time arise in one's mind when one has to say, "All right. One has to exterminate the impossibles?"

'I know all that leads to in one's mind, Nazism, who is it next, the Gypsies, the Tinkers, the Jews, the coloured man. I don't accept that really on these particular...'

Interviewer: 'But exterminate is a terrible word. You can't really mean that?'

Councillor: '... Why not?'

Doctor Farrukh Hashmi has identified five stages of prejudice: antilocution, avoidance, discrimination, physical attack, extermination.

The Gypsy position has for centuries varied between the third and the fourth states. Now the fourth state is becoming more common, and seems, on occasion, to give way to the fifth.

This island becomes more crowded. The shadow of extermination stands round the corner, and has been advocated by a North Country Chief of Police.

Yet Gypsies are more than just a problem. Gypsies have something to give us which may be more valuable than anything which we could ever give them.

Information in Government Reports

Information about English and Welsh Travellers is contained in a document called *Gypsies and Other Travellers*, compiled by the Sociological Research Section of the Ministry of Housing and Local Government (1967).

In a foreword to the document, the Housing Minister, Anthony Greenwood, wrote, 'The world around [the Gypsies] has altered so rapidly that their roving life can no longer be carried on without hardship – indeed the report reminds us of the remarkable fact that for most Traveller families there is nowhere they can legally put their home ...'

'The dictionary definition of *Gypsy*,' says the report, 'is a "member of a wandering race of Indian origin, a Romany".' Although the term has primarily an ethnic meaning, it is often used loosely for all the people described in this report, whether "true Romanies" or not. Since a recent High Court ruling a *Gypsy* is defined, for legal purposes, as a person without a fixed abode who leads a nomadic life dwelling in tents or other shelters or caravans or other vehicles, i.e. as a class of person and not a member of a particular race.

'The first reference to them,' says the report, 'in Britain dates from 1505 (an entry on the accounts of the Lord High Treasurer for Scotland), but they had no doubt crossed over well before then. Although they adopted characteristics from each country through which they passed, they carried with them the language, customs, and occupations of the low caste Indian tribes from which they sprang including fortune-telling, horse-training and dealing, smithery, and entertainment by singing, dancing, playing musical instruments, acting, juggling and acrobatics. In particular, horse-dealing for men and fortune-telling for women were among the occupations of the first Gypsies to arrive in Britain.

'The immigrants also became noted for their wood-carving, from which developed crafts such as peg-making, chair-mending, and flower-making. The Gypsies' occupations were suited to their nomadic life and in the early days they travelled on pack-horses or with horse-drawn trollies, and camped in tents. It was not until the early nineteenth century that they adopted the covered living wagon.

'In the period following their arrival in Great Britain, the Gypsies, or "Egyptians" as they called themselves, travelled in large bands causing consternation among the settled population.'

The researchers found, in March 1965, 13,762 Gypsies in England and Wales. This excluded Kent. Including Kent they reckoned about 15,000 travelling people. They considered these figures to be an underestimate which seems very likely since many Gypsies are very hard to find. Gypsy households were found to be far larger than Gorjio households. There were proportionately ten times as many Traveller families with five or more children.

Ninety-three per cent of the Travellers they found were living in trailer caravans. Twelve per cent had huts, six per cent had horse-drawn caravans, four per cent had tents – but fourteen per cent had these things in combination, thus leaving only eight per cent living in one or other of these things exclusively.

When they researched overcrowding, the authors of the report found that sixty-five per cent of Travellers' families lived at a density of more than two persons per room, compared with less than three per cent of the total population. Over a quarter were found parked on farmland (but it is important to remember that the survey took place in March, at the end of the winter, and it is to farmland that Travellers try to go in the winter).

About an eighth (2,000 people) were on roadside sites and country lanes. Another 2,000 or so were on common or waste-land. Disused pits and quarries, old airfields, yards, car-parks, were other frequent parking places.

Scottish Travellers

Information about Scottish Gypsies is contained in a book published by H.M.S.O. in 1971 called *Scotland's Travelling People*. This is based on research done in 1969. They located about 2,000 Gypsies in Scotland.

They write: 'The predominant type of accommodation in Scotland, as in England and Wales, is now the trailer caravan, used by sixty-three per cent of Scottish Traveller families in March 1969, but the tent is a much more significant feature of Traveller life north of the border than it is in England and Wales and it is used either in conjunction with some other form of accommodation or, more commonly, as the sole habitation. Tents have for many years been much more commonly used in Scotland. In August 1969 thirty-seven per cent of travelling families had tents, with thirty-three per cent of them living in tents exclusively.'

As in England, the percentage of young people in Traveller families was vastly greater than for the settled population. This of course suggests that the Travellers will multiply far faster than the settlers.

Of the tents they write: 'If a good site was secured, a winter tent might have up to forty or fifty boughs placed at only a few inches interval making the tent strong enough to support the weight of a man, and around the tent there would be some form of drainage trench so as to keep the interior of the tent dry, a necessity on peaty or boggy ground. However, a tent of this quality is now a rarity and the insecurity of tenure makes it hardly worth while spending so much time and effort; this itself leads to a loss of pride in the tent and the result is a structure which is very much a patchwork. Problems of life in a tent are much more severe than those of a caravan life. Interiors may often be damp and dark, and the greater overcrowding, the complete lack of privacy and an almost total absence of storage space makes conditions very unsatisfactory on both health and social grounds. Lack of light in tents presents its own problems for children in that it makes any form of homework virtually impossible.'

The research was done at two different moments and sixty-four per cent in March, when questioned, and forty-eight per cent in August said that they'd like to settle all year. Of these, the vast majority thought they would like to settle in a house, three per cent said they'd like to settle but not in a house and three and two per cent respectively wanted to settle but didn't know where.

A further six per cent in March and thirteen per cent in August wanted to settle in winter only, again with the majority wanting to settle in a house. Seventeen per cent on both occasions wished to continue travelling and there was no reply from four and eight per cent on each occasion.

It is interesting that the more affluent Travellers and the more successful Travellers were those less likely to want to settle in a house.

The report concluded that 'in Scotland there are ... just over two thousand persons who spend the winter in a caravan, tent or hut, or on some kind of camping site. The travelling families are unevenly distributed ... more than half of them are concentrated in Lanarkshire and Perthshire and the remainder are scattered in central Scotland and the northern counties.

'The great majority of camping sites are unauthorised and unserviced and they are most likely to be waste-ground or the verge of a minor road.

'The chief occupations of Travellers are dealing, especially in scrap metal, and agricultural work. In the winter months some thirty-six per cent of the men are engaged in dealing and about twenty per cent are employed in agriculture. In the summer the pattern changes, and the proportion employed in agriculture rises to some forty-five per cent.

'Unemployment is very high, especially in winter.'

Northern Ireland

I can find little information about these Travellers. There are thought to be about 2,000 of them, and the pattern of their life is thought to follow that of the Scottish Travellers, but to be more primitive.

Gypsy Lee, the Hertfordshire-based Gypsy evangelist, says that they have been severely hit by the troubles in Northern Ireland and are constantly searched and harassed by troops and others.

Eire

A number of those to whom I talked in this book are Irish Travellers, at the moment living in Britain. They still remain Irish in most of their attitudes. Statistics about what life is like for them back home are contained in a Report called *The Government of Ireland's Report of the Commission on Itinerancy*.

The Report says that there are between forty and sixty families in Ireland who travel with lorries and motor-trailers – far fewer than in Britain. They are described as 'traders and dealers in new mattresses, feathers, horse-hair, ticks, scrap, rags, etc. on a large scale. Some also deal in horses on a large scale.'

The second category in the Irish Report are horse- and other dealers who travel extensively and whose abode is a horse-drawn caravan. In this group they estimate 200–400 families.

The next category of Travellers in the Report is a group who, 'living in horse-drawn caravans, do not travel farther than a small area'. In this group they estimate 350–450 families.

And, finally, they estimate between 300 and 400 families who have only tents for shelter and do not travel far.

The Report gives an estimate as to income and other information about the various Travellers, and of this last group they say: 'The income of the family in this group is estimated to be extremely low, below subsistence level and derived almost entirely from begging. Families in this group have little means of livelihood apart from begging.'

Their figures suggest a Gypsy population of something over 1,000 Gypsy families in Eire. Gypsy families are large, even for Eire where ordinary families are large. So that there are probably at least 6,000 Gypsy people in Eire not in houses, probably many more. Doubling this, to include those Gypsies at the moment in houses, produces the very approximate figure of 12,000 Gypsy people in Eire.

A more recent count done by the National Council for the Travelling People says that there are 302 families recently housed, 230 in chalets on sites, 146 in trailers on sites, and 788 in trailers, tents, wagons, etc., on unofficial stopping places.

This gives a total of 1,466 families. It seems to me that this bears out the total already given, except that there are now a higher proportion of Gypsies in houses.

Assimilation into the housebound population appears, regrettably, to be the aim of the Irish government.

Education

The lack of schooling for most travelling children has only recently been spotlighted, although the problem was recognised as long as a hundred years ago. In the Plowden Report they are named as probably the most severely deprived group in the country. In fact, Lady Plowden was the first chairman of the National Gypsy Education Council.

This organisation has established many teaching points throughout Britain. They have established contact with most local authorities, and have trained volunteers.

Dave Headley, formerly editor of *Romano Drom*, writes: 'The greatest deprivation the Gypsy suffers is from his lack of education. It is rare to find a Gypsy who is able to read and write, and there is a generation growing up which shares its parents' illiteracy. This generation can be saved only by ensuring that families now on the road can have permanent sites which will enable them to stay in one area for a period of months and return there after the seasonal work ends. In this way, Gypsy children will be able to attend local schools full time. The hope that their children will be educated is one that is frequently expressed by Travellers, and even adolescents are anxious to read and write. The Gypsy is acutely aware of his illiteracy, and fears that it makes him appear simple and prevents him giving the best possible account of himself. He is proud of his history and identity, and the self-doubt caused by illiteracy is a source of considerable anxiety.'

The education carried on at the summer schools might not be easily recognisable as such to everybody. It comes closer in some ways to organised play than to education, and the NGEC have even considered whether the word 'school' should be applied to something which is more of an essay in community relationships.

However, the view of Gypsies is that the word 'school' itself excites respect amongst the Gypsy population.

Sister Bertranda, of St Rose's School in Hemel Hempstead, says of one of these places, 'The general attitude in the school is informal – the children are not hemmed in – they have great freedom to wander and to engage in self-chosen activities, without the restraint of a more formal school. Looking back on the days when there was no play group, I can remember how children coming to school for the first time at five presented all kinds of problems, both educational and social. Now they are well able to hold their own.'

Catherine Culpeper-Williams, speaking of other summer schools in the Bromley and Bexley area, says, 'Summer weather enabled teaching to take place in the open at Crittal's Corner and another illegal site where some of the Travellers had moved in June. Teaching in the open has the advantage that everyone could both see and join in if they wished, and we could do messier things involving glue, dough and paint, which were not practical in the family trailer. However, paper and cards tended to be blown about by the wind and small items easily became lost in the grass. The numerous dogs also got in the way, the more savage ones causing a marked reluctance on the part of the teachers to venture into their territories. The numbers at each session varied wildly from two to sixteen and the ages from about two years to adults.

'The teaching side of the sessions consisted mainly of pre-school activities, reading readiness activities, and individual coaching in reading and writing for the older children and adults.'

Venice Manley, who was a founder of the first of all these schools, set up by the Gypsy Council Trust in 1969, had this to say of the London Borough of Redbridge, 'After almost two years, and a hundred children have come and gone, we find that the same rules always apply. The one to fives want to make tea and pour it themselves, cut up their fruit and food, butter their own bread with real knives, wash the dishes, sweep the floors, clean the windows, wash and dress themselves, comb their hair – they want to use real tools with wood and to fix their tractors and bikes. When they play with clay they make plates of sausage and eggs to hand around and their creative play is of ponies and stables, and playing at bedtime and jacking up lorries and changing wheels, and working at tarmacking, going "calling" for old clothes.

'Several of the three-and-a-half to four year olds have developed a means of communication which could not be understood by any but close members of the family, in fact almost all children of four-and-a-half or under have had speech difficulties of one kind or another. This may be because some Gypsy parents speak so quickly and it is difficult for the child to pick up the individual sounds of the language.

'Recently another aspect of the work has developed. Mums and Dads, Aunts and Uncles, Grannies and Grandads have always come and gone as they pleased in the school, but lately they have been spending more time with us, taking part in the work with the children, having tea with us, learning to play the piano, using our materials and so on, and taking a much closer interest in what the children do.'

Mrs Myra Kelly writes: 'If I were asked to recommend any course of action which could help these children it would be that they attend school normally, but that each official site should have a trailer equipped as a schoolroom and that the children be withdrawn to this room for fairly short periods so that they could have extra tuition in language skills.'

A change in public attitudes is still of vital importance in many areas. For instance, in the Birmingham area, police have actually visited schools and removed Gypsy children from them who had turned up asking to be taught.

The problems of lack of education for a Gypsy are described by Mr Johnny Connors as follows: 'When I write something I am very proud when I am writing it, but when I see my own bad writing I get very fed up with the story. You could say I am like the peacock, he displays his lovely feathers with pride but when the peacock looks down at his feet, he gets disheartened because he has the ugliest feet in the world.'

However, Mr Connors consoles himself, 'Anyway, he is a valuable bird and people look on him as a feathered friend.'

Travellers find it hard to understand what is going on in the Gorjio law courts. Their culture is so far from ours that the only way of really securing justice when a Traveller goes to court would be to have an interpreter of some sort, as is used when non-English-speaking people are being brought to trial.

Mr Gordon Boswell, the well-known North Country Traveller, writes about the probems of lack of education when Travellers go to court. 'The Gypsy never says nothing until he's prosecuted, and then he rears up and tries to defend himself—very hasty, very sharp, very sweet. He's only got a few seconds to do it. He loses his temper and he says what he thinks in his uneducated way. If he would have the patience to talk to these people, but without education it can't be put over. The show can't be put over where it comes to prosecution and offence. Against – that is – the educated man.'

Many non-Gypsies became involved in the NGEC. There were various disputes, and in a letter signed by Jim Penfold, circulated shortly before the AGM in 1973, were the words:

'When the NGEC was being set up, we were promised a partnership of Roms and Gaujos. On a fifty-fifty basis. Over the past two years, instead of taking more part, we've seen the management and all the decisions gradually slip out of our hands. It may have been well intended but that doesn't make it right. What must any of our people think when they know that of the invitations for the coming AGM 150 were for Gaujos and only 25 for Roms.

'A few years ago you couldn't get a Traveller to a meeting. Now you can't keep them away. Our movement is growing all the time. That's us getting educated if you like. I know I speak for the majority when I say that I want the NGEC to become again, as intended, a true partnership of equals.'

Relationships between the various groups comprising the NGEC deteriorated and culminated in the resignation of Lady Plowden and many of the officers of the NGEC, prior to the annual general meeting. And the funds were handed by Lady Plowden back to the trustees. There was a good deal of bitterness and Tom Lee's Romany Guild, which has close connections with them, also failed to come to the AGM. Those who resigned formed a new organisation – the Advisory Committee for the Education of Romany and Other Travellers (ACERT).

They claimed that what the Gypsy Council candidates wanted was contrary to the wishes of most Gypsies; and that to be too militant about Gypsy rights might alienate the establishment from which funds must ultimately come.

Donald Kenrick, who became the new chairman, said: 'The new NGEC stands for an equal partnership of Rom and Gorjio.

'We want to build a bridge with one end firmly in the Romany camp – and the other stretching carefully to the State schools.'

Other differences: the 'new' officers of the NGEC felt that Gypsy education should be based more on the actual Gypsy culture and especially should maintain wider contacts with the world Gypsy Community.

Both ACERT and the NGEC have achieved a lot for Gypsy education since then. But, despite their efforts, the vast majority of Gypsy children still are receiving no formal education whatever.

Travellers and Social Security

The section that follows was supplied, at my invitation, by Jane Kingshill of the Kent Gypsy Support Group.

The Gypsy position today

(a) *Employment*
Gypsy families may be dependent on Social Security for long periods. Their traditional livelihood, a mixture of seasonal farm work, horse-trading and various small rural crafts, has almost vanished. Casual labour of any sort is hard to find now and most firms are reluctant to employ itinerants. Out of three jobs offered to one Gypsy who applied at a local Labour Exchange recently, two were refused him on the site for no other stated reason than that he was a Gypsy.

Scrap-metal dealing seems to be the chief source of income for Travellers at present and it is a precarious one. The profits are getting smaller under current market conditions and motor-transport means constant trouble for the impoverished and usually illiterate owner-driver. Though it is worth noting that Gypsies are never (in my experience) charged with drunken or dangerous driving, they are often convicted of faulty vehicle maintenance and because they are unable to manage the paper work connected with licensing and insurance, traffic offences of this kind are innumerable. It is hard to see an end to this situation as long as Gypsies are excluded from further opportunities in education and employment.

(b) *Accommodation*
There is another continuous drain on their resources. Most of them have nowhere to live. The provision of adequate sites is now required in theory but in practice it still seems far off. Meanwhile the great majority of Travellers break the law every time they park their caravans for the night. Yet they do not qualify for housing in the usual way so there is little present chance of escape from this position either. To fines incurred through traffic offences must therefore be

added such penalties simply for existing in any one place at one time as the local courts see fit to impose. Of course Gypsies are seldom legally represented.

Because of their insecure livelihood and the difficulties experienced by an illiterate and distrusted minority in trying to obtain any better jobs or achieve a more stable existence, most of them live near or below the poverty line. Their earnings do not enable them to pay recurring fines. In the end they often have to go to prison.

(c) *Harassment and Criminal Prosecution*
Gypsies are also subject to harassment of a more general sort from the police and from the public too.

The police, accustomed to see them in court on traffic and camping offences, come to regard Travellers as habitual law-breakers, likely suspects for any local theft, burglary or rape. One family I know have been charged with theft six times in the last two years. They have been successively cleared of every charge. But the father and two sons, each without any criminal record have been imprisoned five times on remand during this period. 'We'll get you next time,' a local CID officer is reported as saying.

(d) *Illness*
In addition to these contingencies the father of this particular family (of seven, the youngest of whom is five years old), has spent the last year as an out-patient of Guy's Hospital during which time he has been totally unfit for work and dependent on sickness certificates. The two elder sons make frequent visits to the doctors, they both have stomach ulcers. The mother is permanently affected by shock and burns received when local youths threw a petrol bomb in at the window of her caravan on to the baby's bed. Most adult Gypsies I know are chronically unwell, in fact, and it is not surprising that many of their illnesses are associated with stress: ulcers for example, and migraines and chest conditions resulting from asthma.

Social Security for Gypsies

(a) *Policy*
Help at a subsistence level has always been the policy of the Welfare State towards the needy. Supplementary benefit is designed to prevent

actual want. But the system seems to operate inefficiently where Gypsies are concerned, and I feel there are grounds for considering whether a special directive ought not to be issued to local officers with regard to Gypsy claims. It is not that Gypsies need special treatment – rather that special treatment in an unwelcome sense is what they seem to get. For instance, payment of Family Allowance to itinerants in back-dated lump sums quarterly instead of weekly. This is a disastrous arrangement for mothers whose needs are desperate from day to day, and for families whose 'large' amounts are often swallowed up in fines rather than on children's necessities. There is no discrimination against Gypsies on paper. But their claims are neglected and undervalued in a manner which is so consistent, within my own experience, that it seems to amount to an unofficial policy.

(b) *In Practice*
To begin with, there is almost always considerable delay in the domiciliary visit of the area officer before any payment is made. This is sometimes excused by the fact that Gypsies are nomadic – they may have moved between their application for benefit and the reply. But few families stir beyond a certain radius of about ten miles, say, and the possible sites within their area are so limited as to entail little difficulty for anyone looking for them. Yet large families known to have no other means of support often wait more than two weeks before the officer gets to them. Then there is another wait before the money comes. This second delay occurs, one must remember, after the family circumstances are personally known to the area officer. By then the hungry mouths have actually been seen as well as counted. In the honouring of sickness certificates, not for the first time but after months perhaps of continuous illness, the same kind of delay operates too. What should be an automatic process (after the doctor's signature) almost always involves a wait of not less than two weeks, though it is known that several children as well as at least one invalid adult depend entirely on this source of income for food and warmth. Finally the sum awarded is always less than the standard rate of pay. I have not come across one instance, even allowing for the wages stop, in which the amount has equalled the scale laid down by the Commission.

(c) *The Right to Appeal*

Some payments are so derisory their emendation seems to be a fairly simple matter. The sum of six pounds allotted on Christmas Eve to a married couple with four children who had had no money for three weeks, the husband being just out of prison and severely unwell, was increased to thirteen pounds quite soon after an appeal, a number of solicitor's letters and a direct approach to the Commissioner. Further representations resulted in a back payment of £113 arrears which arrived without comment or apology.

There was a less spectacular deficit in the award of six pounds a week to a young pregnant wife with one three-year-old whose husband was in prison for a year. She received no extra money for three-and-a-half months after her second child's birth though the Social Security authorities did not fail to dock her supplementary benefit of 90p a week in respect of the Family Allowance they knew she was not getting. Nearly a year later her arrears have not been repaid. It can be seen that Social Security is not made available to Gypsies in the humane and flexible manner suggested by the *Social Security Handbook 1971*; that there is a failure to comply even with the legal provisions clearly laid down to protect families against absolute destitution.

(d) *Further Reasons for Breakdown*

The final way in which the system breaks down for the Gypsy claimant is significant. It is a system designed for the literate. The only safeguard against such injustices as I have quoted appears in print on the notice of award telling the claimant how and when he may appeal against the sum awarded. Most communications like this one, arrive by post. Only the visit of the area officer, the man who has the say in how, when and what payment will be made in the first place, and possibly a return visit of the claimant to collect his money from the Labour Exchange or the social security office gives him any chance to participate in the situation. Such interviews as I have witnessed or heard of have not invited participation. A contemptuous, even abusive tone towards and about Gypsy claimants is the rule. One thirty-five-year-old lorry driver with an unusually 'respectable' and articulate background broke down into sobs for twenty minutes when he tried to describe the way an official had talked to him. On all occasions the illiterate claimant is at the mercy of such arguments as those of a local officer who cited a Gypsy's 'signature', a cross on a form she couldn't read as proof that she had misrepresented her own age and circumstances to her own disadvantage thus deceiving the innocent official into paying her less than her rights!

(e) *Discrimination*
It is true that Gypsy claimants are not the only sufferers from this situation. But they are at a particular disadvantage. The age-old prejudice against them as members of an alien, non-conforming race with different traditions and customs makes itself felt most commonly perhaps in the form of a myth which I have encountered at all levels, the belief that Gypsies are, secretly, rich. 'They all have forty pounds in their pockets'; 'Don't worry about them, they know where to put their hands on it – they aren't like you and me'; 'There's no such thing as a poor Gypsy.'

It is this belief that determines the callous behaviour of many Social Security officials towards Gypsy claimants, as far as one can tell, and by excusing delay and neglect in dealing with their claims interferes with the successful administration of the system and gives rise to real hardship, time and time again.

(f) *Desirable Changes*
Any re-alignment of policy towards Gypsies should therefore begin with a statement of fact as regards their social and economic position. A warning perhaps against the type of racist prejudice I have described might help to clear up some misconceptions of this kind.

Having stressed the urgency and credibility of Gypsy claims it would still seem necessary to make a further provision for the needs of the illiterate. Could one Social Security officer in each local office have a specific duty to seek out such claimants as proved unable to read the relevant documents and explain them fully, making sure that the right of appeal in particular was understood? Perhaps help of this kind is offered over the counter in some offices already. But the only official I know who interprets his function in this way has been threatened with dismissal for 'wasting time'. To protect such employees as well as the claimants themselves therefore, the ruling on this point should be made clear. Some kind of periodic check or inspection should follow to ensure that the illiterate really are safeguarded from exploitation along these lines.

If the responsibility for explaining the system were laid down as a statutory duty in all local offices and its performance made subject to inspection from time to time, the discrimination suffered by Gypsy claimants would not vanish overnight but they themselves would be less defenceless against it. So too with the approach to Gypsy claims. A specific directive against delay, neglect, contempt and underpayment, drawing attention to the acutely critical nature of the Gypsy's dependence on Social Security at the present time and describing the severe economic and social hazards to which Gypsy families, through no fault of their own, are exposed would not convert many officials, perhaps. But it would establish as official policy the principles of fair dealing towards this section of the community which at present go by default.

Legal Provision For and Against Gypsies

So many laws have been made which are forgetful of the way that they may affect the Gypsy way of life, that the Gypsy often finds himself in the remarkable position that only when he is drawing his caravan along the road is he not breaking the law. The moment he actually stops it, he becomes a criminal.

Repressive legislation in Acts dated 1530, 1554 and 1562, made all immigrant adult 'Egyptians' and others found in their company liable to be treated as felons, have their goods forfeited, and to be put to death. At York in 1596, 106 Gypsies were condemned to death at one sitting and this grim sentence was in fact carried out in many cases. The first Act repealing this legislation was passed in 1783.

With the nineteenth century, a fresh wave of repressive legislation began to engulf the Gypsies. The Vagrancy Act, 1824, made it an offence, among many other things, to be in the open air or under a tent or in a cart or wagon 'not having any visible means of subsistence and not giving a good account of himself or herself'. Gypsies have gone to prison under this law and still do.

The Commons Act, two years later, enabled local authorities to make by-laws about their commons. Local authorities then framed by-laws which closed the commons to Gypsies.

The Commons Act, 1899, was much the same sort of thing. But it did allow for compensation of those whose rights had been taken from them. As far as I know, Gypsies have never been paid compensation by those local authorities who framed by-laws forbidding them to stop on their commons.

These laws were as nothing, though, to those which have been passed within the last forty years.

The Public Health Act, 1936, makes it an offence to be in a tent or van 'which is in such a state, or so overcrowded, as to be prejudicial to the health of the inmates'. As Gypsies almost always live in conditions which, in terms of house-dwellers, would be considered to be overcrowded, it means that this law can be used against them should a bloody-minded local authority want to harass them or take their children from them.

The Town and Country Planning Act, 1947, says that if a local authority wants to forbid the use of land in some particular way because it is not 'expedient in the interests of the proper planning of their area', then they can by order require the discontinuance of that use. This Act can be used against Gypsies camping on their own land.

The Highways Act, 1959, says that if someone 'wilfully obstructs the free passage along a highway' he's guilty of an offence. And that where a structure has been erected or set up on a highway (structure also means something on wheels), the authority for the highway can order its removal.

It also says that it is an offence if a Gypsy 'without lawful authority ... encamps on a highway ...'

This is the Act, so many people feel, which contains actual racial discrimination. But what is a Gypsy? On 9 March 1967, in the case of Mills versus Cooper, a Gypsy was defined as somebody 'following a particular way of life ... a person without fixed abode who lives a nomadic life, dwelling in tents or other shelters or caravans or other vehicles', i.e. as a class of person and not a member of a particular race.

The Caravan Sites and Control of Development Act, 1960, says that nobody can allow his land to be used as a caravan site unless he's the holder of a licence. It provides further opportunities for local authorities to prevent the camping on commons, farms, or the Gypsies' own land.

The Town and Country Planning Act, 1962, is also sometimes used against Gypsies. 'Enforcement notices' can be served on people using land contrary to the areas' 'development plan'.

The Caravan Sites Act, 1968, says that local authorities must provide sites for Gypsies 'residing in or resorting to' their area. Once they have done this they can apply to become designated areas which means that they have even greater powers to harass Gypsies who are not on the site provided. A recent policy statement by the Gypsy Council outlines some of the attendant flaws (see page 236).

So far, about 120 sites have been created, containing about 1,700 pitches – accommodation for about a quarter of the Gypsy population. And those sites which have been provided are inadequate in their total failure, in most cases, to understand the basic principles of the Gypsy way of life.

The worst thing of all is that local authorities are now applying to become designated areas. Such authorities are given Gestapo-like powers to harass Gypsies. The original verbal undertaking to the Gypsy Council was that such orders would not be made piecemeal, since it would be extremely difficult for those of our illiterate Gypsies to learn which areas were designated and which were not. Now Whitehall has gone back on this undertaking and allowed piecemeal designation to a number of places.

The following changes in the law, or the enforcement of the law, seem to me to be necessary if any dignity or understanding is to be granted by us to our Gypsy people:

VAGRANCY ACT, 1824 – This law should not be used against Gypsies until (i) the rights that have been taken from them are returned by the re-legalising of their traditional stopping places on roadside verges, in lanes, on their own land and on commons, and (ii) adequate local authority transit and permanent sites have been provided.

COMMONS ACTS, 1826 AND 1899 – Gypsies should now be paid compensation, in the same way that Gorjios were, for the rights that were taken from them. With this money they could buy land to make their own stopping places; *or* a responsible body should scrutinise all local legislation framed under the Commons Acts. Wherever feasible, the right to stop there should be returned to the Travellers.

PUBLIC HEALTH ACT, 1936 – A phrase exempting Gypsy caravans should be inserted. Caravans, like boats, are specially designed for living at a density greater than that possible in houses.

TOWN AND COUNTRY PLANNING ACTS, 1947 AND 1962 – These Acts already contain an exemption for showmen and circus people in their winter quarters. Gypsies must also be offered this exemption.

HIGHWAYS ACT, 1959 – The anti-Gypsy discrimination should be reversed. It should be legal for someone 'being a Gypsy' to encamp beside the highway.

CARAVAN SITES AND CONTROL OF DEVELOPMENT ACT, 1960 – Local authorities must be encouraged and, if necessary, forced to grant licences to Gypsies who need to stop on their own land, or on the land of friendly farmers.

CARAVAN SITES ACT, 1968 – Designation, which allows a local authority to fine Gypsies £25 on the first day and £5 on every further day that they are not on the official site, is evil. Something similar was being done in Germany in 1933. It is as well to remember where *that* ended. The only way that we can show respect for the Gypsies and their valuable culture is to build sites as proposed but *also* allow them to camp in their traditional stopping places. Designation has now spread until it covers Manchester, Leeds, Oxford, and many London boroughs and other places.

Effectiveness of the Caravan Sites Act – A Policy Statement by the Gypsy Council in 1972

Two years have now passed since the Caravan Sites Act Part II became law on 1 April 1970. Since that date, less than forty new sites have been constructed in England and Wales (source: Department of the Environment).

This figure is considered by the Gypsy Council to be totally inadequate. Not only were the figures in the original Government census (on which estimates of requirements were made) a grave underestimate. In addition, the Gypsy population is growing by about 1,000 persons each year, and each year sees the usual number of children becoming adults, wanting to marry and start families of their own, and hence requiring additional pitches.

Simultaneously, the number of pitches not on local authority sites continues to be reduced by the denial to Gypsies of their traditional rights and also the closing of commons, destruction of grass verges by roadways, and eviction of Gypsies from land which they themselves own. Thus the provision of sites has not even kept up with the increasing population of the Gypsy people, let alone compensated for the closure of other pitches. The situation is worse than it was since the Act became law, and might be said to be a total travesty of those principles envisaged when the Act was framed.

Not only are these sites inadequate in terms of the number built, they are also inadequate in other ways. The Gypsy Council has produced a document setting out the minimum requirements for a Gypsy site. So far few local authorities have followed or made use of this document.

Most of the sites provided since the Act, and the twenty-eight provided before the Act became law, are criticised on one or more of the following grounds:

The rent demanded is too expensive.
Rules restricting the number of pets strike a blow at this traditional aspect of Gypsy life.

Rules against the open fire (where Gypsies' social life traditionally took place) are similarly inimical to the Gypsy life style.

Local authorities do not seem to take seriously the fact that the breaking, sorting, storage and dealing in scrap is now the basic livelihood of most Gypsies. Few sites have provision for these activities.

There are inadequate washing or toilet facilities.

They are too small.

They are too far from any place where a Gypsy can gain a living.

They are a long way from the nearest telephone (necessary in case of fire or other emergency).

They have inadequate sewage facilities.

No community centre.

No play place.

No education whatever – or are very slow in providing any form of education – or even, on some sites, Gypsy children have been refused entry to the local school.

They are inappropriately sited. The majority are near or on top of one of the following: rubbish tip, canal, sewage bed.

There are no arrangements for refuse collection.

They are too far from shops and schools.

Gypsies are sometimes inspected before being allowed to enter the site in a way which is out of keeping with human dignity.

There is harassment of Gypsies on these sites by the police. Gypsies often feel apprehensive that being on such sites makes it easier for the police to indulge in harassment.

The type of warden, often an ex-policeman, is often inappropriate in that he shows little knowledge or respect for the Gypsy way of life.

There is an illegal neglect of facilities for fire prevention.

The local authorities providing the site have failed to liaise with the Gypsy Council as they were recommended to do in a Government circular.

On the positive side it can be mentioned that Bedfordshire County Council and Chesterfield Rural District Council and other local authorities have accepted the principle of providing transit sites in addition to permanent sites. This shows an understanding of the nomadic nature of the life led by many Gypsies and it is to be commended.

Also, the Gypsy Council has had six meetings with the Local Authority Association and a joint working report has been drawn up which has been sent to all local authorities.

However, it is the experience of the Gypsy Council that harassment is being intensified and is in many areas worse than it has been for some years, as local authorities attempt to drive Gypsies from their area in an effort to evade their responsibilities under the Caravan Sites Act by claiming that they have no Gypsies in their vicinity.

The Gypsy Council learns with regret that some local authorities have applied for exemption under the Act from their statutory duties, on the grounds that they have no land and/or Gypsies in their vicinity. The Gypsy Council has knowledge of some places, where there is both land available and a large Gypsy population, where this is done.

We also learn with regret that a number of local authorities have applied to become designated areas on the grounds that they have now provided adequate provision for Gypsies residing in or resorting to their area.

The Gypsy Council has opposed all such applications except Stoke on Trent, St Helens and Plymouth. We trust that designation status will not be granted by the Government to any other local authority. Provision in all other places of which we have knowledge is inadequate, and the granting of designation status would be in contravention of an agreement between the Gypsy Council and the Department of the Environment that designation would not be applied piecemeal (partly because this would be very confusing to Gypsies and partly because it would involve many Gypsy families in a poor-law-style rat-race whose misery would be even greater than that of those Gypsies being harassed at the moment).

The Gypsy Council further learns with regret that all forms of obstacles are still being placed in the way of Gypsies who wish to buy their own land to camp on, or who apply for planning permission to camp on their own land (on which they often have been camping for many decades already). Obstacles are also being placed in the path of farmers who, out of generosity or for any other motive, offer their land for Gypsies to camp on.

The Story Brought Up to Date

Some good books by Gypsies have appeared since the original edition of this book came out, among them *In the Life of a Romany Gypsy* by Fred Wood, and *The Gypsy*, a collection of poems by an anonymous Gypsy writing under the name of Petulengro.

Meanwhile, although in some areas conditions have got better for Gypsies, in most there seems all too little change in the realities of life on the road. At a recent NGEC meeting it was claimed that there were 4,200 Gypsy children resident in the five counties of the West Midlands. Only 430 were receiving formal education – about one in ten.

Other recent events, noted by the Gypsy Council:

In Kent, Mrs Evans was moved from private land after an enforcement order had been served on the owner. She left her premature baby behind in a hospital oxygen tank. In the following week she was moved three times, while a social worker tried to find her to tell her the baby was fit to be taken out. The morning after she collected the baby she had to move again – and as a special favour was allowed to stop for seven days on an old rubbish tip in Rochester.

In Walsall, the first action of the new Labour council was to stop work on the half-built Gypsy site. One year later, while her parents were stopping on the unfenced bank of a canal in Walsall, Amanda Walsh, aged three, was drowned.

In Surrey, police and council employees came to a field in Esher where three caravans were stopping. They arrested the two men on the site and then towed the caravans on to a main road, leaving them with the doors opening into the traffic stream. Damage worth £200 was done to the caravans during this operation and no compensation has been paid.

The father of one family was due to go into hospital for a major operation, but felt he could not leave his family in these circumstances. He lost his place on the hospital waiting list.

Meanwhile, Bedfordshire has legalised stopping places for every Gypsy in the county. Surrey and Somerset have almost reached this stage. What has been done by some could be done by all.

As Gypsies become more aware of the need to take control of their own destinies, so there is political intrigue and much alignment and re-alignment between Gypsies and those Gorjios who try to be of help. Often the Gorjios squabble amongst themselves in a way which cannot give the Gypsies a good impression of us. It seems to be difficult to be impartial about Gypsies – Gorjios either love them or hate them. Those who love them are racked with violent passions which often seem to make them behave unreasonably and childishly, believing that they are the only ones who should relate to Gypsies.

Some of those offering help have few, if any, social contacts with Gypsies. This may help them to be more objective but of course does not lead to an atmosphere of trust.

The divisions are tragic at a time when there is so much else that is tragic about the Gypsy situation, because of the consequent loss of power through divisiveness, and also the lack of credibility through in-fighting.

There was a time when Johnny Connors appeared to be going to emerge as a great Gypsy leader. Regrettably, he seems for the moment to have retired from both writing and politics, saddened and disheartened perhaps by his experiences in prison, and prey perhaps to the Irish foe. This is a very great loss.

Hughie Smith of Leeds, with Tommy O'Doherty, dominates the Gypsy Council in the North.

Roy Wells has emerged as a powerful London figure, and has fought in many campaigns in the London area aimed to force London boroughs to provide sites.

Gaining in political skill and acumen all the time is Tom Lee of the Romany Guild, although there are those who say that the effect of the Romany Guild is divisive and that he should bring it back into the Gypsy Council from which he resigned, so that the Gypsies can speak more with one voice. This has on occasion seemed likely to happen. Others allege that the Romany Guild is somewhat of a puppet organisation, too close under the wing of ACERT.

Jim Penfold has worked hard for the Gypsy cause and so have a large number of other Gypsies.

I do not propose to single out particular Gorjios for mention; there are so many involved and this could be invidious. The sheer volume of work put in entitles the Gorjio (now married to a Gypsy girl), Grattan Puxon, to a mention. Many friends of the Gypsies, alienated by him, have departed from the Gypsy scene, never to return. In his faith in his own destiny to help the Gypsy people to forge the Gypsy Council into a body capable and worthy of representing the Gypsy people of Britain, he has alienated people by the way. Sometimes the alienation can seem to have been arbitrary, and to have served no useful purpose.

Besides his belief in total Gypsy autonomy, another of his most important beliefs concerned the relationship of British Gypsies to Gypsies in other parts of the world. Most British Gypsies are distrustful of foreign Gypsies and generally, so it seems to me, would prefer to have nothing to do with them. But Puxon's attitude was that the Gypsies will never be considered more than a social problem in Britain unless they are understood to be a part of the world Gypsy community.

In the past, many liaison groups and pressure groups have been more efficient than the Gypsy Council. Puxon's insistence that Gypsy participation must be put ahead of efficiency was seen by many to be misguided.

Perhaps, though, now that the system is coming to produce Gypsies able to parley with the Gorjio on the Gorjio's own terms, the system may be seen to have been justifiable, and Puxon, now working far away on the world Gypsy scene, can look back in greater perspective on what he did in Britain.

Matters which go on and on being discussed at meetings of the various organisations:

How important is the Romani tongue? Should Gorjios be encouraged to learn it? Should spelling follow that of European Romani or should it follow a pattern easily recognisable to British Gypsy children? Should it be kept as a 'secret tongue' or should it be taught in school? Should semi-legal and illegal action be part of the campaign for Gypsy rights, or does this alienate the general establishment and make provision for Gypsies slower rather than faster?

Should Gypsy affairs be run more by Gypsies who are, to a certain degree, unfamiliar with the procedures necessary to get one's way in a Gorjio world, or by Gorjios with the consequent dangers of paternalism?

Should Gypsy children be educated in the State system or in a parallel system?

Should Gypsy children be educated (in the formal sense of the word) at all?

Is the aim to force the Government to make local authorities provide the sites they are legally bound to provide the best way of fighting for Gypsy rights? Or is to do this to fall into a trap; should the fight be to annul the Caravan Sites Act and fight for the legalisation of all traditional atchintans?

How much should the campaign for Gypsy education be seen as part of the campaign for stopping places? How far may the fight for the first be hampered by a fight for the second?

How much should the Christian churches be asked to take part in such campaigns or how much might this alienate helpers?

How much encouragement should be given to organisations which study only the Gypsy culture and give little or nothing back to the Gypsies?

Is it reasonable to waive some of our laws concerning land planning as they relate to Gypsies' land? Such laws are already waived for showmen, and there are other examples of laws being waived for minority groups, for example, for Jewish people in laws concerning ritual slaughter.

Should inability to write or read be accepted as a defence for not filling in a licence application form?

What advice should we give to a Gypsy who's thinking of going into a house because it's become too hard on the road? Can we honestly tell him that things will ever be better?

Is nomadism a basic feature of Gypsy life or, as some aver, only an economic necessity for some Gypsies?

How far should Gypsy children be educated past their parents (in Gorjio terms) with the resultant loss of respect and confusion that that may involve for the teenage children?

How much money should be spent on long term research? On immediate succour of Gypsies in the mud by the road?

How can Gypsies and pro-Gypsy Gorjios learn to forget their squabbles and work towards a common end?

A note on the question of extermination. Some reviewers found my reference to this possibility for British Gypsies far-fetched. I do not mean that there is a danger of *mass* extermination but I do feel that isolated occurrences of extermination have already taken place. (Careful readers of this book will recognise the events I am referring to.)

Extermination has been attempted more often than carried out. There is a possibility that Britain could move further in this direction. Public figures who should know better have advocated it.

In 1967, Councillor Barry Smith of Hitchin called for a 'concentration camp for Gypsies'. A report of the Hampshire Association of Parish Councils in 1960 says 'they (Gypsies) are faced with the problem that besets a decadent stock. They belong to neither past nor present.' The arguments about 'decadent stock' were used as justification for the German exterminations.

The Guardian reviewer wrote:

'... More than once he (Sandford) refers, darkly, to an unnamed councillor and unnamed police chief who, he says, have urged "extermination" of gypsies, but it is hard to believe this was meant in the Hitlerian sense.'

The North County chief of police, Mr Alec Muir, was actually quoted in *The Guardian*. He advocated extermination of Gypsies and undesirables generally.

As for the councillor: Charles Parker, the well known ex-BBC producer, replied to *The Guardian*:

'... The Councillor was Alderman Harry Watton, then leader of the Birmingham City Council. I recorded him in 1963 for the Radio Ballad "The Travelling People", and the passage in question can be heard on the LP of the programme, Argo D.A.133 ...
'... This was the only time in the Radio Ballads that we included the interviewer's question, anticipating disclaimers such as Mr Turner's that the Alderman didn't really mean it. But as the pas-

sage reveals it was not a slip of the tongue, and in what *other* sense than the Hitlerian can the word be understood?

'Surely the use of such a word cannot but have the most sinister implications – not least that of conditioning the public to an ultimate acceptance of the actual inhumanity which underlies the word, but which such use seemed to drain from it! a technique which can make possible the acceptance by decent people of every process up to Hitler's "Final Solution". And as the recent ruthless evictions in Birmingham give evidence, the Alderman seems to have worthy successors.'

The Guardian did not print this letter.

The Romany Guild has stated the following aims:

1 To get more and better permanent and transit sites. The latter should include traditional stopping places.
2 The Romany Guild wants education for all our children, because they are our future. We shall work in co-operation with the Advisory Committee for the Education of Romany and other Travellers (ACERT) and its chairman, Lady Plowden.
3 The Romany Guild is concerned at designations and exemptions. To agree to designation would be to condone the outlawing of our own people. No other section of the community is outlawed in any part of the country. Until there are sites for every Travelling family based on an accurate and current count there can be no question of any town being exempted from providing space for us to stop. And there is the question of sites for our children when they marry and the right of our relatives to visit us.

One of the resolutions of the NGEC has been:

'That the Caravan Sites Act, 1968, for all its limitations, should be put into practice. At the same time the Act be also reviewed in order to: oblige local authorities to provide for a larger number of Travelling families if they are in excess of fifteen families; oblige local authorities to provide working space for Travelling families;

oblige local authorities to complete permanent sites by a specified date. It further considers that, where local authorities have disregarded their obligations under the 1968 Act without due cause, legal action should be *considered* to obtain what is the Travellers' due at law.'

The Gypsy Council has formulated this six-fold campaign:

1 End to harassment by councils and police.
2 1,000 legalised temporary pitches by Christmas.
3 All permanent sites to have working space and all animals.
4 Amnesty for past motoring and stopping offences.
5 All Gypsy children to get suitable education supported by local authority funds.
6 Encouragement for private site owners.

The West Midlands Gypsy Liaison Group recently sent this letter to Birmingham councillors:

'... You will I hope share our deep concern at the state of affairs which now exists in Birmingham with regard to the Gypsies.
'We are aware of the problems which exist in the fields of planning and public health; we recognise the pressures of general prejudice and political expediency; but we dare to assert that the plight of the gypsy families concerned must surely now take precedence and a civilised solution be found.
'It must surely tarnish the city's image to have scenes such as those at King's Norton on the 10 July in the national press and on television screens. In common humanity these should surely now belong to the past, and in the name of practical commonsense and good government such harrying of human beings and waste of resources must surely be stopped.'

The letter produced precious little change in official attitudes in Birmingham.
Meanwhile, at a time when the Gypsy world is particularly beset with infighting, Donald Byrne, a Gorgio, has been appointed as 'Adviser on Gypsy Encampment', a new post, at the Department of the Environment. Let us hope that he gives good advice and that it will be listened to.

And there is talk among some M.P.s of trying to amend some of the worst provisions of the 1960 Act where it concerns Gypsies. Let us hope that they will carry the day.

Gypsies from Ireland and Gypsies from houses continue to move onto the official sites. The Gypsy population continues to increase from natural causes. One area which had been granted designation because of its Gypsy site has now closed that site. Indeed, at the present rate of progress, we may well be into the 2000s before there is a place on a site for every British Gypsy.

Just a few changes in the law – and a diversion of the vast sums spent on harassing Gypsies into the building of permanent and transit sites – is that too much to ask as a mark of respect to our Gypsy population?

Meanwhile the majority of British Gypsies on the road still live in a world in which they are confused by Gorjios' language and deeply suspicious of us. They are cynical of ways that are devised to help them, shattered by designation and do not, most of them, even now realise the extreme gravity of the future that lies before them, a future in which, more and more, unless they're able to get on a site, they will be shifted and lifted, shifted and lifted, shifted and lifted.

Select Bibliography

Acton, T. A., *Gypsy Politics and Social Change*. Routledge and Keegan Paul, 1974

Adler, Marta, *My Life with the Gypsies*. Souvenir Press, 1960

Berlin, Sven, *Dromengro*. Collins, 1971

Boswell, Gordon, *The Book of Boswell*. Gollancz, 1970; Penguin, 1973

Clebert, Jean-Paul, *The Gypsies* (translated by Charles Duff). Studio Vista, 1963, and Penguin (mainly about Continental Gypsies, inaccurate on British Gypsies)

Dodds, Norman N., *Gypsies, Didecois and Other Travellers*. Johnson Publications, 1966

Lavengro (pseud), *The Gypsy*. Midas Books, 1974

Puxon, Grattan, *On the Road*. The National Council for Civil Liberties, 1967

Puxon, Grattan, and Kenrick, D. *The Destiny of Europe's Gypsies*. Heinemann Educational, 1972

Reiss, Christopher, *Education of Travelling Children*. Macmillan Education, 1975.

Rishi, W. R., *Romani Dictionary*. Romanestan Publications

Webb, G. E. C., *Gypsies: the Secret People*. Herbert Jenkins, 1960

Wood, Manfri Frederick, *In the Life of a Romany Gypsy*. Routledge and Keegan Paul Ltd, 1974

Yoors, Jan, *The Gypsies*. Allen & Unwin, 1967

Gypsies and Other Travellers. HMSO, 1967

Scotland's Travelling People. HMSO, 1971

Report of the Commission on Itinerancy, Government of Ireland, 1963

ACERT Newsletter. The journal of the Advisory Committee for the Education of Gypsies and Other Travellers

Romano Drom. Newspaper for Gypsies and their Gorjio friends, from the Gypsy Council

The Journal of the Gypsy Lore Society. University Library, Liverpool. (back numbers) C. Beresford-Webb, Coutts House, Sandon, near Stafford. (new series)

The Romany Guild Looks at the Caravan Sites Act – five years after. The Romany Guild, 1973

Towards a Rational and Humane Policy for the Accommodation of the Gypsy Community in Kent. Kent Gypsy Support Group

Travellers' Education. A tri-annual Report on Gypsy Education. NGEC

The Travelling People. A gramophone record by Charles Parker with contributions by many Gypsies. Argo Records, 1970

Some Useful Addresses

Researchers and students writing theses should be aware of the shoestring funds of many of these organisations. It is unfair to ask for help without sending money.

Advisory Committee for the Education of Romany and other Travellers (ACERT), 204, Church Road, London W7 (01 597 5108)
Bedfordshire Gypsy Council, c/o G. & M. Marriott, My Folly, Dunstable Road, Caddington, Bedfordshire (a branch of the Gypsy Council)
Comité Internationale Rom, Leulea Rouda, Residence Les Fougeres Bt D5, Avon 77, France
Departmental Advisory Officer on Gypsy Sites, Donald Byrne, Department of the Environment, 2 Marsham Street, London SW1
Gypsy Council, Cottingley Springs, Geldard Road, Leeds 12
Gypsy Council (Southern Branch), 61 Blenheim Crescent, London W11 (01 727 2916)
Gypsy Lore Society, University Library, Liverpool
Institute of Race Relations, 74, Shakespeare Road, London SE24
Kent Gypsy Support Group, c/o Brian Richardson, Greenways, Knockholt, Sevenoaks, Kent
National Council for Civil Liberties, 186 Kings Cross Road, London WC1
National Gypsy Education Council (NGEC), 61, Blenheim Crescent, London W11
Register of Gypsy Support Groups, Diana Allen, The Grey House, Kitsbury Road, Berkhampstead, Hertfordshire
Romanestan Publications (Gypsy Book Centre), 61, Blenheim Crescent, London W11
Romany Guild, Folly Lane Caravan Site, Waltham Forest, London E17 (01 531 6394)
Romani Institute, 61 Blenheim Crescent, London W11
West Midlands Gypsy Liaison Group, 72 Woodfield Road, Birmingham 13

Glossary

This glossary is included at the request of those Gypsies who used Gypsy words when talking to me.

Romany is not usually written down, so opinions about the pronunciation, spelling and sometimes meaning of words, vary in different parts of the country. The reader may already have noticed that the Romani Institute is spelt with an 'i' and the Romany Guild with a 'y'.

atch	to stop or camp
atchintan	a camping place
barons	frontier guards (Irish)
camp	where Gypsies are stopped (Scottish)
Cant	a secret Gypsy language
caer, ker	house
ceili, ceilidh	a get-together
chal	man
chavvy	child
chored	stolen
chuchi	rabbit
conya	a term of endearment/abuse (shit)
cosh	firewood
Countryman, Country Handle	non-Gypsy (Scottish)
crush comra	go dog (Irish)
cushti	good, nice
Didecoi	form of Gypsy (definitions vary)
drom	road
duckering	fortune-telling
Espanolo Gitano	Spanish Gypsy
fannie, fawnie	ring
gavmush, gavver	policeman
Gorjio (s, is, ios)	non-Gypsy(ies)

grai	horse
hatch	to stop or camp
hatchintan	a camping place
Hedgecrawler	inferior form of Gypsy
hotchiwitchi	hedgehog
jogray	Gypsy stew (possibly originally Joe Gray, a cockney stew)
joller, joll, jell	variations of the verb, to go
jukel	dog
ker	house
landings	lead or metal piping
lifted	arrested (Scottish)
moulder	lorry
Mumpley	inferior form of Gypsy
mush	friend, man
muskra (musgro)	policeman
nupe	a term of endearment/abuse (piss)
Pav (pavee)	Irish Gypsy
peg	sell
Pikie	inferior form of Gypsy
poove	a field, and hence, to graze
poppys	soup (Irish)
rackley	woman or girl
ragging	dealing in old clothes
rokra	speech
rocker	speak
Rom	Gypsy
Shelta	a secret Gypsy language
shifted	evicted (Scottish)
shirted	taken by the police
starry	prison
scholar	a person who can read or write
skiving	dealing in ...
tan	camping place
Tinker	Scottish or Irish Gypsy
tooken away	sent to prison
totting	dealing in junk or scrap
trailer	motor-drawn caravan
trashed	frightened

Traveller	Gypsy
varda	horse-drawn caravan
vass	hand
yog	open fire
zetterings	guttering (Herefordshire)

HUMAN TYPES
RAYMOND FIRTH

A revised, illustrated edition of the classic introduction to social anthropology, which explains its main principles, examines its role in the modern world, and serves as a fascinating and informative aid to understanding the diversities of human behaviour.
95p *Illustrated*

OPEN MARRIAGE
NENA O'NEILL and GEORGE O'NEILL

'*Open Marriage – A New Life Style For Couples* plants a sizeable time-bomb under traditional concepts without denying the necessity of marriage itself. . . . I guarantee that every marriage has something to learn from the O'Neills'
Daily Express
90p

SMALL IS BEAUTIFUL
A Study of Economics as if People Mattered

E. F. SCHUMACHER

'The basic message in this tremendously thought-provoking book is that man is pulling the earth and himself out of equilibrium by applying only one test to everything he does: money, profits, and therefore giant organisations. We have got to ask instead, what about the cost in human terms, in happiness, health, beauty and conserving the planet?'
Daily Mail
75p

THE PRIMAL REVOLUTION
ARTHUR JANOV

Author of the bestselling *The Primal Scream*, Arthur Janov presents Primal Therapy, a revolutionary method for curing neuroses which has shattered traditional ideas of psychoanalysis.
'Dr Janov is a compelling and articulate writer who comes through as the sort of fiery humanitarian we can well do with. . . . Dr Janov does not paint a picture of glittering euphoria, but sketches a person who can live without neurotic anxiety, tensions and blocked out emotions'
The Guardian
90p

TOTAL MAN
STAN GOOCH

'Drawing on literature and legend, on science fiction, mythology, history, physiology, psychology, linguistics and art, British psychologist Stan Gooch has written a daring new interpretation of the human psyche. . . . His book, which contains what may be the best defence of the "I Ching" as a way of knowledge since Carl Jung, presents a rare attempt at providing a complete system of thought aimed at fostering the evolution of a "new consciousness"'
Publishers Weekly
£1·60

ONE DIMENSIONAL MAN
HERBERT MARCUSE

'A "classic" of social criticism. . . . The analysis he presents is impressive without doubt . . . for the ferocity and power with which he reveals the pervasive alienation and un-freedom of modern technological society'
Peace News
75p

SCOTT JOPLIN AND THE RAGTIME ERA
PETER GAMMOND

An exploration of Scott Joplin's life from his birth in 1868 in the small city of Texarkana, Texas, to his death in a mental institution in 1917, which describes his family background, the music he would have been influenced by, the beginnings of his career playing in the brothels and gaming halls along the Mississippi, his rise to fame as 'King of Ragtime' and his subsequent decline. Peter Gammond then discusses ragtime's influence on the worlds of jazz, popular and classical music, and shows why Joplin must now be reckoned as one of the world's great popular composers.
£1·25 *Illustrated*

LADY SINGS THE BLUES
BILLIE HOLIDAY with WILLIAM DUFTY

Lady Sings The Blues is the tragic autobiography of Billie Holiday, the brilliant blues singer who fought her way from poverty in the ghettos and brothels of black America to stardom and her triumphant concert at Carnegie Hall.
£1·00 *Illustrated*

BESSIE
Empress of the Blues
CHRIS ALBERTSON

'A definitive biography of the woman they billed as Empress of the Blues. . . . Mr Albertson has created a fascinating account of a stormy and ultimately tragic life, an overdue record of a neglected artist'
Sunday Times
£1·00 *Illustrated*

All Sphere Books are available at your bookshop or newsagent, or can be ordered from the following address:

Sphere Books, Cash Sales Department,
P.O. Box 11, Falmouth, Cornwall.

Please send cheque or postal order (no currency), and allow 15p for the first book plus 5p per copy for each additional book ordered up to a maximum of 50p in U.K. or Eire. Overseas customers and B.F.P.O. please allow 20p for the first book and 10p per copy for each additional book.